Understanding
Microsoft® QuickBASIC

Related Titles

Understanding C
Carl Townsend

Understanding HyperTalk™
Dan Shafer

Understanding Local Area Networks
Stan Schatt

Understanding Microsoft® Windows 2.0
Katherine Stuart Ewing

Understanding MS-DOS®
Kate O'Day and John Angermeyer,
The Waite Group

**Understanding OS/2™
with Presentation Manager** *(forthcoming)*
Daniel Paquette and Kathleen Paquette

Understanding WordPerfect®, Version 5.0
Vincent Alfieri

Understanding dBASE IV™ *(forthcoming)*
Judd Robbins

Mastering Turbo Assembler®
Tom Swan

**The Waite Group's Turbo C®
Programming for the PC,
Revised Edition**
Robert Lafore

The Waite Group's Turbo C® Bible
Naba Barkakati

C: Step-by-Step
The Waite Group

**The Waite Group's Microsoft® C
Programming for the PC,
Revised Edition**
Robert Lafore

*For the retailer nearest you, or to order directly from the publisher,
call 800-428-SAMS. In Indiana, Alaska, and Hawaii call 317-298-5699.*

Sams
Understanding
Series

Understanding
Microsoft® QuickBASIC

Judd Robbins

HOWARD W. SAMS & COMPANY

A Division of Macmillan, Inc.
4300 West 62nd Street
Indianapolis, Indiana 46268 USA

To Marriage, and Family
To Love, and Life
To Balance, and Health
To Kids, and Wife

International Standard Book Number: 0-672-27287-3
Library of Congress Catalog Card Number: 89-60587

Acquisitions Editor: *Richard K. Swadley*
Development Editor: *James Rounds*
Manuscript and Production Editor: *Amy M. Perry*
Illustrator: *Wm. D. Basham*
Cover Art: *DGS&D Advertising, Inc.*
Cover Photo: *Cassell Productions, Inc.*
Indexer: *Sherry Massey*
Compositor: *Shepard Poorman Communications Corp.*

Printed in the United States of America

Contents

Chapter 7 Controlling File and Device Input/Output, 151

Chapter 8 Processing Character Strings, 179

Chapter 9 Developing Graphics Programs, 207

Part 3 Designing Useful Application Programs, 229

Chapter 10 Building a Strong Foundation, 231

Chapter 11 Programming Tips and Techniques, 257

Acknowledgments

Thanks to all the hard working people behind the scenes at Sams: Richard Swadley, Jim Rounds, and Amy Perry. Their commitment to quality makes me proud of the final product you are now reading.

And thanks to Laura, for making the rest of my life work while I write these books!

Trademarks

All terms mentioned in this book that are known to be trademarks or service marks are listed below. In addition, terms suspected of being trademarks or service marks have been appropriately capitalized. Howard W. Sams & Company cannot attest to the accuracy of this information. Use of a term in this book should not be regarded as affecting the validity of any trademark or service mark.

dBASE III Plus, dBASE IV, and Framework III are trademarks of Ashton-Tate.
Epson is a registered trademark of Epson America, Inc.
HP LaserJet is a registered trademark of the Hewlett-Packard Corporation.
IBM, IBM AT, IBM PC, and PS/2 are registered trademarks and OS/2 and XT
    are trademarks of International Business Machines Corporation.
Lotus 1-2-3 is a registered trademark of Lotus Development Corporation.

Introduction

Congratulations! Your decision to learn Microsoft QuickBASIC puts you at the leading edge of software development. As the 1990s take shape before us, operating systems like UNIX and OS/2 will extend the power of DOS. They will also share the limelight with advanced programming languages like QuickBASIC. Any programming language offers you the ability to write instructions for your computer to follow. You can initiate groups of instructions, called *programs*, to accomplish specific business or personal tasks.

You can write a program to manage your business contact list, doing such things as printing out mailing labels or typing personalized letters. You can also write programs to store and retrieve student class lists, calculate grades, control automated tutorials, prepare payroll, and analyze pharmaceutical drug interactions. The list of possible applications is endless. QuickBASIC is one of the best choices for a computer language to do these types of jobs.

Why QuickBASIC over Other Computer Languages?

In short, QuickBASIC symbolizes the kinds of glimmering advancements in computer science which have all been founded on one successful equation:

1

New Software = Old Software + Enhancements

Microsoft QuickBASIC 4.5 applies this equation in two significant ways. First, QuickBASIC provides you with an unusually rich set of development capabilities. QuickBASIC is a major improvement over the more simplistic and limited BASIC language developed at Dartmouth College 20 years ago. QuickBASIC features range from a built-in language editor, to automatic syntax checking, to state-of-the-art debugging support.

Part 1 of this book is about the development environment. It concentrates on QuickBASIC windows, menus, and files, the numerous ways in which the QuickBASIC environment enables you to write, test, debug, and run programs easily and efficiently. Part 1 also helps you install and set up your own QuickBASIC system.

A second way that QuickBASIC applies the above equation is by providing distinct improvements to earlier versions of BASIC. In Part 2 of this book you will explore the greatly enhanced power of Quick-BASIC itself. This part will focus on the programming language elements. As you will see, many of these features are more powerful than earlier, simpler versions of BASIC. In addition, QuickBASIC 4.5 offers tools which were previously unavailable even in competitive computer programming languages.

Parts 1 and 2 explain the tools at your disposal in QuickBASIC. But a desk, pen, and paper alone are insufficient to produce a literary work of art. Similarly, QuickBASIC only provides the computer tools with which you can write powerful computer programs.

Part 3 ensures that you understand the computer equivalent of a creative writing class. You will learn fundamental techniques of structured and modular programming for the QuickBASIC programming environment. These techniques are blended with a rich array of tips and design methods that will ensure that your programs are individually sound. Lastly, you will learn how the most experienced programmers test and debug their programs so you can immediately begin to apply those techniques to your own programming.

Required Hardware and Software

Learning QuickBASIC with this book requires that your computer system consist of an IBM PC or compatible. Version 4.5 of QuickBASIC requires also that your system have at least 384 Kb (kilobytes) of random access memory (RAM). You can run QuickBASIC from any hard disk system, any 3.5-inch disk drive, and any high-capacity (1.2 Mb) 5.25-inch disk drive. (Or, if you have *two* low-capacity (360 Kb) 5.25-inch disk drives and do not have a hard disk built in, you can install and run QuickBASIC from it using five disks.) You can install QuickBASIC onto any hard disk using any disk drive; yes, a system with a 360 Kb drive is sufficient to read the QuickBASIC diskettes to install it onto a hard disk. Chapter 1 shows you how to install QuickBASIC in the various configurations.

Naturally, a hard disk system offers the highest performance capability of all these alternatives. You must have at least 1.8 Mb of disk space available in order to install copies of all the QuickBASIC files. Diskette systems with multiple drives offer the next best choice, since you will be required to do the least amount of disk swapping during the operation of QuickBASIC. Of course, higher capacity diskette drives will allow more of the QuickBASIC files to be stored on each diskette; hence, you will be required to swap disks even less frequently.

Additionally, a Microsoft mouse or compatible is supported, but is optional. It offers convenience, but no features beyond those available through a variety of keystrokes.

The Best Way to Use This Book

This book presents a highly organized introduction to the Microsoft QuickBASIC language. It is appropriate for first-time users of Quick-BASIC and first-time programmers in any language, as well as experienced programmers in other language environments. This book is a wise choice for even BASIC programmers with experience in another version of BASIC.

All first-time users of the QuickBASIC language should read Part 1, "Using The Development Environment," carefully. Chapter 1 presents the fundamental issues and concerns of a first-time user. You will learn about the different installation options for the software and the mouse hardware. Importantly, if you bring any existing BASIC programs with you, this chapter will explain how to convert these earlier BASIC programs (BASICA or GW-BASIC) to the new QuickBASIC format.

Chapter 2 gets all users up and running. You'll learn options for starting QuickBASIC, and you'll come to understand the menu structure of the main QuickBASIC screen. You'll also discover the proper way to use either a mouse or a keyboard, or both, for controlling everything that you do in the QuickBASIC environment.

Chapter 3 introduces QuickBASIC windows. You'll learn about the different types of windows and how to use them effectively. You'll also see the various ways in which QuickBASIC uses them to communicate with you during program development. Chapter 4 rounds out your understanding of the overall development environment by explaining how to manipulate files. You'll learn the various menu commands for accessing and controlling different types of data and program files.

Part 2, "Understanding the Programming Language," explores the range of programming language features seen in QuickBASIC. It is required reading for novice programmers, beginning in Chapter 5 with the basics of syntax, data types, and programming conventions. Experienced programmers need not read some of the material in this part as carefully. Assuming that you understand similar issues from some other language, you only need to look for the differences between Quick-BASIC and the language you already know.

Chapter 6 addresses the concept of flow of control. Every language contains compound structures that allow for decision making and repetition. Experienced programmers need discover in this chapter only how QuickBASIC implements these fundamental programming techniques.

Chapter 7 discusses the different types of data files you can create and manage with QuickBASIC. This chapter also explains how a Quick-BASIC program can connect to these files during both input and output operations. The tutorial section on the nature of data files is a good refresher treatment of the topic even for experienced programmers.

Chapters 8 and 9 present two major topics that vary dramatically in their treatment by different programming languages. You will see how character strings are created, manipulated, and updated using a host of different techniques. All readers can benefit from reading in Chapter 8 how QuickBASIC deals with this fundamental area of computer processing.

Since graphic screens, graphic environments, and graphic software are at the leading edge of development, much of what is in Chapter 9 may be new to all readers. Although graphic presentation is not always necessary, it always provides an opportunity to dress up the appearance of your output. Even more than that, Chapter 9 shows how QuickBASIC contains commands which allow for types of graphic output that you can't even obtain with many other languages.

Part 3, "Designing Useful Application Programs," is still another part that is helpful for all readers. The beginning programmer, the experienced BASIC programmer, and even the programmer most experienced in alternate languages (COBOL, FORTRAN, Pascal, etc.) can all benefit from the information in these chapters.

In Chapter 10 the most important elements of software development coalesce. Understanding these methods for program construction and for module and system development will give you a sturdy foundation on which to construct your QuickBASIC applications. If you are an experienced programmer, you can only benefit from confirmation and reiteration of the techniques that you presumably have been using in your other languages.

Chapter 11 extends the general approaches of Chapter 10 into a host of explicit tips and techniques applicable to writing programs with QuickBASIC. You will learn the specific guidelines and design methods that come from my years of experience with program and system development. And Chapter 12 pulls together this same experience into a focused approach to effective testing, debugging, and running of your QuickBASIC programs. You will even learn how to produce Quick-

BASIC programs that can later run independently of the QuickBASIC development environment.

The three appendices are designed to make your experience with this book and with QuickBASIC a little easier. Appendix A contains a glossary of computer terms used in the DOS and QuickBASIC environments. Appendix B includes a summary and explanation, with detailed language references, of all QuickBASIC statements and functions, even those that are too advanced to be included in the main chapters of the book. And Appendix C shows the complete menus, called Full menus, containing all possible development environment commands. Only the most needed of these commands are described in the other parts of this book. These last two appendices make *Understanding Microsoft QuickBASIC* a more complete text for advanced as well as for beginning and intermediate users. Following the appendices are the answers to all the quiz questions that are included for your benefit at the end of each chapter.

1 | Using the Development Environment

QuickBASIC offers powerful tools for helping you to write new programs or adjust old ones quickly and easily. The four chapters in this part introduce you to QuickBASIC itself and explain how to use these development tools most effectively when you work with your Quick-BASIC programs.

Chapter 1 explains how to install QuickBASIC in your individual system. For those of you who have programs written in other dialects of BASIC, this chapter explains how to convert those programs to run under QuickBASIC. If you are a new user of both DOS and QuickBASIC, this chapter also shows you how to produce backup copies of your original QuickBASIC diskettes.

Chapter 2 shows you how to start QuickBASIC on your system. You will learn how to use the powerful menu structure for creating, accessing, and managing all your files. You will see how to control all system capabilities through your keyboard, and with your mouse if you have one.

Chapter 3 introduces the concept of windows. All features of QuickBASIC are presented visually via screen windows. You will learn here of the many different types of windows used in Quick-

BASIC. You will discover when and why they are used and how to use them effectively yourself.

Chapter 4 will concentrate on explaining files in the Quick-BASIC environment, because files are the fundamental repository of information, whether it be your programs or your data. You will learn about the different kinds of files that are commonly used by QuickBASIC, as well as the various types of files that you can create and manage during your operation of QuickBASIC.

Chapter

1 | Fundamentals of QuickBASIC

QuickBASIC is one of the most advanced computer programming languages. It blends the simplicity seen in the original BASIC (*Beginners All-Purpose Symbolic Instructional Code*) language with a variety of advancements incorporated in newer languages like Pascal, C, and FORTRAN. It remains easy to learn and use, yet it has acquired a host of powerful features that now make it the first choice of many experienced programmers.

You can install QuickBASIC with either the Easy menus or the Full menus option.

QuickBASIC offers you numerous choices. During installation, you can choose between *Easy menus* or *Full menus*. Easy menus present the simplest possible interface for your development environment, and full menus present you with the most complete access to all of QuickBASIC's powerful capabilities. This chapter shows you how to manage all possible choices offered during installation of QuickBASIC. Chapter 2 will explain how to adjust each of these choices once your system is running.

Since Microsoft QuickBASIC is designed to be compatible with both IBM's BASICA and Microsoft's GW-BASIC, this chapter also explains how to convert existing programs in those languages to work properly in this new environment. Throughout this chapter, and for the rest of this book, you should have QuickBASIC available for use. Follow along in this chapter if you are installing QuickBASIC for the first time. And in all later chapters, you should immediately try out what you read in this book. By practicing as you go, you will be sure to reinforce the lessons of the chapters.

9

Back up your original
diskettes using DOS's
diskcopy command.

For those of you with limited experience in DOS, you should precede all programming work by first backing up your original QuickBASIC diskettes. Refer to your DOS user's manual for the necessary procedures. DOS's DISKCOPY command is the correct command to use before continuing on with your QuickBASIC study.

What Is QuickBASIC?

QuickBASIC is a computer programming language. Just as French lets you speak to Frenchmen, and Dutch lets you speak with Dutchmen, so does QuickBASIC facilitate conversations with your computer. And just as French and Dutch have their own vocabulary and grammatical rules, so does QuickBASIC have its own vocabulary (called *reserved words*) and its own rules for constructing proper sentences, or commands.

For a summary of all
QuickBASIC commands,
including detailed
language references, see
Appendix B.

QuickBASIC's vocabulary consists of a fixed set of commands (statements and functions) that direct your computer to perform specific tasks. Appendix B provides capsule summaries of all possible commands. In that Appendix, you will also find the formal syntax, or grammatical construction, which must be followed when you use these individual statements or functions in a QuickBASIC program.

When you speak to someone, you combine your words into sentences and paragraphs. This conveys meaning, and can be used to explain as well as to guide or direct others. Putting multiple commands together in a computer programming language provides the same result. However, it is only a means to direct the computer to perform a series of instructions sequentially. A QuickBASIC program is only a collection of these instructions, logically organized to perform an overall chore.

Just as you might organize your personal writing into sentences, paragraphs, sections, chapters, and parts—much like this book—so can a QuickBASIC program be organized into similarly structured modules. Part 2 of this book will teach you about the individual instructions you can use in your programs, and then Part 3 will ensure that you effectively structure these instructions into well documented, easily understood and updated, and correctly working programs. But first, Part 1 will show you how to use the QuickBASIC environmental tools to make all of your developmental efforts both quick and easy. Begin now by installing the QuickBASIC development environment on your system.

Installing QuickBASIC on Your System

Installing QuickBASIC 4.5 on your system is easy. Installation procedures may vary slightly, depending on whether you plan to run Quick-

BASIC from a hard disk, a 3.5-inch floppy, or a 5.25-inch floppy. This section will take you through the process of preparing your system to run QuickBASIC, regardless of what kind of disks you use.

QuickBASIC is provided for you on five 360 Kb 5.25-inch floppy diskettes. Table 1.1 describes these five diskettes and their contents.

Table 1.1 Contents of QuickBASIC Installation Diskettes

Disk Label	Contents
Setup/Microsoft QB Express	Installation and training files
Program	QuickBASIC development environment and help files
Utilities 1	Compilation and library support routines
Utilities 2	Special purpose system support routines
Microsoft QB Advisor	Help files and example programs for QuickBASIC language topics

A completely automated installation program is included on the SETUP disk. This program will take you through the easy sequence of steps required to install QuickBASIC on your choice of system disks. You only need to respond to a series of specific questions by the SETUP program. SETUP will then properly configure QuickBASIC and copy the necessary files onto your destination disk(s).

Assuming that you have your DOS system up and running, you should first place the disk labelled *Setup/Microsoft QB Express* into your drive A. Then, enter the following command:

A:SETUP

The SETUP program guides you through the entire installation process.

The SETUP program will take control, beginning its interaction with you as seen in Figure 1.1. This is the opening SETUP screen. It is representative of all screens in the complete SETUP sequence. You receive a brief description of what is about to be done, as well as directions concerning your choices. As suggested on this screen, if you have a hard disk you might want to terminate the SETUP process now if you realize that your hard disk does not actually have 1.8 Kb of available space.

Other keys on your keyboard play special roles during this SETUP process. The keys and the jobs they perform are always displayed for you on the individual screens. For example, you have only two choices here; you can *Continue* the SETUP program (press C) or *Exit* the program (press X) and return to DOS. Alternatively, you can press the Up or Down arrow keys to highlight your choice, then press the Enter key to actually make the highlighted selection.

In this example sequence, I installed QuickBASIC onto my hard disk. If you wish to install QuickBASIC onto a set of diskettes, you can

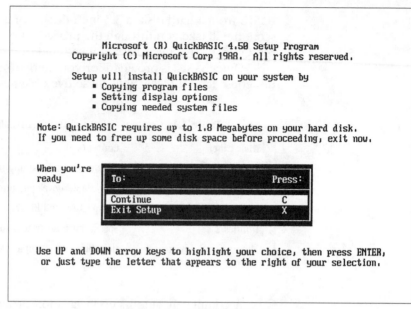

Figure 1.1 Initial SETUP Screen

adjust the default options. You will soon see precisely how to do that. When you perform these steps on your computer, you may notice minor differences between your screens and the figures in this chapter.

The sequence seen in this chapter represents the most common set of installation options; your system and your responses may differ slightly from mine. Concentrate primarily on the automatic flow of questions and answers, and on how they enable you to control the overall environment within which you will be writing your QuickBASIC programs.

You can always rerun the SETUP program from DOS at any time in order to reinstall QuickBASIC with a different configuration. Or, you can go through the same sequence to install QuickBASIC onto a different set of diskettes, or even into a different directory of your hard disk.

SETUP includes a complete QuickBASIC tutorial program, the QB Express.

Continuing with the installation begun above brings you to the SETUP main menu screen, seen in Figure 1.2. You can always return to this menu from any step in the installation process. When this screen is being displayed, you can terminate the setup process without actually installing QuickBASIC; simply press the letter X on your keyboard. Selecting T on this menu brings you to a lighthearted introduction to the QuickBASIC environment. Because it only takes a few minutes, you should spend the time to review this training material. It can complement the instruction that Part 1 of this book provides. Particularly effective would be to review this QB Express disk-based tutorial *after* you install QuickBASIC on your system but before you continue your study of the following chapters.

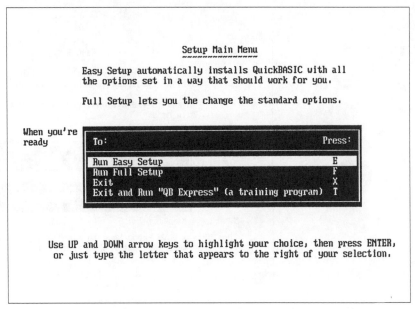

```
                          Setup Main Menu
                          ~~~~~~~~~~~~~~~
            Easy Setup automatically installs QuickBASIC with all
            the options set in a way that should work for you.

            Full Setup lets you the change the standard options.

 When you're
 ready       ┌──────────────────────────────────────────────────────┐
             │ To:                                             Press:│
             ├──────────────────────────────────────────────────────┤
             │ Run Easy Setup                                     E  │
             │ Run Full Setup                                     F  │
             │ Exit                                               X  │
             │ Exit and Run "QB Express" (a training program)     T  │
             └──────────────────────────────────────────────────────┘


            Use UP and DOWN arrow keys to highlight your choice, then press ENTER,
            or just type the letter that appears to the right of your selection.
```

Figure 1.2 SETUP Main Menu Screen

If you continue with the normal installation of QuickBASIC at this point, your primary choice is whether to tell SETUP to run the partial version (called Easy Setup) or the complete version (Full Setup) of QuickBASIC. This decision can be changed later with a selection from the QuickBASIC *Options* menu.

Installing QuickBASIC with Easy Setup

Easy Setup automatically provides defaults for all installation values.

If this is your first time running QuickBASIC, you should select Run Easy Setup, as shown in Figure 1.2. Among other options, this choice means that all QuickBASIC menus will include only the most fundamental commands needed to develop and work with programs. When Easy Setup is installed, more sophisticated menu alternatives are not displayed. Those will be presented on screen only when you select *Full Menus* during Full Setup (see the following section and Chapter 2, which deals with the menu structure in depth). Although this book will concentrate on the fundamental Easy menus, at appropriate points it will describe the more advanced features, which can be accessed at any time from the Full menus.

The Easy Setup menu is shown in Figure 1.3. Your SETUP choices are limited here to viewing the default options (the *Show Options* choice), performing the actual installation (*Perform Easy Installation*), or returning to the SETUP main menu (*Do Not Install—Return to Setup Main Menu*).

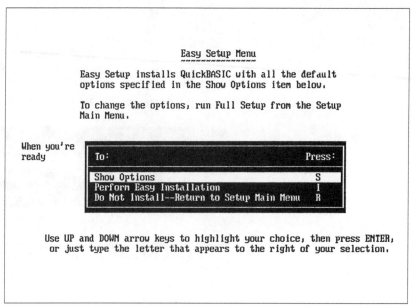

```
                        Easy Setup Menu
                        ~~~~~~~~~~~~~~~
                 Easy Setup installs QuickBASIC with all the default
                 options specified in the Show Options item below.

                 To change the options, run Full Setup from the Setup
                 Main Menu.

When you're
ready        ┌──────────────────────────────────────────────────────┐
             │ To:                                           Press:  │
             │┌────────────────────────────────────────────────────┐│
             ││ Show Options                                    S    ││
             ││ Perform Easy Installation                       I    ││
             ││ Do Not Install--Return to Setup Main Menu       R    ││
             │└────────────────────────────────────────────────────┘│
             └──────────────────────────────────────────────────────┘

             Use UP and DOWN arrow keys to highlight your choice, then press ENTER,
             or just type the letter that appears to the right of your selection.
```

Figure 1.3 Easy Setup Menu

The following will describe the four screens you will see if you choose *Show Options*. It shows the additional screen possibilities presented by the Full Setup menu. For now, during Easy Setup, you can only view, but not affect, these four pages of default options, seen in Figures 1.4 through 1.7. During Full Setup, you can actually adjust the individual settings.

Figure 1.4 shows the default hard disk paths for the four principal types of files installed during the QuickBASIC setup. Diskette users typically will see `A:\` for these entries. Easy Setup places all files into one hard disk directory named QB45 that is located in the root directory (\) of the boot drive (C:).

Installing QuickBASIC to diskettes requires that you select Run Full Setup.

In order to formally install QuickBASIC in any other directory, or onto a set of diskettes, you must select *Run Full Setup* from the SETUP main menu screen shown in Figure 1.2. Hard disk users must specify the desired drive and path for the QuickBASIC files. You can use DOS to install and set up QuickBASIC as well. For diskette-based systems, using DOS is even easier than running the SETUP program. DOS installation is explained later in the section *Installing QuickBASIC onto Diskettes.*

Even though this first screen in the Show Options section suggests that all files are copied to the C:\QB45 directory, that is not completely true. It is only true for the various executable, library, and system (include and help) files. Two subdirectories located in QB45 are also created that contain a wide range of example and utility programs. The .BAS files placed in the EXAMPLES directory are excellent demonstration programs for you to run and study, especially when you read the chapters in Part 2 of this book. The other .BAS files located in the

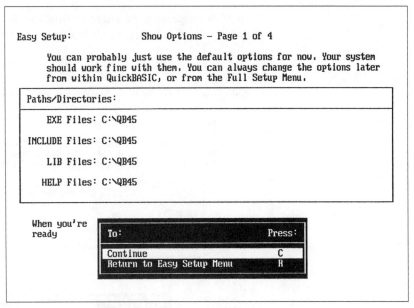

```
Easy Setup:               Show Options - Page 1 of 4

        You can probably just use the default options for now. Your system
        should work fine with them. You can always change the options later
        from within QuickBASIC, or from the Full Setup Menu.

    ┌─────────────────────────────────────────────────────────────┐
    │ Paths/Directories:                                          │
    │                                                             │
    │    EXE Files: C:\QB45                                        │
    │                                                             │
    │ INCLUDE Files: C:\QB45                                      │
    │                                                             │
    │    LIB Files: C:\QB45                                        │
    │                                                             │
    │   HELP Files: C:\QB45                                        │
    │                                                             │
    └─────────────────────────────────────────────────────────────┘

    When you're
    ready        ┌──────────────────────────────────────────┐
                 │ To:                           Press:     │
                 ├──────────────────────────────────────────┤
                 │ Continue                        C        │
                 │ Return to Easy Setup Menu       R        │
                 └──────────────────────────────────────────┘
```

Figure 1.4 Default Path/Directory Settings

QBADV_EX subdirectory are small samples used by the on-line help facility (QB Advisor).

The second page of options (Figure 1.5) contains a list of important QuickBASIC support executables. The SETUP program checks both your hardware configuration and your specified installation paths (from Option page 1) to determine which files should be copied from the installation diskettes. For example, as Figure 1.5 shows, the three files for link, library, and mouse support do not currently exist, but will be copied from the installation diskettes. The file for Hercules support (MSHERC.COM) is not required, and will not be installed.

Earlier QuickBASIC versions can be quickly updated.

If you later decide to reinstall QuickBASIC in the same directory, the middle column would show **Yes** across from the names of the first three files. This indicates that an earlier version of each file was found to exist in the specified installation directory. If a version number is identifiable in the earlier version, it will also be shown to you.

You can use different colors to highlight different portions of your programs.

The succeeding screen of options concerns the color and emphasis shown for different aspects of your program listings. Figure 1.6 shows the assignments given to the three different facets of QuickBASIC programs. When I am viewing QuickBASIC programs in the development environment, all *Normal Text* lines are shown on my color monitor as white letters against a blue background. The default values for your monitor may be different. Since only one statement can be worked on at a time, that *Current Statement* is emphasized by bright (bold) white letters on the same blue background. (Chapter 5, on QuickBASIC statements and commands in general, discusses displays in more detail.) *Breakpoint lines* (lines that allow you to temporarily and automatically pause your program as an aid to testing and debugging) are highlighted differently; in my system, they are shown as white letters on a red background.

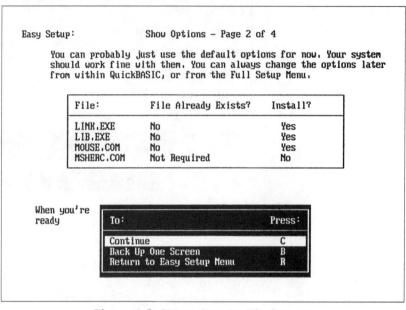

Figure 1.5 System Support File Options

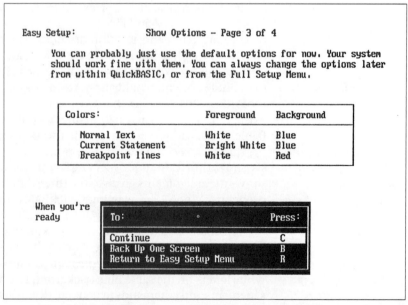

Figure 1.6 Options for Displaying QuickBASIC Program Code

Always keep Syntax Checking turned on to get instant feedback.

The final Options screen is seen in Figure 1.7. Each of these options will be discussed later in the necessary detail, but for now here is a brief look at them. Easy Setup assumes that you would like to see *Scroll Bars* on your screen windows. Using scroll bars, explained in Chapter 3, makes it easy to view and edit large programs. You should always have *Syntax Checking* turned on when you are writing or editing your QuickBASIC programs. This provides instant corrective feedback about each new program line that you type.

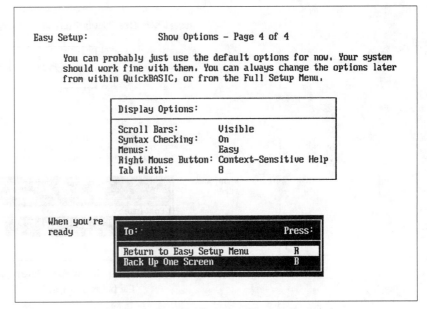

Figure 1.7 Miscellaneous Display Options

As you might expect, the Easy Setup sequence assumes that you will be using the Easy menus. In this case, only the minimum yet essential choices are displayed on the various pulldown menus for you. You can perform all required program development chores with this minimum set of menu choices.

You can set up the right mouse button to provide instant help information.

If you have a mouse, it can be set up to provide context-sensitive help by merely pressing the *Right Mouse Button*. On my Microsoft mouse, pressing the right button produces a window containing help text. The contents of this help window are directly relevant to whatever phrase, expression, or portion of my QuickBASIC screen is being highlighted at that moment.

Finally, when you write your QuickBASIC programs, you can significantly help the readability and apparent structure of those programs by the position of the words on the screen. Setting the *Tab Width* merely sets the number of spaces that are skipped when you press the Tab key. The conventional number of spaces assumed by most programming languages is 8. You can now return to the Easy Setup menu by pressing R, as Figure 1.7 shows.

Easy Installation instructs you which diskettes to place in drive A.

Whether or not you have viewed the default options, you can begin the *Easy Installation* of QuickBASIC using these defaults by selecting *I* on the screen in Figure 1.3. You are then directed to insert each of the five installation diskettes in turn (see Figure 1.8).

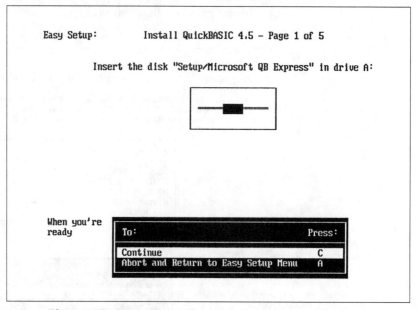

Figure 1.8 Screen Seen When Easy Setup Copies Files from Each Installation Disk

As each file is copied from an installation disk, the SETUP program checks to ensure that the destination directory exists. If it does not, SETUP asks if you would like the directory to be created or not. This gives you an opportunity to return to the main menu and exit the program if you have a hard disk and wish to make some directory adjustments at this time. Or, you can respond positively, and SETUP will create the directory and continue the installation process.

Do not update QuickBASIC system files unless you are absolutely certain that the earlier versions are not somehow and uniquely tied to your hardware configuration, or to other software products on your disk.

Furthermore, if you are running SETUP to install an update of an earlier QuickBASIC installation, SETUP will warn you when it finds existing copies of critical files already in your destination paths. At that point, SETUP will provide you with the new version number and ask you to specifically direct it to replace your current disk version or not. For example, version 4.5 of QuickBASIC contains the most current versions 3.14 of LIB.EXE and version 6.24A of MOUSE.COM.

After all five installation disks have been read, and all required directories have been created, your default QuickBASIC directory structure looks like the one in Figure 1.9. The main and support files for the QuickBASIC environment are all placed in the QB45 directory, and the various .BAS sample programs are placed in the EXAMPLES and ADVR_ EX directories.

After SETUP completes the QuickBASIC installation, you are given one last chance to view the QB Express tutorial. Spend a few minutes doing so if you haven't done so yet. It will complement material presented in the following chapters.

At this point, you also receive a confirmation screen, shown in Figure 1.10, indicating that the installation was completed successfully. This screen appears primarily for information purposes only. It confirms the destination drive/directory where QuickBASIC was installed, and explains that typing **QB** is all that is necessary to now enter the QuickBASIC environment. Naturally, you must either be in the \QB45 directory, or the destination directory must be included on the DOS PATH list. Chapter 2 will take you from this point forward, actually bringing up QuickBASIC itself and exploring the menu structure and the possibilities you can develop from the QuickBASIC environment. But now is a good time to look at Full Setup.

Installing QuickBASIC with Full Setup

Full Setup allows you to adjust all installation options.

Running Full Setup from the screen shown in Figure 1.2 results in the Full Setup menu seen in Figure 1.11. It is similar to the Easy Setup menu seen in Figure 1.3, but you can now individually specify values for all options before actually installing QuickBASIC. If you are a diskette user, you should use the DOS installation described in the following section. However, you still should read this section lightly. It offers new and useful information for you as well. Choosing the first entry on the Full Setup menu allows you to set the complete paths for your QuickBASIC files. Four successive screens are displayed, each of which looks similar to Figure 1.12. In the screen shown in this figure, you can tell SETUP the drive (and directory) to which it should copy the various executable program files. This includes such files as the QuickBASIC environment

You can organize your QuickBASIC files in several diskettes or in several directories.

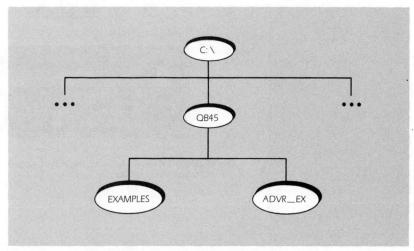

Figure 1.9 Final Hard Disk Directory Structure

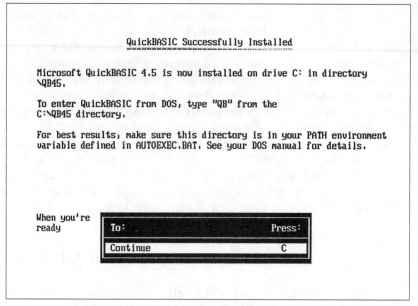

Figure 1.10 Installation Confirmation Screen

manager (QB.EXE), the compiler (BC.EXE), the linker (LINK.EXE), and the library manager (LIB.EXE). The remaining three screens in this sequence enable you similarly to set the path for the QuickBASIC Include, Library, and Help files (see Figure 1.4).

At this point, it's necessary to explain something that is unique to

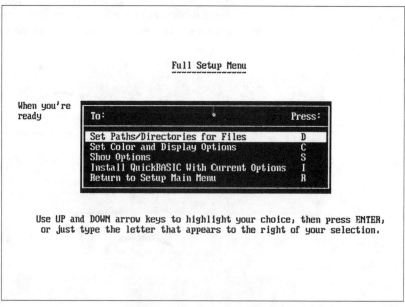

Figure 1.11 Full Setup Menu

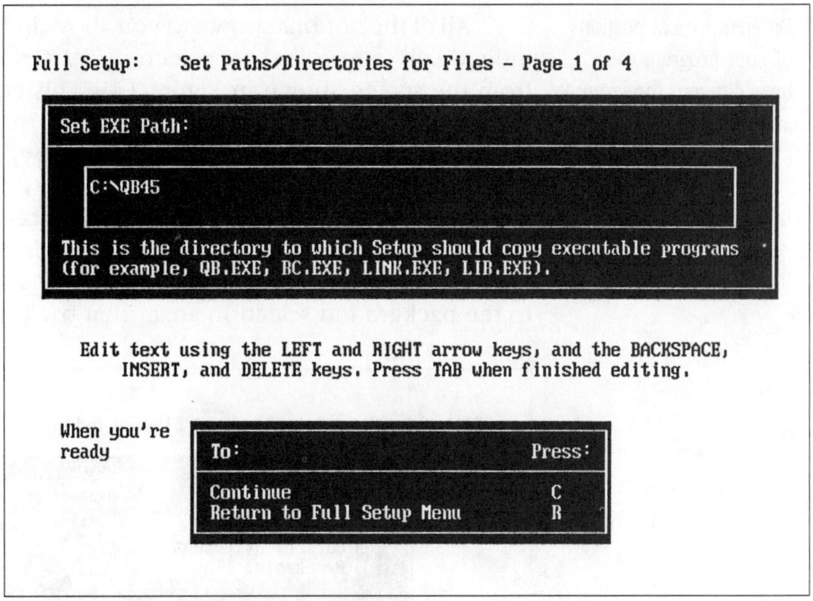

```
Full Setup:    Set Paths/Directories for Files - Page 1 of 4

  ┌─────────────────────────────────────────────────────────────┐
  │ Set EXE Path:                                                 │
  │                                                               │
  │  ┌──────────────────────────────────────────────────────┐   │
  │  │ C:\QB45                                               │   │
  │  └──────────────────────────────────────────────────────┘   │
  │                                                               │
  │ This is the directory to which Setup should copy executable programs
  │ (for example, QB.EXE, BC.EXE, LINK.EXE, LIB.EXE).            │
  └─────────────────────────────────────────────────────────────┘

         Edit text using the LEFT and RIGHT arrow keys, and the BACKSPACE,
           INSERT, and DELETE keys. Press TAB when finished editing.

   When you're
   ready        ┌──────────────────────────────────────────────┐
                │ To:                                  Press:   │
                ├──────────────────────────────────────────────┤
                │ Continue                                C     │
                │ Return to Full Setup Menu               R     │
                └──────────────────────────────────────────────┘
```

Figure 1.12 Setting the Path for QuickBASIC .EXE Files

many of Microsoft's software packages: multiple data entry groups on the same screen. So far, you've seen screens asking for only one type of input—in this case, menu choices. Logically, only one thing can be done on a menu screen; that is, you can select one of the menu entries. You do this either by pressing a particular letter key (like C for Color, I for Install, etc.) or by highlighting an entire choice with your arrow keys and then pressing Enter.

The Tab key cycles the input focus among various data entry and selection windows on your screen.

Figure 1.12 is the first example of a screen that contains multiple logical areas, that is, areas that require different types of input on the same screen. A menu selection area (or window, if you like) appears near the bottom of your screen. And a data entry area, in which you can type the EXE path, appears nearer to the top of your screen. When two or more windows such as these appear on one screen, only one of them can be focused on at a time. The TAB key controls which area receives what is called the *input focus*.

In Figure 1.12, I've already pressed Tab once. This switches the input focus from the menu at the bottom of the screen to the data entry window at the top. At this point, you can use the various keyboard editing keys along with any alphabetic keys to type in a new path for EXE files. When done with any changes, you can return to the menu at the bottom of the screen by pressing Tab once again. Only then can you once again select a menu item and control the overall flow through the SETUP program. In fact, as you'll see throughout your work with QuickBASIC, pressing Tab will cycle you and the input focus among all individual window areas on a screen. You'll explore this in more depth in Chapter 3.

Different logical portions of your program can have different foreground and background colors.

All of the options shown to you above in Figures 1.6 and 1.7 can be individually controlled by selecting *Set Color and Display Options* from the screen shown in Figure 1.11. This choice provides you with two successive screens controlling all of those options. In the first screen shown, Figure 1.13, I've already pressed Tab once. In this screen, there are three logically separate data entry areas, in addition to the menu area at the bottom. Pressing Tab successively moves the input focus from the menu area to the text selection area (*Normal Text, Current Statement*, or *Breakpoint lines*), to the foreground selection area, to the background selection area, then back to the menu area.

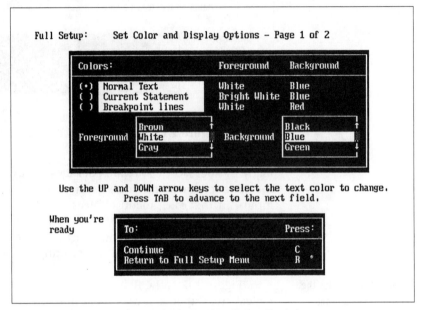

Figure 1.13 Setting Color Options

A parenthetical bullet symbol is shown beside the currently selected data entry field. You must first select the field to modify by using the Tab key. When you have tabbed to this text selection area, you can then press the arrow keys to change your selection from *Normal Text* to *Current Statement* to *Breakpoint lines*. Once you've selected one of these, pressing Tab brings you to the *Foreground* window. Pressing Up or Down arrows then will change the color of the text selection. You will see the results of a new color choice immediately on your screen. For instance, if you had selected *Current Statement*, then pressed Tab and selected brown letters, the formerly white lettered phrase, *Current Statement*, would be redisplayed in brown letters.

Similarly, pressing Tab once more will bring the input focus to the *Background* window. You can now change the background color for the selected type of text lines. Moving back to the menu area and choosing *Continue* will bring you to the screen seen in Figure 1.14. Here is

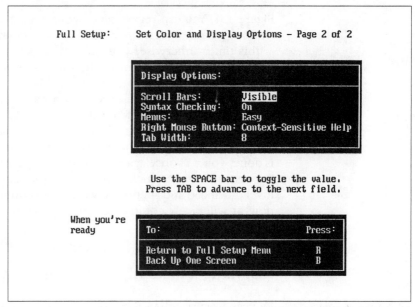

Figure 1.14 Setting Miscellaneous Display Options

where you can adjust a variety of other display options. There are six separate input areas on this screen. The menu area receives the input focus when the screen is first displayed. Pressing Tab successively will highlight the five display option fields: *Scroll Bars, Syntax Checking, Menus, Right Mouse Button*, and *Tab Width*. You must first select the option to change by tabbing to it. Then, for the first four of these, you can press the spacebar on your keyboard to *toggle* between the two possible values. (A *toggle switch* flips back and forth between two possible values.) The last option, *Tab Width*, can be entered as a number of spaces from 0 to 99. Table 1.2 shows the possible choices for each of these five options.

The right mouse button can be set up to provide rapid debugging control of execution flow. See Chapter 12 for more details.

Table 1.2 Possible Display Option Values

Display Option	Possible Values
Scroll Bars	Visible or Hidden
Syntax Checking	On or Off
Menus	Easy or Full
Right Mouse Button	Context-Sensitive Help or Execute To This Line
Tab Width	0 to 99

After adjusting any or all of these option values, you should Tab back to the menu section and return to the Full Setup menu seen in

Figure 1.11. You can review all of your adjustments by selecting *Show Options* (choice *S*). If further changes are necessary, you can make them at this time. Otherwise, you can direct SETUP to install QuickBASIC using the current values of all the various option fields. Select *I* to do this now.

As seen above in the section on using Easy Setup, you will be directed to place each of the five installation disks successively into drive A. SETUP will create directories as necessary and copy files from these disks to the disks/directories you specified. When the installation is done, you will once again be given the opportunity to review the QB Express, an on-line QuickBASIC tutorial program. If you haven't viewed it yet, go ahead and spend a few minutes running this training program now. It will nicely complement the upcoming material in this book.

Installing QuickBASIC onto Diskettes

It is easier to use the DOS COPY or XCOPY command to create a diskette-based QuickBASIC system than to use the SETUP program.

You can use QuickBASIC 4.5 on any system with at least 720 Kb capacity. This means you can use low or high density 3.5-inch disks, as well as low capacity (360 Kb) or high capacity (1.2 Mb) 5.25-inch disks. If you have a two-diskette system with 360 Kb drives, you can make your own five copies from the original five diskettes and run QuickBASIC. To get started, put the program disk in drive A and type **QB**.

In order to run the QuickBASIC development environment with disks containing at least 720 Kb, use DOS commands to copy files from your installation disks to three newly formatted disks, organized as seen in Figure 1.15. Even though you can use the SETUP program to help prepare these disks, that method will result in a cumbersome sequence of disk swaps.

The first diskette of your three should be a DOS system disk, containing the standard DOS system files (two hidden files, plus COMMAND.COM). Except for the files named below, all of the files from your five QuickBASIC distribution disks should be copied to this first and primary disk. This constitutes the primary development environment, exclusive of QuickBASIC programs, libraries, and compilation support.

Your second disk, whether you are using a high capacity 1.2 Mb 5.25-inch system, or any 3.5-inch based system, should contain the following four files: BC.EXE, LINK.EXE, LIB.EXE, and BCOM45.LIB. Your third and last diskette should contain all the initial .BAS files provided on your distribution diskettes, as well as any .QLB library files.

If your system includes two disk drives, you will be able to run QuickBASIC with the fewest interruptions by placing disk 1 in your drive A, and placing disk 3 in drive B. In this way, you will only occasionally be required to swap disk 2 in place of disk 1 in drive A. This second disk contains the four primary files responsible for making Quick libraries and independently executable DOS programs. When

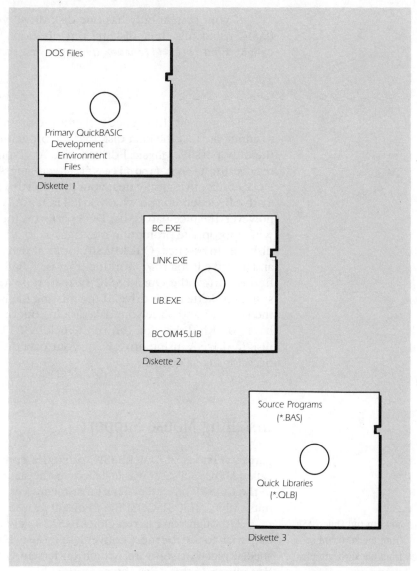

Figure 1.15 Diskette-Based QuickBASIC Development
Environment

you ask QuickBASIC to create one of these types of files, you will receive the following message:

```
Cannot find file <filename>
```

Whenever you receive this type of message, you must put into drive A
the diskette containing the indicated file. Pressing Enter will then allow
QuickBASIC to continue its processing.

If your system only has one disk drive, you can still run Quick-BASIC using this three-diskette organization. When you receive the `Cannot find file <filename>` message, first type

`B:`

Then, insert the needed diskette and press Enter. This directs DOS to anticipate that the next disk that the program needs can be found in the only possible physical drive (drive A). Typing `A:` or `B:` when you receive the `Cannot find file <filename>` message takes advantage of DOS's ability to logically treat your physical drive A as either a drive A or a drive B, depending on what you tell it. It's only mental sleight of hand; however, the nice part is that DOS performs the magic, presenting you with appropriate prompting messages as to when to insert the correct diskette. In essence, QuickBASIC looks at drive A for *its* working files and at drive B for *your* working (that is, *.BAS) files. If the file it can't find is part of the QuickBASIC system, type `A:` and place the proper system diskette in the drive. If the missing file is one of your .BAS files, then type `B:` and place your data disk in your one and only drive. If you have 360 Kb disks, you can run QuickBASIC by putting the program disk in drive A, using drive B for your data disks, and swapping disks occasionally as needed.

Installing Mouse Support

Earlier versions of QuickBASIC offered a conventional mouse driver called MOUSE.SYS. It was installed via the standard DEVICE command in the CONFIG.SYS file. This most recent version of QuickBASIC permits only a MOUSE.COM file to install mouse support.

You can run QuickBASIC from the keyboard or from the keyboard plus the mouse.

Although you can run QuickBASIC solely from the keyboard, you may wish to use the more convenient mouse. If so, you must install this special piece of software, which understands the mouse electronics. You must run this driver by executing

`MOUSE`

from the DOS command prompt. Also, you must either be in the Quick-BASIC directory, or this latest mouse driver file must be available via the DOS PATH.

If you will be using your system primarily to run the QuickBASIC development environment, you can automate the installation of this mouse driver by including a line such as

`C:\QB45\MOUSE`

in your AUTOEXEC.BAT file. Diskette users must update the AUTOEXEC.BAT file on their system disk to include a line like

```
MOUSE
```

The MOUSE.COM file should be included on this boot diskette.

You can reclaim the space taken up by the mouse driver only if you haven't subsequently loaded other memory-resident programs.

This latest mouse driver, Version 6.11, consumes about 10 Kb of memory. If you are doing other work with your system, and wish to recapture this space, you can enter the command:

```
MOUSE OFF
```

at a DOS prompt. This applies only if you haven't followed the mouse driver installation with any other memory-resident program installations!

Running BASICA and GW-BASIC Programs

Programs written in either IBM's BASICA language, or in Microsoft's GW-BASIC language, are stored in a special format called *binary*. The BASIC statements are not readable by you except when you are using one of those languages, and have loaded your program statements. If you use the DOS TYPE command, for instance, you will see only a meaningless collection of symbols and characters.

QuickBASIC, on the other hand, uses two different types of storage formats. One of those two is a proprietary format designed to permit rapid storage and retrieval of your programs. It is the standard method used. The alternative format is the simple and easily readable storage format called ASCII. This is the format you need to use when transferring files from other dialects of BASIC.

Suppose you have a program called EXAMPROG.BAS written and stored in ASCII format. If you enter the DOS command

```
TYPE EXAMPROG.BAS
```

you will see all the instructions exactly as they were typed when you wrote the program. Running a program under QuickBASIC that was written in BASICA or GW-BASIC requires only that you first convert the other system's .BAS file from binary to ASCII format.

You cna easily convert and run BASICA and GW-BASIC programs in QuickBASIC.

Converting between formats requires a two-step sequence in either BASICA or GW-BASIC. First, bring up your other system. For example, you start IBM's BASICA program by entering

```
BASICA
```

at a DOS prompt. Once your other BASIC system is up and running, you must use it to convert an existing binary program into ASCII format (see Figure 1.16).

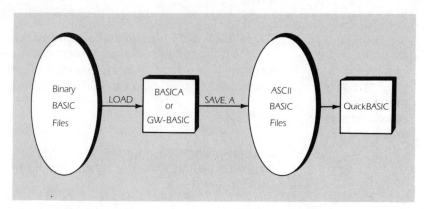

Figure 1.16 Converting Binary .BAS to ASCII .BAS Files

Step One: Load the Binary Version of the BASIC Program

Assume that your binary file is named *EXAMPLE.BAS*. You first load it into your alternative BASIC system with the LOAD command:

```
LOAD "EXAMPLE"
```

Step Two: Store the File in ASCII Format

The standard BASICA and GW-BASIC command used for storing your program files is SAVE. It allows a special parameter (*A*) that overrides the default binary format and directs that the file be stored in ASCII format. Enter

```
SAVE "EXAMPLE",A
```

You only need to exit that other BASIC program with the SYSTEM command, then begin the QuickBASIC environment with the QB command. Loading and working with the program is the subject for Part 2 of this book.

Review

You took your first critical steps with QuickBASIC in this chapter. You learned several important points:

1. What the QuickBASIC development environment is and how it differs from other BASIC programs.

2. What a program is and what can you do with QuickBASIC programs.

3. That DOS's DISKCOPY command should be used to back up your original QuickBASIC installation diskettes.

4. How to install QuickBASIC on your hard disk system.

5. How to organize the QuickBASIC files on multiple diskettes for a floppy-based QuickBASIC setup.

6. How to use the SETUP program to customize directories, colors, and display options in your QuickBASIC development environment.

7. How to install mouse support in your QuickBASIC system.

8. How to prepare existing BASICA and GW-BASIC programs to run in your QuickBASIC environment.

Quiz for Chapter 1

1. Backing up your QuickBASIC diskettes is best done with which of the following DOS commands?

   a. DISKCOMP
   b. DISKCOPY
   c. BACKUP
   d. BASICBAK

2. Microsoft QuickBASIC is designed to be compatible with which of the following specific BASIC implementations?

   a. BASICA
   b. BASICB
   c. BASICC
   d. BASICD

3. BASIC is an acronym for which phrase?

   a. Beginner's Advanced Storage Information Code
   b. Beginning Approach to System Integration Commands
   c. Beginner's All-Purpose Symbolic Instructional Code
   d. Best Approach to Symbolic Information Construction

4. QuickBASIC 4.5 comes to you on how many separate diskettes?

   a. Four
   b. Two
   c. Three
   d. Five

5. What is the name of the QuickBASIC installation program?

   a. INIT
   b. START
   c. SETUP
   d. INSTALL

6. What is QB Express?

   a. A dial-up information service for QuickBASIC
   b. A fast mode for QuickBASIC programs
   c. A training program included with QuickBASIC
   d. An updating service from Microsoft

7. Easy Setup enables you to adjust which system values?

   a. Directories and paths
   b. Colors and display options
   c. Both (a) and (b) above
   d. Neither (a) nor (b) above

8. On which of the following can you not install QuickBASIC 4.5?

   a. 3.5-inch 720 Kb drives
   b. 3.5-inch 1.44 Mb drives
   c. 5.25-inch 180 Kb drives
   d. 5.25-inch 1.2 Mb drives

9. What is the *input focus*?

   a. Another name for the keyboard
   b. Another name for the mouse
   c. The screen section receiving keyboard input
   d. The screen window displaying a menu

10. Which of the following cannot be separately colored or high-lighted during QuickBASIC operation?

    a. The current statement
    b. A program's normal text
    c. A watch statement
    d. A breakpoint line

11. Which key cycles the input focus among all eligible screen areas?

    a. Spacebar
    b. Tab
    c. Enter
    d. PgDn

12. What is the control mechanism called that switches between two and only two different values?

    a. Flipper
    b. TwoFer
    c. Toggle
    d. GoBetween

13. You install mouse support in QuickBASIC 4.5 with which of the following?

    a. MOUSE.SYS in the CONFIG.SYS file
    b. MOUSE.SYS in the AUTOEXEC.BAT file
    c. MOUSE.COM in the CONFIG.SYS file
    d. MOUSE.COM in the AUTOEXEC.BAT file

14. On a diskette-based QuickBASIC system, which message will you receive when you must swap diskettes?

    a. Error: Missing disk
    b. Please swap disk ⟨*diskname*⟩
    c. Cannot find file ⟨*filename*⟩
    d. System paused. Swap disk.

15. GW-BASIC and BASICA binary files can be stored in QuickBASIC ASCII format with which of the following commands?

    a. STORE ⟨*filename*⟩

    b. STORE ⟨*filename*⟩,A

    c. SAVE ⟨*filename*⟩

    d. SAVE ⟨*filename*⟩,A

Chapter

2 | Up and Running

In Chapter 1, you learned the fundamentals of QuickBASIC. You also installed the QuickBASIC development environment on your system. If you had previously written programs in a BASICA or GW-BASIC system, you learned how to convert those programs to work in your new Quick-BASIC system. Now it's time to actually begin working with the Quick-BASIC development environment.

This chapter will explain the screen layout you see when the QuickBASIC development environment first appears. All elements of the screen will be explained, from main menu selections to pulldown menus. Since windows are such a significant aspect of graphics-intensive systems like QuickBASIC, explaining the various types of screen windows forms the basis of the entire next chapter. In this chapter, however, you will first learn how to control the many aspects of your development system, regardless of whether you are using a mouse or your keyboard. Lastly, you will learn how this latest version 4.5 differs from and improves upon earlier versions.

The QuickBASIC Screen Layout

To start the QuickBASIC program, you must enter:

QB

at the DOS prompt. Hard disk users should remember that the current directory must contain the QB program, or that directory must be included in the DOS PATH list. For example, a typical PATH list might include the root directory, the DOS utility directory, and the Quick-BASIC directory:

```
PATH C:\;C:\DOS;C:\QB45
```

This produces the opening QuickBASIC screen seen in Figure 2.1.

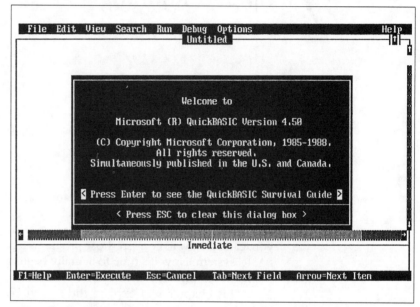

Figure 2.1 Opening QuickBASIC 4.5 Screen

The QB Advisor is an advanced on-screen help mechanism available only in QuickBASIC 4.5. See Chapter 3 for a detailed explanation.

The most visually dominant portion of this display is the welcome message seen in the center window. Pressing Enter at this point will lead you into the QuickBASIC Survival Guide, an advanced on-screen help mechanism. It is sophisticated and extensive, and is one of the major window-oriented features of QuickBASIC 4.5. Seen for the first time in version 4.5, it is one of the significant enhancements to Quick-BASIC. Consequently, Chapter 3 covers it in depth, along with other types of window mechanisms used in QuickBASIC.

Pressing the Esc key removes the bold rectangular welcome window from your screen, leaving the skeletal screen seen in Figure 2.2.

The major portions of this screen remain visible throughout all your development work, but the content of each section changes according to your work. The *reference bar* at the bottom provides dynamically varying information about which keys are active, and what they will do for you when pressed. It often displays a small textual description of the next menu choice that will be activated if you press Enter.

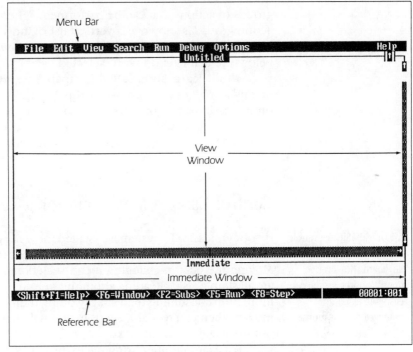

Figure 2.2 Typical QuickBASIC Development
Environment Screen

Just above the reference bar is a small area called the *Immediate window*. You can try out programming ideas here by entering individual lines of BASIC code. They are executed immediately, giving you instant feedback on what they will do in a program. This is covered in more detail in Chapter 3.

Your program appears in the center portion of the screen, called the *View window*.

The largest area of the screen, just above the Immediate window, is called the *View window*. Nearly all of your programming development, editing, and testing takes place here. Naturally, since most development takes place here, it will be the principal focus for most of the work and examples throughout this book. The top line of the View window contains the name of the current program being worked on. When no program is being worked on, as is the case now, this line shows the phrase *Untitled*.

The top line of the QuickBASIC development environment screen is called the *menu bar*. It lists horizontally the eight main menu choices; selecting any one will display another set of subordinate choices. All subordinate choices are grouped according to the type of role they perform. Whenever you are working in the development environment, these eight choices and the secondary commands shown on the subordinate menus provide all the tools you'll need to write, edit, test, and run your programs.

The single words visible in the menu bar represent the major groups of actions that can be performed. When selected, each of these action groups is shown as a vertical list of individual choices. This secondary vertical list, known as a *pulldown menu*, is displayed directly below the main action word selected.

You'll learn about all the capabilities available through these menus at appropriate points in this book. But to effectively explore these possibilities, you must first learn how to use your keyboard and mouse (if your system has one) to make selections and move around the screen. The following section focuses on these fundamental skills.

Control Using a Mouse and/or a Keyboard

All QuickBASIC features are obtainable with your keyboard. However, many features are more easily accessed and managed with a mouse.

If your QuickBASIC system is installed, now is a good time to bring it up on your machine and try the various things presented in this section. Moving the cursor, changing menu selections, and running programs are all simple tasks. Reading about the steps required to do them may be more time consuming than simply doing them. Use your keyboard and mouse when you read this section; you will then be able to instantly try out the examples in the text.

For example, after bringing up the QuickBASIC development environment screen seen in Figure 2.2, you can use a number of special keys on your keyboard. Some key names are displayed in the reference bar at the bottom of your screen. Other key combinations may also be active, but you must learn about them. You'll learn about many of these optionally available keystrokes at appropriate times throughout this book. For now, you must learn that selecting one of the main menu choices requires using the Alt key.

Press the Alt key on your keyboard now. You'll notice that the first letter of each of the main menu choices becomes highlighted, using either color or reverse video, depending on your monitor. You only need to press one of these highlighted letters now to select that menu choice. For example, pressing F opens up the pulldown menu containing the *File* menu choices (see Figure 2.3). This menu contains the four primary commands that relate to files, as well as the *Exit* command to return to DOS from the QuickBASIC environment.

On systems with a properly installed mouse, a moveable solid rectangle represents the mouse pointer on screen.

If your system has a mouse installed, you can control just about everything with it. Figure 2.3 shows a small, solid rectangle in the middle of the View window. This symbol represents the *mouse pointer*. It moves around the screen as you move your mouse on its table surface. If you want to select something, like a menu choice, with your mouse rather than with your keyboard, you first move the mouse pointer to the desired item, then press button one (the left button) on the mouse. This is called *clicking* your mouse. Try selecting the File menu with your mouse now.

Once you've selected a main menu choice, the pulldown menu

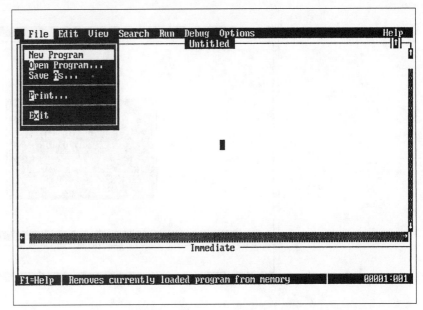

Figure 2.3 File Pulldown Menu

appears. If you are using keyboard controls, the Up and Down direction arrows are active. You can choose a command from the pulldown menu by first highlighting it with an arrow key, then pressing Enter. Or, as you did with the main menu selections, you can simply press the single keyboard letter that is highlighted or shown in a different color. Alternatively, mouse users can simply move the mouse pointer to the desired command choice, and click button one. Go to the File menu now, and select the *Print* command.

The pulldown menu disappears and the *Print* command takes effect. You see the screen appearing in Figure 2.4. This represents a special kind of window, called a *dialog box*, which requires further input from you. Chapter 3 explains dialog boxes in more depth.

You can ask QuickBASIC to *Print* any portion or all of your programming work.

Typically, you would invoke the *Print* command only when you are actually working with program text. As you can see, you could ask QuickBASIC to print selected portions of your program code, or just the active window's contents, or the current module being worked on. These choices will be valuable during the program development you'll be doing in Part 2 of this book.

For now, you need to know only how to backstep during menu selection processing. Pressing the Esc key now will cancel the *Print* request. In fact, when you pull down any menu erroneously, you can always cancel that request by pressing the Esc key. Mouse users can move the mouse pointer to ⟨*Cancel*⟩ and click button one to achieve the same effect. When commands have been selected, no *Cancel* choice is displayed, so mouse users can simply move the mouse pointer outside the menu to a blank area of the screen, and press button one. Other

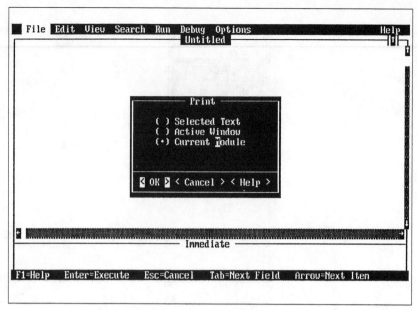

Figure 2.4 The *Print* File Dialog Box

possible key and mouse options are shown on this screen, but will be discussed in more depth in Chapter 3.

The QuickBASIC Menu Structure

Now that you've seen how to open up all of the main menus, and how to back out of any choice, spend a few moments looking through these menus now. Remember the discussion in Chapter 1 about Full menus versus Easy menus. What you are seeing here is the Easy File menu. A Full menu shows additional and more sophisticated command possibilities. Appendix C shows what each Full menu looks like and describes each of its possibilities briefly; the principal ones included on the Easy menus are dealt with throughout this book.

Working with Complete Files

The File menu is used to perform common actions on entire files.

This section provides brief explanations of the various Easy menu possibilities. More extensive details appear when appropriate in this book. Open up the File menu now. From this menu, you can *Exit* from the QuickBASIC environment, or you can perform the four most common tasks designed to act on an entire file. You can clear any existing program and begin to write new programs (that is, select *New Program*). You can list file names in any directory on any disk drive, then view and edit any existing program (that is, select *Open Program*). When done working with a file, you can save it to disk (select *Save As*). And, lastly, you can print your entire program or any part of it (select *Print*).

Moving Text Around in Your Programs

The *Edit* menu can be seen in Figure 2.5. There are three choices presented here: *Cut, Copy,* and *Paste.* These three actions are performed with text only. Hence, you only need this pulldown menu when you are entering new program lines, or modifying old lines. The *Cut* option enables you to temporarily remove specified sections of your program, while *Paste* enables you to insert the text that was cut at a new location in your program.

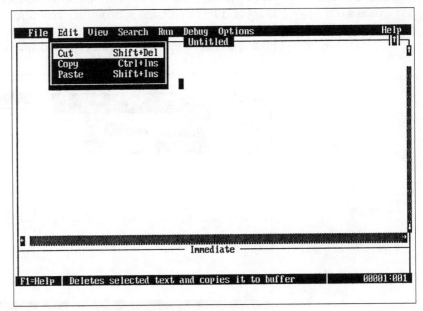

Figure 2.5 Edit Pulldown Menu

The Edit and Search menus contain text manipulation commands only. See Chapter 5 for further details.

This Cut and Paste tandem parallels the concept of a file Move in DOS 4, while the remaining command, *Copy,* parallels the command of the same name in DOS 4. These QuickBASIC commands do not move and copy files, but allow you to easily move and copy blocks of text in the program you are working on. Chapter 5 discusses techniques surrounding these text manipulations in more depth.

Shortcut keys save time by doing two steps at once: pulling down a menu and choosing an individual action.

One additional thing to point out here is the inclusion of *shortcut keys.* Listed on this pulldown menu, as well as on others for which shortcut keys exist, you see the immediate keyboard equivalents of the pulldown menu functions. After selecting text in your program to be copied, for instance, you can pull down the Edit menu, then select *Copy* to manage the operation. Alternatively, you can select the program text, then simply press the Ctrl-Ins key combination. Pressing this shortcut keystroke, then, takes the place of pulling down a menu and choosing the desired operation.

Viewing Your Modules, Routines, and Code Groups

The View menu controls viewing access to your application system's modules, routines, and code groups. See Chapter 10 for further explanation of these program elements.

The third main menu choice, *View*, appears in Figure 2.6 and also shows three choices: *SUBs*, *Output Screen*, and *Included Lines*. You use this menu during program development to see different parts of a group of program modules. The *SUBs* choice relates to information presented in Chapter 10, which covers modular design and shows how to structure your code to successfully segment and organize your development work. Some code modules are memory resident, such as a main program and its referenced subroutines and functions. You use the *SUBs* choice to select among the currently loaded subordinate, yet still complete, program files. Your choice is then displayed in the View window.

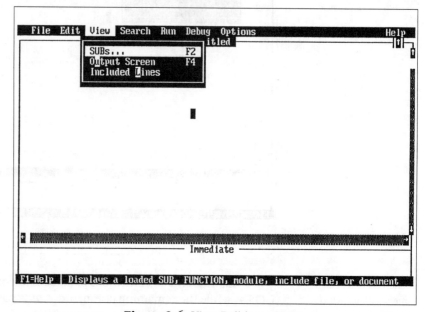

Figure 2.6 View Pulldown Menu

Switch quickly and efficiently between program development and output by pressing the F4 key.

You can always execute a program through the Run menu (see below). The *Output Screen* choice on this View menu lets you visually switch between the QuickBASIC development environment screen, and the program's output screen. Pressing the shortcut key, F4, instead of pulling down this menu and choosing *Output Screen*, is considerably more efficient.

Chapter 10 also explains how, when, and why to use the $IN-CLUDE programming command. When you take advantage of this programming technique, you can use the toggle command, *Included Lines*, to view (only!) the contents of referenced Include files.

Searching for and Replacing Text Strings

Prior to doing any text manipulation at all, you must first find the correct place in your program that contains the desired text. Two searching mechanisms are included in QuickBASIC's Search menu. This menu, seen in Figure 2.7, contains the two most common operations used to locate and modify existing program text. *Find* locates any specified string of characters, while *Change* performs automatic replacing of one set of characters with another.

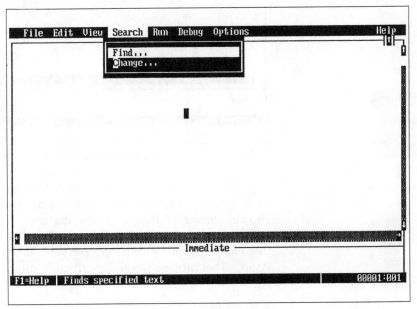

Figure 2.7 Search Pulldown Menu

Running Your QuickBASIC Programs

The Run menu contains options for controlling program execution. See Chapter 12 for more advanced uses of this menu.

The Run menu, appearing in Figure 2.8, contains the necessary commands to execute your programs. Anytime you wish to try out your program, you can press the shortcut key Shift-F5. This is equivalent to selecting the first choice on the Run menu, *Start*. This runs the currently loaded main program. The second choice, *Restart*, actually only prepares to rerun your program. Any variables used by your program are set to zero, any string expressions are set to null (zero-length) strings, and the next instruction to be executed is reset to your program's first statement. The third choice, *Continue*, is used both from this point and during debugging to continue execution from the point it was last paused. A detailed differentiation among these alternative execution methods can be found in Chapter 12.

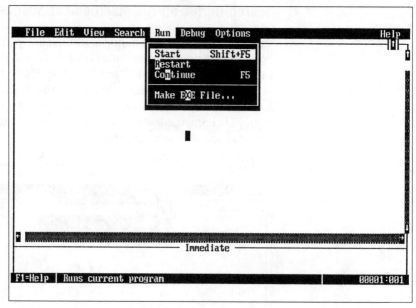

Figure 2.8 Run Pulldown Menu

Lastly, you can produce a stand-alone DOS-executable (.EXE) file from your QuickBASIC code by selecting the last pulldown menu choice, *Make EXE File*. This is an extremely powerful, and extremely easy, way to convert your developed QuickBASIC code into a program that can be used by other people who know nothing about Quick-BASIC. This process is also described in more depth in Chapter 12.

Debugging Your QuickBASIC Programs

Debugging is, in my opinion, the single most important factor in rapid and effective computer programming. Chapter 12 concentrates on the best way to use the various QuickBASIC debugging tools. There are more tools than the Easy Debug menu shows.

The Debug menu seen in Figure 2.9 contains five choices for identifying and correcting errors in your program logic. Choice one, *Add Watch*, asks QuickBASIC to display a window containing selected variables and expressions while your program runs. Choice two, *Instant Watch*, is one of the features unique to QuickBASIC 4.5. Using this feature, you can instantly display the value of any desired variable, or the true/false value of any expression. This is a tremendous convenience for program debuggers. When a debugging watch mechanism is no longer needed, you can remove its entry from the specially displayed window by using choice three, *Delete Watch*.

A breakpoint is a specified location in your program where you would like execution to pause, as described earlier. The *Toggle Break-*

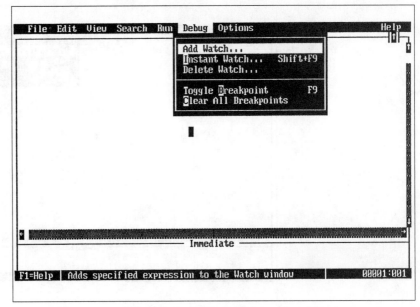

Figure 2.9 Debug Pulldown Menu

point choice turns on or off a QuickBASIC breakpoint. It affects whichever line your cursor happens to be on when you make this choice on the Debug menu. When later viewing your program text, a line at which a breakpoint has been set is displayed in reverse video or in a specified color combination. (Recall that this is one of the installation parameter settings.) The *Clear All Breakpoints* option is used only after you no longer need any of the currently defined breakpoints.

Customizing Your QuickBASIC Development Environment

The Options menu tailors the QuickBASIC development environment to your special and advanced needs.

You can turn on Full menus at any time through the Options menu. Refer to Appendix C for explanations of each choice available through the Full menus.

The main Options menu contains three primary choices. They control a miscellaneous set of special QuickBASIC features. The *Display* choice provides you with on-line control of the various color and display settings originally initialized during installation. Figure 2.10 shows the three choices on the Easy Options menu.

Selecting the first choice on this pulldown menu, *Display*, brings up the screen seen in Figure 2.11. This screen is another example of a dialog box. In this case, you can change any of the values for the displayed variables. Remember to use the Tab key to switch between the various logical portions of this dialog box. Switching with the Tab key is similar to the procedure used to adjust grouped values during the original installation.

The Tab key is used throughout QuickBASIC when multiple logical display areas are presented to you. First, you tab to the section you want to influence. Mouse users need only move the mouse pointer to

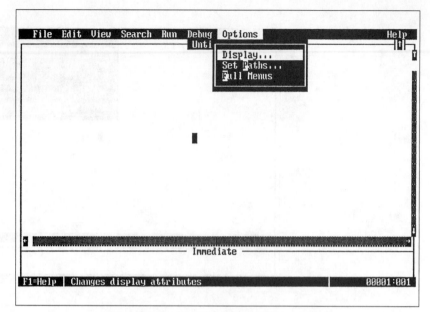

Figure 2.10 The Options Pulldown Menu

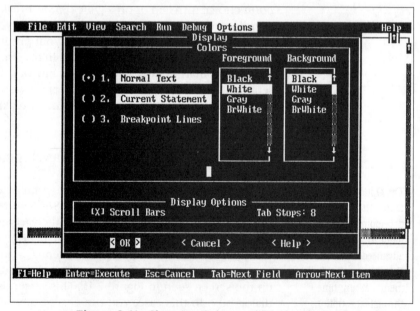

Figure 2.11 Changing Colors and Display Options

the desired area and click button one. Then, you can take one of several steps: on this screen, for example, you might press Enter to make a choice, as in the *OK, Cancel,* and *Help* entries at the bottom of the dialog box. Or, you might press the Spacebar to toggle a setting, as in the *Scroll Bars* entry. Or you might enter a completely new value, as can be done for the *Tab Stops* entry. Lastly, you might use the arrow keys and Enter to select a new choice from among many, as in the *Text, Foreground,* and *Background* listings in the *Colors* area.

For hard disk users, the second primary option on the Options pulldown menu that you can adjust during on-line operations is the file paths. Introduced for the first time in Version 4.5, the values for the default file search paths are initialized during installation (see Chapter 1). QuickBASIC will look for its four needed types of files according to the values you set during installation, or the values you reset through the *Set Paths* choice on the Options menu.

Selecting this menu choice produces the display shown in Figure 2.12. You can tab to one of the fields for the four file types, and type in a new directory path. When required, QuickBASIC will hunt later through your new directory entries for any referenced executable, include, library, or help file. Naturally, as with other screens like this, you can select ⟨*OK*⟩ when you are done entering search paths, or ⟨*Cancel*⟩ to back out without making any changes, or ⟨*Help*⟩ to access the Help text associated with this *Set Paths* process.

Version 4.5 introduces separate search paths for different QuickBASIC files for hard disk systems. You can use the DOS directory structure more effectively to organize your QuickBASIC files by setting default paths through the Options menu.

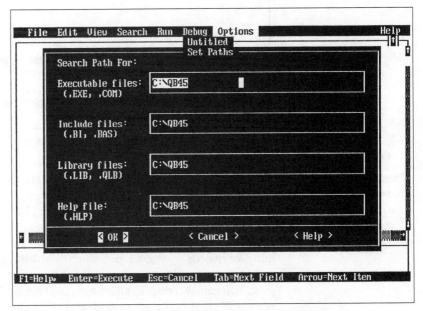

Figure 2.12 Adjusting Default File Search Paths

The third choice is a simple toggle switch. Selecting it switches between Easy and Full menus. Although you will be using Easy menus through most of this book, this option allows you to turn on the advanced Full menu capability at any time. If you want to explore the more sophisticated capabilities available through Full menus, simply turn this toggle switch on and refer to the explanations in Appendix C.

Obtaining Context-Sensitive On-Line Help

In fact, help is never more than a keystroke away in QuickBASIC. The results of the last choice on the Options main menu, *Help*, are seen in Figure 2.13. This on-line help has been dramatically enhanced in Quick-BASIC 4.5 and is explained in depth in Chapter 3. For the moment, let's take a brief look at the four choices seen on the Help menu.

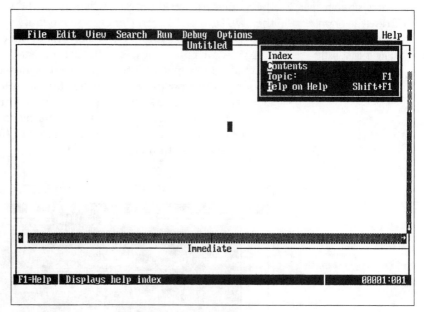

Figure 2.13 Help Pulldown Menu

Press F1 to obtain context sensitive help about the currently highlighted screen item.

The QuickBASIC Help feature is *context-sensitive*. This means that you only need to select *Topic* from this menu to obtain the help text associated with whatever topic happens to be currently highlighted on your QuickBASIC development screen. Help text is available here about a host of varied topics, such as commands, menu items, and programming keywords. However, pressing the shortcut key F1 is much easier, so I recommend you use it.

You can also display an alphabetical list of all possible QuickBASIC keywords (that is, select *Index*), and then choose any one of them to receive the relevant help screen. Additionally, for those of you who like to browse around this type of information garden, the *Contents* choice presents a visual tree outline of all the on-screen topical areas. You can use your keyboard or mouse to find a topic of interest. And, lastly, you can even obtain a help screen about the Help facility itself, including a listing of the available keyboard shortcuts. Pressing Shift-F1 will produce this *Help on Help* display without your even having to pull down this menu.

What's Available in the Different Versions of QuickBASIC?

QuickBASIC 4.5 adds significant new features and improves old ones.

Table 2.1 summarizes the evolution and availability of many features of QuickBASIC. The table deals only with special features that are not found in the fundamental product, and that therefore are not available in all versions. It is easy to see from the table the first QuickBASIC Version that included the listed feature.

Table 2.1 Evolution and Availability of Special
QuickBASIC Features

Special Feature	Version(s) in which Available		
	3.0	4.0	4.5
Support for IEEE data format	X	X	X
Support for math coprocessor	X	X	X
Compatibility with ProKey, SideKick, and SuperKey	X	X	X
Insert/overtype modes	X	X	X
Compilation error listings	X	X	X
Assembly language compilation listings	X	X	X
User-defined types		X	X
On-line help		X	X
32-bit integers		X	X
Fixed-length strings		X	X
Automatic syntax checking		X	X
Binary file I/O		X	X
User-defined functions		X	X
Support for CodeView		X	X
Compatibility with other languages		X	X
Multiple modules in memory		X	X
WordStar keyboard interface		X	X
Recursion		X	X
On-line QB Advisor (extensive help text)			X
Instant Variable/Expression Watch			X
Setting default search paths			X
Assignable right mouse button			X

As you can see, Version 3.0 first included support for IEEE data format and math coprocessor functions. This represents an expansion of the possible application areas for QuickBASIC to a broader range of engineering users. In an effort to reduce problems with certain popular memory-resident programs, this version also ensured that ProKey, Side-kick, and SuperKey users would no longer experience any compatibility difficulties when running QuickBASIC.

The standard keyboard convenience of insert/overtype modes was also included in Version 3.0. Most common PC programs assume this common usage of the Ins key. Lastly, two improvements to the program compilation phase were introduced. Error listings and separate assembly language listings became available in this version as well.

Version 4.0, available since the fall of 1987, was another leap forward for QuickBASIC. In the area of improved development features, Version 4.0 first introduced on-line help, a WordStar keyboard interface, and support for CodeView, the extremely popular debugging program from Microsoft. In addition, multiple modules could be maintained simultaneously in memory, and program statements could be checked automatically for correct syntax at entry time.

In the area of program code itself, Version 4.0 introduced compatibility with other languages, as well as the sophisticated ability to support recursion. Other miscellaneous features were introduced at the same time, including user-defined types, user-defined functions, binary file I/O, fixed-length strings, and long integers.

As you learned in this chapter, Version 4.5 now includes a state-of-the-art help facility called the QB Advisor, a hypertext-based help text feature described in depth in Chapter 3. Also introduced in this current version is the special new debugging tool called Instant Watch for either individual variables or expressions.

Version 4.5 also introduced assignable roles to the right mouse button.

As testimony to the value of good file and directory organization on hard disks, QuickBASIC 4.5 also enables you to set up default search paths for the four primary types of files used by the QuickBASIC system. And, lastly, Version 4.5 allows you to assign different roles to the right mouse button. The standard role is to provide rapid context-sensitive help, but during active debugging work you can reassign it to a special execution role. Chapter 12 explains this possibility in greater depth.

Review

You brought up your QuickBASIC 4.5 development environment in this chapter. You learned the following points about this software environment:

1. A reference bar is always visible on the bottom line of your Quick-BASIC screen. It shows active keys and describes the action that will occur when the Enter key is pressed.

2. A menu bar is always visible at the top line of the screen. It displays the names of the main groups of actions possible with the Quick-BASIC development environment.

3. You can immediately execute individual QuickBASIC program statements in the Immediate window, or you can group many statements into a program using the View window.

4. Standard keystrokes for list selection are the arrow keys and the Enter key. Alternatively, a mouse can be used to make menu selections, by clicking button one (the left button).

5. The Tab key cycles among multiple fields or logical screen areas. This cycling is similar to the mechanism seen earlier during Quick-BASIC installation.

6. There are many shortcut keys that can replace the double action of pulling down a menu and selecting an action. F1, for instance, always calls for the display of a context-sensitive text screen. F4 always switches your monitor between the QuickBASIC development environment screen and the standard program execution output screen.

7. Each main menu choice can be selected to display a pulldown menu of secondary choices. These various subordinate menu choices are grouped according to functional areas that encompass file-oriented actions, editing and text searching methods, module viewing and execution, display and system options, and help screens.

8. QuickBASIC 4.5 is the most recent of a series of QuickBASIC releases. It includes significant enhancements in the various areas of sophisticated help, selectable mouse button functionality, and instant variable/expression watches for debugging. Also, DOS search paths can be set on-line for better file organization.

9. Easy menus can be expanded to Full menus at any time with a simple toggle switch on the Options menu. This makes available a host of advanced features not visible on the more fundamental Easy menus. Appendix C provides details on these additional capabilities.

Quiz for Chapter 2

1. You can begin the QuickBASIC development environment from the DOS prompt with what command?

   a. QBASIC
   b. BASICA
   c. QB
   d. QB45

2. The reference bar displays what information?

   a. Help text
   b. Active keys
   c. Drink recipes
   d. Spell checks

3. You do your principal programming in what area?

   a. Immediate window
   b. View window
   c. Dialog boxes
   d. Watch window

4. You can enter and instantly execute trial QuickBASIC commands in what portion of the environment?

   a. Immediate window
   b. View window
   c. Dialog boxes
   d. Watch window

5. Where do major groupings of QuickBASIC environment commands appear as one-word entries?

   a. Reference bar
   b. Menu bar
   c. Choice list
   d. Pulldown menu

6. You can open up a main menu with what keystroke?

   a. Alt-letter
   b. Ctrl-letter
   c. Shift-letter
   d. Tab-letter

7. You can make menu selections with a mouse and what technique?

   a. Clicking button two
   b. Double clicking button one
   c. Clicking button one
   d. Double clicking button two

8. With which key can you cycle among screen fields or logical data areas?

   a. Enter key
   b. Tab key
   c. Ins key
   d. Alt key

9. You cancel a request by pressing what key?

   a. Del
   b. Alt-letter
   c. Tab
   d. Esc

10. Which menu performs common actions on entire files?

    a. Edit
    b. View
    c. Debug
    d. File

11. Which two menus contain the primary text manipulation commands?

    a. Debug and File
    b. Edit and Search
    c. View and Run
    d. Options and Help

12. Customizing your QuickBASIC environment is done with the commands on which menu?

    a. Run
    b. Edit
    c. File
    d. Options

13. Which of the following is not uniquely new to Version 4.5 of the QuickBASIC development environment?

    a. QB Advisor help mechanism
    b. Instant debugging watches
    c. Assignable right mouse button
    d. Math coprocessor support

14. What is a keystroke called that takes the place of pulling down a menu and making a choice?

    a. Toggle key
    b. Function key
    c. Shortcut key
    d. Assigned key

15. Full menus include all possible QuickBASIC features and can be activated by a choice from which main menu group?

    a. File menu
    b. Options menu
    c. View menu
    d. Search menu

3 | Introducing QuickBASIC Windows

In the previous two chapters, you took a first look at QuickBASIC's fundamental features. You saw an environment rich in helpful development tools. And you learned how to traverse various menus to initiate QuickBASIC environment commands. You also began to develop a sense of the graphic appearance and control mechanisms presented by the QuickBASIC interface.

Windows are the basis of the newest graphic user interfaces.

This chapter takes you a step further toward understanding the graphic face of QuickBASIC. You'll explore windows in greater depth, concentrating on the various kinds of windows used in QuickBASIC. I'll explain and demonstrate how to expand, contract, and use the contents of the View window, the Immediate window, the Watch window, and the Help window. You'll also revisit the information presented in various special purpose windows called dialog boxes.

What Makes up a QuickBASIC Window?

There will be times during your use of QuickBASIC when questions will arise. You may want additional information about menus or commands, or you may need further explanation about a programming construction. Since *Help* is readily available, you should know as much as possible about obtaining this textual help. But first, you must understand how to easily use and manage the fundamental mechanism for obtaining information in QuickBASIC: the window.

Your first contact with the QB Advisor was an invitation on the opening QuickBASIC screen (see Figure 2.1) to press Enter to see the QB Advisor Survival Guide. Bring up QuickBASIC again at this time and press Enter when invited to do so. You will receive the screen seen in Figure 3.1.

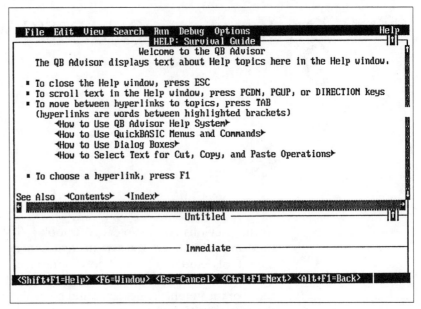

Figure 3.1 First QB Advisor screen

Using Scroll Bars to Control Window Displays

Scroll bars appear whenever there is more data to display than fits in a window.

The text information being displayed is entitled *HELP: Survival Guide*. It is being shown in a Help window that is squeezed in between the menu bar and the untitled View window. This new window demonstrates a visual technique called *scrolling*, which uses *scroll bars*. Scrolling is a fairly common aspect of screen windows whenever the information to be displayed exceeds the size of the window. As Figure 3.1 shows, a vertical scroll bar appears on the right side of a window, while a horizontal bar appears on the bottom line of a window.

In order to see information not currently being shown in the window, you can scroll through the text. Keyboard users can simply press the up and down arrow keys to move the cursor one character at a time. As is common, you can also use the PgUp and PgDn keys to view additional information, one screenful at a time, in the vertical direction. The right and left arrow keys, as well as the Home (to beginning of line) and

End (to end of line) keys provide similar motion control in the horizontal direction.

You can combine the Ctrl key with the right and left arrow keys, as well as with the Home and End keys, to produce greater incremental movement of the cursor. When writing programs, as with writing text with a word processor, you often want to move the cursor by whole words. Ctrl-Right Arrow moves the cursor to the first letter of the next word. Ctrl-Left Arrow moves the cursor to the first letter of the preceding word. These movements work the same way even if the next or preceding word is on a separate line.

Ctrl-Right Arrow moves the cursor to the first letter of the next word.

The greatest amount of movement is possible with the Home or End keys. Pressing Ctrl-Home moves the cursor to the first letter on the first line of the current window; this is commonly the beginning of your program. Pressing Ctrl-End moves the cursor to the very end of your current window; this is usually the end of your program. Furthermore, these cursor movement controls apply to any windows, whether they are programming text, help text, or otherwise.

Mouse users have more and better control than keyboard users do over the display of additional information. You can position the mouse pointer over either one of the arrow symbols at the end of either scroll bar, then press button one. This has almost the same effect as pressing the similar arrow key on your keyboard. In fact, when you use your mouse to select the up or down arrows on a scroll bar, all the lines in the window scroll along with the cursor. Pressing an Up or Down arrow key only moves the cursor, except when the cursor reaches the bottom or top line in the window. Try this now if you have a mouse.

The left and right arrows also produce a somewhat inconsistent response. While a right or left arrow key moves the cursor in the indicated direction, selecting the visual arrow symbol at the left or right of the horizontal scroll bar actually causes the entire body of text in the window to scroll left or right, while the cursor remains fixed in one spot in the screen window. Windows in QuickBASIC can actually contain up to 256 characters on each horizontal line, with no limit on the number of lines. However, for the sake of readability, you will rarely find help or program text lines that exceed the standard 80-character lines found on a typical display monitor.

Mouse users gain more control over scrolling with slider boxes.

On a system with an installed mouse, an additional visual element appears. The *slider box* is a white rectangle appearing inside a scroll bar. You can see a slider box at the left side of the horizontal scroll bar, and in the center of the vertical scroll bar in Figure 3.1. The slider box moves proportionately inside the scroll bar, providing you with visual feedback as to how far along in the entire information contents you've progressed with your cursor movements.

You can manipulate the slider box itself by positioning the mouse on it, pressing button one, then moving the mouse without releasing the button. When you finally release button one, the window contents are redisplayed beginning at a new, proportionately located position in the text.

All help screens operate this same way, offering a consistent interface between both keyboard and mouse operations. As you'll see in Chapter 4, working with your program files is made easier by using similar scroll bar controls.

Clarifying Your Requests with Dialog Boxes

Explore the demo programs included in QuickBASIC 4.5 to learn new programming techniques.

Your QuickBASIC system comes with a variety of example programs. Use your File menu now to select the *Open Program* choice, bringing up a screen similar to Figure 3.2. DEMO3.BAS is one of the many example programs included with your QuickBASIC 4.5 system. Keyboard users can open the DEMO3 program by first highlighting it with the use of the cursor keys, then pressing Enter. Remember to tab to the appropriate field first. The Tab and Shift-Tab keys jump forward and backward respectively between successive entry and selection areas of your screen. If your system has been customized, you should first tab to the *Dirs/Drives* section to select the drive or directory where the example programs were installed on your system. Once you do this, all of the *.BAS files that are located on the selected drive and in the selected directory will be displayed in the *Files* section of the dialog box.

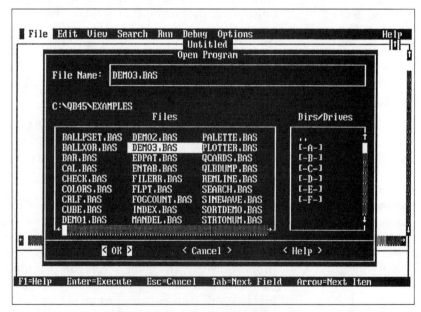

Figure 3.2 Opening a BASIC Program

Double clicking a mouse button (rapidly pressing

Mouse users can go directly to any section of this dialog box by moving the mouse pointer and pressing button one. This highlights a

it twice in succession) selects an entry from a list. If this is not successful, simply double press the button again, but more quickly.

choice, but does not actually select it, as was done with menu items. To select a directory or drive from the list of possibilities, a mouse user must *double click* button one. This means to press the button twice in rapid succession.

This overall *Open Program* operation results in a QuickBASIC dialog box. A dialog box is a special type of window, designed to solicit further information from you in order to continue with the process of opening a file. This procedure is used to load the desired program into memory so it can be edited and run.

Dialog boxes contain several standard QuickBASIC mechanisms that you will see frequently during your program development. One of them is a *text box*. The thin wide horizontal area (Figure 3.2), labelled *File Name* and containing the initial value `*.bas`, is an example of a text box. A text box appears when QuickBASIC expects you to type in some text from your keyboard, such as the name of a desired file. If you highlight a file name from the *Files* area of the screen, QuickBASIC does the typing for you by entering the highlighted name in the text box.

In this example, you really don't even need to select a file name or drive/directory entry first. You could have just typed in the complete path name of the BASIC program you wanted to load, and then pressed Enter. However, personally speaking, the less typing I do, the fewer errors I can make, so I almost always display file names first, then select from the choices displayed.

A *list box* is a dialog box that permits one choice from a list of items.

As far as choices go, QuickBASIC often presents you with a group of items from which you must choose one. The *Files* and *Dirs/Drives* portions of the dialog box are both called *list boxes* (another standard QuickBASIC mechanism) because they display a list of choices, allowing you to choose one item from each list. A mouse offers the fastest means of selection, enabling you to directly specify the desired item in the list (by double clicking on the item).

Pressing the arrow keys is the next most obvious method, once you've tabbed into the list box. However, a less obvious but faster method of selection is to press the first character of the desired choice, such as the letter *D* in *DEMO3*. When multiple choices exist beginning with the same letter, simply press that letter repeatedly until the item you desire is highlighted.

When all your data entry, or list selection, is completed, you can use your mouse to select ⟨*OK*⟩ at the bottom of the screen. Or, you can tab to it with the keyboard, then press Enter. This confirms to QuickBASIC that all data entry is complete, and that processing can be continued.

Selecting ⟨*OK*⟩ when done is especially important when multiple data entry areas appear on a screen. First, you use the Tab key or your mouse to switch from one area to the next. Then, you enter the desired information or make the desired selections. Lastly, you select ⟨*OK*⟩ to confirm that you're done.

Command buttons are another frequently encountered mechanism in QuickBASIC. The ⟨*OK*⟩, ⟨*Cancel*⟩, and ⟨*Help*⟩ entries in a typi-

Command buttons appear in dialog boxes and are the graphic equivalents of the Enter, Escape, and Help (F1) keys.

cal dialog box are called *command buttons*. Sometimes, they are also referred to as *pushbuttons*. These command buttons are similar to function keys; they perform certain frequently occurring actions instantaneously, ending in a single result. In this case, the result is to confirm your data entry (⟨*OK*⟩), or to enable you to back out of the dialog box without continuing processing (⟨*Cancel*⟩), or to provide context-sensitive help text (⟨*Help*⟩). Selecting the ⟨*Help*⟩ command button here would cause QuickBASIC to display another window of information about the Open Program dialog box itself (see Figure 3.3).

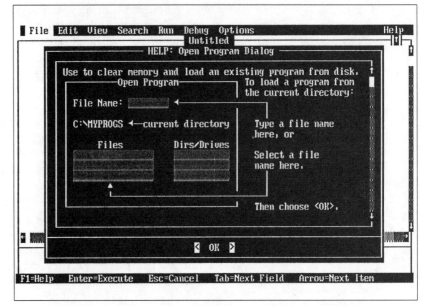

Figure 3.3 Help Window for the Open Program Dialog Box

After you have read the Help information, or after you've simply opened DEMO3.BAS, your screen should look like Figure 3.4. The former Help window and the temporarily displayed dialog box have both been cleared, and the specified program has been loaded into the QuickBASIC development environment. The former label for the View window, *Untitled*, is now replaced with the actual name of the program that you've opened and can now use. We'll use it for a variety of demonstrative purposes in the remainder of this chapter.

Using View Keys to Control Window Relationships

Certain keys offer immediate results that affect your screen's windows. For instance, you can run the currently loaded program by opening up the Run menu (press Alt-R) and selecting *Start*. DEMO3.BAS is a simple program for creating a variety of sound effects. Run it now on your

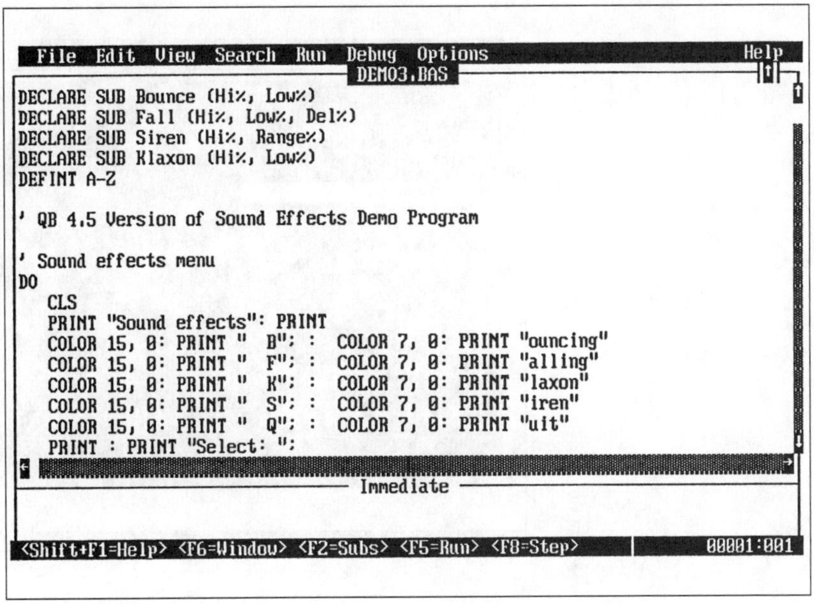

```
 File  Edit  View  Search  Run  Debug  Options                    Help
                            DEM03.BAS
 DECLARE SUB Bounce (Hi%, Low%)
 DECLARE SUB Fall (Hi%, Low%, Del%)
 DECLARE SUB Siren (Hi%, Range%)
 DECLARE SUB Klaxon (Hi%, Low%)
 DEFINT A-Z

 ' QB 4.5 Version of Sound Effects Demo Program

 ' Sound effects menu
 DO
   CLS
   PRINT "Sound effects": PRINT
   COLOR 15, 0: PRINT "  B": :   COLOR 7, 0: PRINT "ouncing"
   COLOR 15, 0: PRINT "  F": :   COLOR 7, 0: PRINT "alling"
   COLOR 15, 0: PRINT "  K": :   COLOR 7, 0: PRINT "laxon"
   COLOR 15, 0: PRINT "  S": :   COLOR 7, 0: PRINT "iren"
   COLOR 15, 0: PRINT "  Q": :   COLOR 7, 0: PRINT "uit"
   PRINT : PRINT "Select: ";

                            Immediate

 <Shift+F1=Help>  <F6=Window>  <F2=Subs>  <F5=Run>  <F8=Step>        00001:001
```

Figure 3.4 Example of How Loaded Programs Reside in the
View Window

system to see what it does. Note that you must type the letter **Q** to eventually quit the program.

To manage all the different sound effects, the program is organized into a main controlling program and several smaller single-task modules. Pressing F2 displays the names of all loaded programs and support modules (see Figure 3.5). This dialog box offers a host of possible actions to take, from changing the module you want to edit (see Chapter 4) to manipulating complete modules of QuickBASIC code. Some of the options shown in Figure 3.5, such as ⟨Edit in Split⟩, are only shown if you installed QuickBASIC with Full menus. With this useful option, you can even split the View window into two separate smaller windows by selecting ⟨Edit in Split⟩ here. If you installed your system with Full menus, try this feature now. You can select among the different modules in the list seen in Figure 3.5; your selection will be shown and can be edited in a different view window from the main module.

The Full menus setup offers to advanced users the ability to split the View window into two functioning program development areas.

An alternative way to obtain a split screen for program development is to switch directly to Full menus from the Option menu, then choose *Split* from the View main menu. This is an advanced toggle switch you can use as you become progressively more comfortable with the QuickBASIC development environment (see Appendix C). You should realize by now that the Full menus setup goes beyond simply presenting additional choices on the menus themselves. You will also see extra options during a variety of advanced situations requiring QuickBASIC to display dialog boxes.

Try highlighting one of the SUBs listed in Figure 3.5, such as

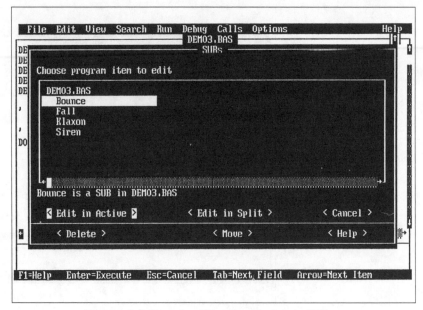

Figure 3.5 Pressing F2 to Display Loaded Files,
Modules, and SUBS

Use a split screen to see and edit two groups of code at one time.

Bounce, and then choose ⟨*Edit in Split*⟩. You now have three separate windows visible, as in Figure 3.6. Chapter 4 will demonstrate how you can use split windows efficiently to edit multiple modules of code. When multiple windows appear on your screen, you can change the

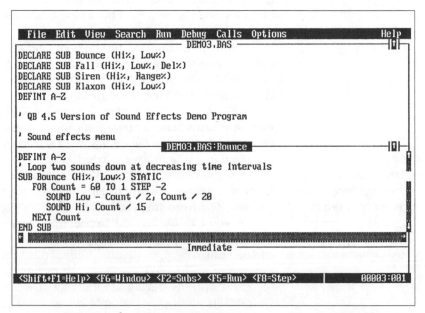

Figure 3.6 Splitting the View Window to Edit Two Files

active window from one to the other by pressing F6 (or pressing Shift-F6 to change to the previously active window). Do that now several times in succession. When the input focus shifts from one window to another, the title of the window becomes highlighted and the cursor shifts to that window. Whatever keystrokes you enter are applied to that window, either as text to appear, or as control characters to cause some action in the text.

When you are looking at a particular module in an active window, pressing the Shift-F2 key combination changes the window display to show the contents of the next entry in the SUBs list. Pressing Ctrl-F2 reverses this, and displays the text of the previous procedure in the SUBs list.

Although it is often advantageous to view multiple windows simultaneously, it is also often advantageous to work with as many lines of text in a file as possible. QuickBASIC recognizes certain key combinations that allow you to adjust your environment to suit your particular needs. Pressing the Alt and the plus sign keys will enlarge the size of the active window by one line; pressing Alt and the minus sign key will shrink the active window by one line each time you press that key combination.

Ctrl-F10 toggles between multiple smaller windows, and single large (full-screen) active window modes.

If you are not concerned with viewing information in other windows than the active one, you can press Ctrl and F10 together to enlarge the active window (one of the two text View windows) to the size of a full screen. This key combination acts as a toggle between a full-screen active window and a multiple window display. Mouse users can activate this toggle by clicking on the vertical arrow shown on the title line of a View window.

Using the QB Advisor Hypertext System

Get help fast in QuickBASIC with *hypertext*.

Hypertext is one of those avant-garde computer terms that insidiously become commonplace. Analyzing the Latin roots of this coined phrase simply leads you to a meaning of "super-fast words." In fact, this is the meaning—it does represent the result you see when you use this latest in retrieval techniques for extensive reference text. Other help systems manifest noticeably slower response when you request help; QuickBASIC's help displays are virtually instantaneous.

In Figure 3.1, you saw four main entries displayed between highlighted arrow brackets. If you move the cursor to any position between these brackets, then press F1, you will automatically receive the hypertext display window containing relevant text. In fact, the Enter key will do just as well; many people have a feel for where the Enter key is, but have to look down at the keyboard to locate the F1 key.

As before, the Tab key can be used to move you rapidly from one logical portion of the screen window to the next. In this case, pressing

Tab successively brings you from ⟨*How to Use QB Advisor Help System*⟩ through ⟨*How to Use QuickBASIC Menus and Commands*⟩ and on down to the ⟨*See Also*⟩ choices, ⟨*Contents*⟩ and ⟨*Index*⟩, then back again to the first choice.

Using a mouse for hyperlink selection requires that you double click button one on the desired entry. However, mouse button two is assignable in QuickBASIC 4.5 and is usually assigned to the task of providing hyperlink help with a single click.

Any topic for which a hypertext entry exists will appear between highlighted brackets such as these. Each entry is called a *hyperlink*. Hyperlinks are thus named because they are linked, or connected, together into an elaborate and extensive series of informational screens. The display of information is nearly instantaneous after you make your selection. Note that selecting a hyperlink with your mouse requires that you double click button one on the hyperlink entry.

If you explore the QB Advisor hypertext help screens, you will see some hyperlinks that are identical to the entries on the Help menu. Opening up this menu, for instance, and selecting ⟨*Contents*⟩ produces the screen seen in Figure 3.7. Note that QuickBASIC uses a portion of the screen for this new Help window information, and has compressed the other windows in order to do this. The amount of visual compression that you will encounter in QuickBASIC will vary in general according to the nature and number of windows appearing on your development screen. In all cases, however, the title bar of each window will always remain visible so you can know which windows are in fact available for use.

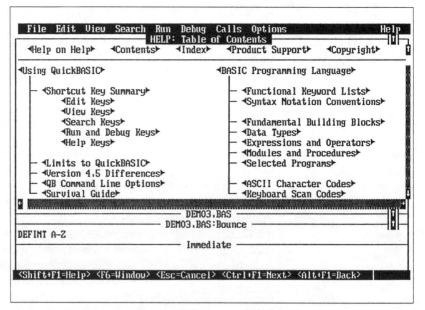

Figure 3.7 The Help System Table of Contents

All of the entries on this Help screen are hyperlinks and lead to the display of additional help screens, as well as additional hyperlink choices. This screen also has its own main menu of topical help areas, in addition to the two principal groupings seen here. Hypertext help from this screen concentrates on help for using the QuickBASIC development environment and on the QuickBASIC programming language. You should take a few minutes now to explore these screens further.

In addition to the QB Advisor hypertext screen hierarchy that is accessible from the Help menu, you can instantly tap into the hypertext system when you are writing programs. You only need to press F1 to obtain hypertext help for whatever BASIC keyword the cursor happens to be on.

Pressing F1 when the cursor rests on a BASIC keyword immediately invokes the hypertext text related to that keyword.

In Figure 3.6, let's assume that the cursor happens to be on the reserved BASIC keyword SUB. Pressing F1 at this moment, or moving the mouse pointer to this word and pressing button two, brings up the screen shown in Figure 3.8. This screen provides information about the SUB statement that includes a brief definition and a complete specification of required syntax. Because it is immediately displayed, this help screen is called a *QuickSCREEN*. As you can see, additional hyperlinks appear at various positions on this QuickSCREEN. These references are to other statements or subjects that provide relevant additional information. The main Help menu at the top of this QuickSCREEN enables you either to obtain more detailed information about the SUB command, or to wend your way to other unrelated areas in the hypertext system.

QuickSCREENs offers screenfuls of help text as well as additional hypertext links.

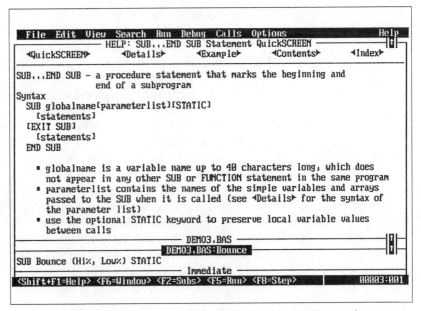

Figure 3.8 Hypertext Help for a QuickBASIC Keyword

The main menu choice ⟨*Details*⟩ offers extended explanations about the selected BASIC keyword, while the choice ⟨*Example*⟩ will show you the keyword in the context of an actual programming example. Choosing ⟨*Contents*⟩ returns you to the Table of Contents screen seen in Figure 3.7, while choosing ⟨*Index*⟩ will display an alphabetized list of all BASIC keywords (see Figure 3.9).

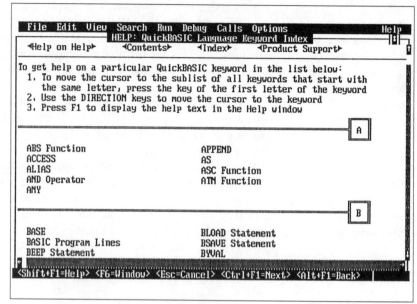

Figure 3.9 Index Hyperlinks for All QuickBASIC Keywords

All entries in the Index are hyperlinks and can be selected directly. Because the list is very large, it is set up so that you can move directly to any of the 26 alphabetical groups by pressing the desired letter and then selecting the individual entry you want further information about. In this screen, the full screen mode has been toggled using Ctrl-F10. Note the two-way vertical arrow symbol on the title line of the window in Figure 3.9; this indicates that full screen mode is active.

You can take a second look at recently referenced hypertext screens by pressing Alt-F1 successively (up to a maximum of 20 times).

QuickBASIC retains a table of up to 20 successively referenced hyperlinks. You can always look at the most recently chosen hyperlink screens (up to a maximum of 20) by pressing Alt-F1. Since all hyperlinks are stored alphabetically, you can also ask QuickBASIC to show you the next hyperlink screen by pressing Ctrl-F1. This displays the screen topic stored next in the HELP file. You can also go backwards to look at the previously stored topic by pressing Shift-Ctrl-F1.

Figure 3.10 summarizes the principal access mechanisms for obtaining hypertext help in the QuickBASIC development environment.

Previewing Instruction Results

You can experiment with QuickBASIC commands by using the Immediate window. As discussed in Chapter 2, this window serves a utility role

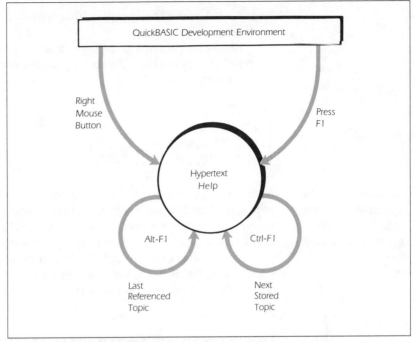

Figure 3.10 Obtaining Hypertext Help Screens

in QuickBASIC, offering you a place to execute individual commands as soon as you type them and press Enter. When trying out particular variations of a single command, you can quickly determine the correct syntax, as well as try out a set of different parameter values.

Experimenting with the Immediate Window

Press F6 to reach the Immediate window, and use Alt-Plus to expand its size.

To understand the Immediate window, you must try it out. Make the Immediate window into the active window. Do this by pressing F6 until the title line, *Immediate*, becomes highlighted. Then, expand this window by pressing Alt-Plus several times. You can open up the Immediate window to a maximum size of ten screen lines, although you can actually enter more than ten lines of immediate instructions. QuickBASIC allows you to scroll up or down through these lines of experimental code. The next section, which is on cutting and pasting, will even show you how to avoid retyping instructions when you want to incorporate into a program the lines of code you tested in the Immediate window.

Suppose you wanted to draw a circle with a partially removed pie-shaped wedge. If you were unsure of the required parameters, you could spend time using the QuickBASIC documentation or the hypertext mechanism. Or, you could forge rapidly ahead by using the Immediate window. Enter a command or two and see what happens; if it's not what you want or expect, then simply adjust a value or two and try it again.

Chapter 9 presents graphic programming techniques in depth, so for now, just try entering the following four commands in your Immediate window:

```
CLS
SCREEN 2
CIRCLE (320,100),160,,-3.00,-2.00
CIRCLE (260,80),160,,-2.00,-3.00
```

A *message box* appears that explains an error or problem and offers hypertext help about it.

After you type each instruction, the entire typed line is verified for correct syntax and immediately executed. If anything is wrong, you will receive a *message box* such as can be seen in Figure 3.11. You will either recognize and correct the typographical error instantly (you select ⟨OK⟩ to continue), or you can obtain context-sensitive help text for the particular error situation identified by QuickBASIC. The error in Figure 3.11 is a missing extra comma in the second CIRCLE statement.

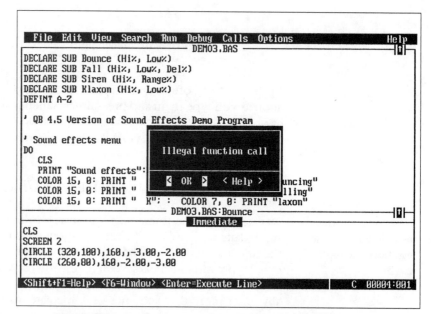

Figure 3.11 Encountering an Error in the Immediate Window

After each instruction is executed, your video monitor is automatically switched from the QuickBASIC development environment screen to the QuickBASIC programming output screen so you can see the results of the instruction. You only need to "press any key to continue," as is noted at the bottom of the output screen. Figure 3.12 demonstrates this situation after the four lines above have been successfully entered into the Immediate window.

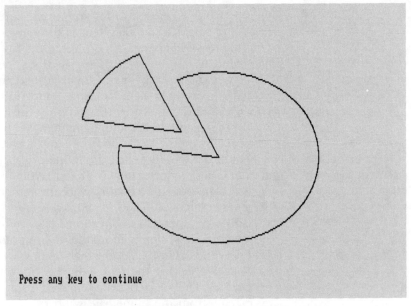

Press any key to continue

Figure 3.12 Output Screen Showing Immediate
Instruction Results

Try this sequence yourself for a few minutes. Use these four instructions to begin with, varying the parameters to explore how the CIRCLE command works. Basically, CLS clears the output screen once, while SCREEN 2 sets the monitor into a high resolution graphic mode (see Chapter 9 for more details). The first CIRCLE command draws the primary circle, while the second CIRCLE command draws the wedge.

Remember that pressing F4 while you are in the QuickBASIC development environment switches your monitor to display the last output screen. Pressing F4 again toggles you back to the development screen. Since this key works this way at all times, you can use it from the Immediate window and—during program development later—from the View window(s).

Press F4 to toggle between the QuickBASIC development screen and the output screen.

Cut and Paste to Avoid Retyping

As you develop instructions that work correctly in the Immediate window, you will notice several things about this window. First, an instruction line is executed whenever you place the cursor anywhere on the line and then press Enter. Second, after returning from the output screen, the cursor is automatically moved to the next line in the Immediate window. This is helpful when you are trying out several lines of code sequentially.

No line is erased from the Immediate window until you actually type over it or press Ctrl-Y when the cursor is on the line. In addition, for this window as well as for any other window, Ctrl-Home always resets the cursor to the first line. In the Immediate window, you may want to press Ctrl-Home frequently in order to execute each of your test lines successively, beginning with the first.

After you've experimented with several lines of code, you may be ready to incorporate them into a program you are developing in one of your View windows. Rather than retyping the lines, you can take advantage of the main Edit menu to literally move the desired lines from the Immediate window to the appropriate place in the View window.

Cut and *Paste* effectively move text from one place to another.

In order to remove text from one place (that is, *Cut* the text) and insert it in another place (that is, *Paste* it), you must first identify or select the text to be treated. To do this, place the cursor on the first character of the text to be moved. Then, keyboard users should hold down the Shift key and press appropriate directional keys to highlight and select text. Mouse users must simply move the mouse pointer while button one is held down to achieve the same highlighting and selection effect.

After selecting the text, you can open up the Edit menu and choose *Cut*. The selected text is removed from the screen; in this case, it disappears from the Immediate window. Try this now. Next, switch your active window from the Immediate to a View window. If you have any text there already, move the cursor to the desired point of insertion. Open up the Edit menu again, and choose *Paste*. The text formerly cut from the Immediate window now appears in your View window.

You can easily begin to appreciate the development possibilities of writing many of your program statements in the Immediate window. After you've tested the statements and are comfortable with how they work, you can move them all into the actual program area. As you'll find in the next chapter, program code can be eventually saved to disk files only when the instructions appear as a named group in a View window.

Cutting and Pasting works just about anywhere in QuickBASIC. You can move or copy text to and from any windows, including the split View windows, the Immediate window, and even the Help windows. Some Help screens contain sample code segments that can be copied into either the Immediate or a View window. You can then slightly adjust the sample code to suit your purposes, rather than redevelop the code from scratch.

Use *Copy* and *Paste* between split View windows to build on previously written code. Use *Cut* and *Paste* to build on new instructions entered in the Immediate window.

When you use sample code from a Help window, make sure that you use the Copy command from the Edit menu, and not the Cut command. In this way, you will be working with a copy of the sample code; the original will still remain in the Help file for later reference. Furthermore, this technique can just as readily be used with your own programs. You may have previously written some code that is similar to what you must now write. Use the Copy and Paste technique between split View windows to obtain a block of starter instructions that then only needs to be appropriately modified.

Monitoring Program Execution with a Watch Window

Chapter 12 discusses debugging techniques in depth, but in this chapter, you will learn about one last type of window that is useful in debugging. The *Watch window* is a rectangular portion of your screen that is placed just above your View window. It contains variables and expressions that you specify by selecting *Add Watch* from the Debug main menu.

A maximum of eight variables and expressions can be monitored in the Watch window.

When you develop programs, things don't always go as you plan. Sometimes, results are not as desired and the incorrect statements are not immediately obvious. Specifying program variables to observe as the program progresses can be helpful in identifying why a program is working incorrectly. For example, Figure 3.13 depicts a Watch window containing two variables, X and Y. These two variables are both used and located in the program SINEWAVE.BAS, which can be seen in the View window. As you will learn in more detail in Chapter 12, you can use the Watch window to monitor variables from both main programs and subordinate modules. As you add entries to the Watch window, a separate line is displayed in the automatically expanding Watch window. Up to eight separate variables or expressions can be monitored simultaneously in this Watch window.

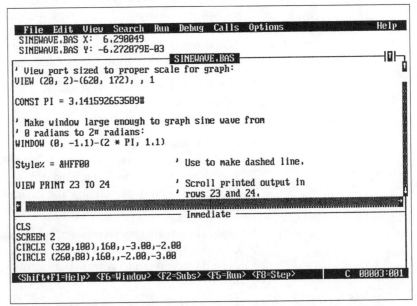

Figure 3.13 Monitoring Variable Values in the Watch Window

In other programming systems, you are often forced to debug your programs by incorporating PRINT or WRITE statements into the code. These statements also obtain the values of specified variables and expressions, making them a part of your output. In this way, you obtain the same assistance in debugging your programs, but at a considerably greater expense. Not only must you spend time editing these commands into your code, but when your debugging job is over, you must edit them out again. With QuickBASIC, you only need to Add the Watch; you needn't affect your program code at all.

Furthermore, the printed values from the older technique often merge with your output and make normal results more difficult to interpret. And, even more importantly, in order to be sure of the value of certain variables and/or expressions at different points in your program, you must incorporate multiple PRINT statements into other languages' code. With QuickBASIC's Watch window, the displayed value changes as the expression changes value during program execution. In fact, since the results of all monitoring appear in this Watch window, they become even easier to interpret. All relationships between variables and expressions become immediately obvious.

Review

1. Modern programs all seem to be leaning toward graphic interfaces. They offer a consistently easier means to tap into the power of the computer software. This chapter concentrated on the graphic windows used by the QuickBASIC development environment. You learned about the different types of windows, as well as the different means at your disposal for manipulating these windows.

2. Scroll bars enable you to scroll up and down, as well as left and right, through your text. A variety of Ctrl-other key combinations exist that move you through your text incrementally.

3. A slider box provides visual feedback about how far into the text you've actually moved. This white rectangle slides along the horizontal or vertical scroll bar, and can actually be manipulated directly with a mouse to change the current cursor position in your text by large amounts at once.

4. Dialog boxes are special types of windows used by QuickBASIC to establish two-way communication with you. Information is displayed for you, and various data entry requirements are solicited from you.

5. A list box is a dialog box mechanism for providing you with a list of items from which to choose. It is a smaller rectangle window contained in the dialog box.

6. A text box is another window contained in a dialog box that allows for your typed input.

7. Command buttons also appear in a dialog box. They are selectable by mouse or keyboard and are used to confirm your entry, cancel your request, or obtain help about the dialog.

8. A host of special key assignments exist in QuickBASIC. Among them:

> Pressing F6 switches the active window among all possible screen alternatives.

> Pressing F4 toggles between the QuickBASIC development screen and the program output screen.

> Pressing F2 displays a dialog box containing a list of all modules and submodules currently loaded in memory.

> Pressing Alt-Plus or Alt-Minus expands or contracts the active window to suit your tastes.

> Many other keys serving special purposes are discussed in this chapter, as well as throughout the rest of the book as appropriate.

9. The QB Advisor is the main controlling program that supplies instant help screens, which are called hypertext. An elaborate series of connected help screens, called hyperlinks, can be called up readily.

10. Pressing F1 displays instant context-sensitive help about any BASIC keyword on which the cursor is resting. Mouse users can press button two to obtain help about whatever topic lies under the mouse pointer.

11. You can also use the Alt-H Help menu to directly enter the Help system via a Table of Contents or an alphabetized list of keywords.

12. Programs are typically written in the View window. This window can be split into two parts—either through the F2 key's dialog box, or through the View menu when Full Menus has been activated.

13. You can enter individual commands in the Immediate window to test out their results one at a time.

14. You can use Cut and Paste techniques on the Edit menu to move type bodily from the Immediate window to a View window, thus avoiding retyping code.

15. You can use Copy and Paste techniques to bring sample code from a Help window to a View window, or even from one View window to another on a split screen.

16. A watch window provides a state-of-the-art method of monitoring variables and expressions during program execution.

Quiz for Chapter 3

1. Which of the following are not QuickBASIC windows?

   a. View and Immediate
   b. Watch and Help
   c. Dialog boxes
   d. Insets

2. Which of the following never appear in a dialog box?

   a. List box
   b. Text box
   c. Data box
   d. Command button

3. What does pressing F6 do?

   a. Enlarges the active window
   b. Shrinks the active window
   c. Switches the active window
   d. Displays loaded module names

4. What does pressing F2 do?

   a. Enlarges the active window
   b. Shrinks the active window
   c. Switches the active window
   d. Displays loaded module names

5. What does pressing Ctrl-F10 do?

   a. Splits the View window
   b. Toggles full screen mode
   c. Switches to the Immediate window
   d. Switches to the View window

6. What is a hyperlink?

   a. Fast compilation mode
   b. A Help dialog box
   c. Topical entry in a Help file
   d. QuickBASIC Help file name

7. Which pair of keystrokes enlarges and contracts the size of the active window?

   a. Alt-F10 and Alt-F9
   b. Ctrl-Plus and Ctrl-Minus
   c. Alt-Plus and Alt-Minus
   d. Shift-Plus and Shift-Minus

8. Which technique is typically used to move fully tested text from the Immediate window to the View window?

   a. Copy and Paste
   b. Cut and Paste
   c. Cut and Copy
   d. Divide and Copy

9. Which key enables you to switch instantly between the Quick-BASIC development environment screen and the QuickBASIC program output screen?

   a. F2
   b. F4
   c. F6
   d. F8

10. Which keystroke combination moves the cursor to the first line and to the last line in a window, respectively?

    a. Home and End
    b. Ctrl-Home and Ctrl-End
    c. Shift-Home and Shift-End
    d. Alt-Home and Alt-End

11. How is the Watch window used?

    a. To watch your program's progress
    b. To watch your program's compilation
    c. To watch your program's variables
    d. To watch your program's code

12. Which feature most clearly reflects the portion of a file that is being displayed in a window?

    a. Scroll bar
    b. Slider box
    c. Hypertext indicator
    d. Hyperlink

13. Mouse button two is typically used for what purpose?

    a. Changing the active window
    b. Obtaining hypertext help
    c. Equivalent to Esc key
    d. Equivalent to PgDn key

14. A dialog box that requires no list selection or keyboard data entry is called a:

    a. Text box
    b. Message box
    c. Error box
    d. Display box

15. Mouse button one selects menu items with single clicking. What requires double clicking with mouse button one?

    a. Items in a list
    b. Hyperlinks
    c. Both of the above
    d. Neither of the above

4 | Manipulating and Editing Files

In the first three chapters, you learned about many of QuickBASIC's fundamental development tools. You learned how to maneuver around QuickBASIC's Easy and Full menus. And you learned how to use a variety of QuickBASIC windows in an efficient manner. This chapter rounds out your knowledge of this powerful programming environment.

This chapter concentrates on the View window, which is primarily used for creating and editing program code. When you complete this chapter, you will have all the tools you need to begin to write QuickBASIC programs. Part 2 of this book then introduces you to the features, syntax, and requirements of the QuickBASIC programming language itself.

Understanding the Life Cycle of a Computer Program

Programmers follow identifiable patterns during development.

Programmers quickly learn that there is a pattern to their computer work. Once in a while, they write a completely new program from scratch. Then, they work and rework the code involved until they are satisfied that it performs properly. If there is time left, they add documentation to the code. They may also improve certain lines of code so that the program works faster or the output is presented in a more attractive manner. Ultimately, if the program is for someone else, the end user may request that improvements, corrections, or additions be made.

Figure 4.1 represents the life cycle of a computer program. Ninety percent of the total time spent in developing a program is probably spent in the cyclic development phase of this figure. Chapter 12 concentrates on the testing and debugging portions of this phase. In this chapter, you will hone your editing skills. They are your bread and butter skills, which ensure smooth and fast development of QuickBASIC programs.

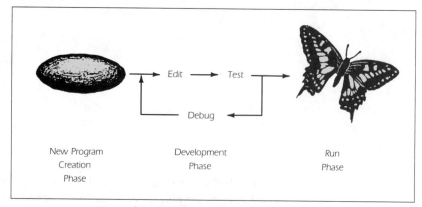

Figure 4.1 Life Cycle of a Computer Program

Writing a New Program from Scratch

When the QuickBASIC development environment first appears on your screen, the View window is ready for your first program effort. If you simply begin to type lines of QuickBASIC code, they will appear in the View window as you type. The window retains its untitled nature until you decide to pull down the File menu and give your program a name. After writing several lines of code for a new program, you can name your program by saving it. Figure 4.2 shows the dialog box that appears after making the *Save As* choice.

The minimum you must do here is type in a name for your program. As you will see in Figure 4.3, I typed in STYLE.BAS as the program's name; that new name appears subsequently in the title bar of the View window. You can save your program under any name you like, and also ask QuickBASIC to store it in any available directory on any available system disk drive. You do this by entering a full path name in the *File Name* box. For example, to store the STYLE.BAS program in the directory called WORDS on drive E you would enter

`E:\WORDS\STYLE.BAS`

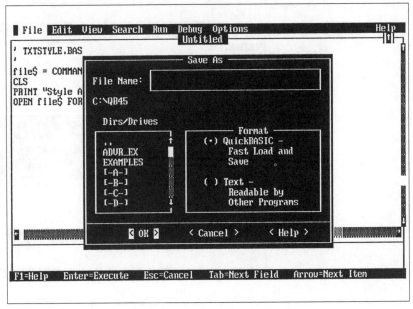

Figure 4.2 Naming Your New Program

as the full path name in the *File Name* box.

If you only enter a simple file name, then the current system directory and drive are used. Alternatively, you can modify the directory/drive for the duration of this file saving operation only. Simply press Tab (or use your mouse) to switch the input focus to the *Dirs/Drives* list box, and select the desired drive or directory to receive your new program file.

QuickBASIC binary storage format is faster for both program storage and retrieval, but it cannot be read by other programs, or easily transferred to other BASIC systems.

QuickBASIC usually stores its files in a unique binary format that is easily and quickly manipulated by the computer. When this default format is used, QuickBASIC requires less time to save your programs to disk, and less time to later retrieve them for continued development. You may wish to save your file in the alternative, and somewhat slower, text format. This choice is necessary if you must have a readable version of your program for word processing, for DOS print spooling, or for a colleague who uses a different vendor's version of BASIC.

Once your file is saved, it is safe to continue working on it. This is a form of ongoing backup. If the power fails during an 8-hour program development session, you only lose the QuickBASIC instructions that you typed in since the last Save As operation. Try to take a couple of seconds every 15 minutes to save your ongoing work.

QuickBASIC has a built-in safety feature that comes into play if you forget to save your code while working in the View window. Figure 4.3 shows the special protective dialog box that appears whenever you are in danger of losing your work through a failure to save it (not from a power failure).

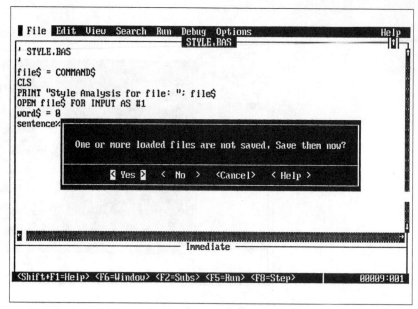

Figure 4.3 Automatic Protection Against Inadvertent File Loss

QuickBASIC reminds you when you haven't saved a file.

This dialog box appears under three conditions, and all three conditions result from choices made on the File pulldown menu. You may tell QuickBASIC that you wish to begin writing a *New Program*, or that you wish to load into memory a copy of an existing program (*Open Program*), or that you're done for the day and wish to *Exit* back to DOS. In each case, QuickBASIC checks to see if you have made any adjustments to any of your loaded files (including the main program, support procedures, and other possible files to be discussed in later chapters). If you have, it asks if you want to save them.

You can select 〈*Yes*〉 to ask QuickBASIC to automatically save current versions of all loaded files. If a file in a View window is still untitled, you will receive a dialog box equivalent to the *Save As* box seen above. Otherwise, your files will be saved and then your requested operation (*New Program, Open Program,* or *Exit*) will be performed.

If you are completely sure that you need not save your work, you can select 〈*No*〉. But this means that no files, neither those visible in View windows nor those not visible, will be saved. Hesitate and be sure before making this selection. As always, you can *Cancel* the requested operation or obtain *Help* about it.

Running Your QuickBASIC Programs

The example program in the previous section is called STYLE.BAS. This chapter focuses on the various editing techniques and capabilities of QuickBASIC that will result in the final STYLE.BAS program shown in

Listing 4.1. The individual lines of code in STYLE.BAS are explained at appropriate points during later chapters in Part 2. For now, you simply need to understand how to run a program. You must do this repeatedly during program development, and typically, a useful program is run repeatedly after it is completed as well.

Listing 4.1 A Completed QuickBASIC Example Program

Analyze your own
writing skills with
STYLE.BAS.

```
'* Main program module STYLE.BAS
'*
'* Purpose: Analyze any text file for stylistic
    characteristics
'*
CLS
INPUT "Please enter file to analyze: "; file$
CLS
PRINT "Style Analysis for file: "; file$
OPEN file$ FOR INPUT AS #1
  word% = 0
  sentence% = 0
  fog% = 0
DO
  eachchar$ = INPUT$(1, #1)
  SELECT CASE eachchar$
    CASE " ", CHR$(13)
      word% = word% + 1
      IF wordlength% > 7 THEN
        fog% = fog% + 3
      ELSE
        fog% = fog% + 1
      END IF
      wordlength% = 0
    CASE "."
      sentence% = sentence% + 1
    CASE ";", ",", ":", CHR$(10)
    CASE ELSE
      wordlength% = wordlength% + 1
  END SELECT
LOOP UNTIL EOF(1)
averagefog% = fog% / sentence%
PRINT "Total number of words is "; word%
PRINT "Total number of sentences is "; sentence%
PRINT "Average fog count is "; averagefog%
END
```

STYLE.BAS performs a useful task, and this task will be expanded

Assess the quality and readability of your writing with STYLE.BAS's fog count.

to do even more useful work during later chapters of this book. As it is presently written, it analyzes any text file and determines the number of words and sentences in that file. It also computes what is sometimes called a Fog Count. A variation on this number is used by the U.S. Air Force and a number of large corporations, to analyze the quality and readability of various written documents.

STYLE requires that you specify the DOS filename of the text file that you wish to analyze. It then scans the file, character by character, and computes the three pieces of output information (number of words, number of sentences, and Fog Count). To have some fun while gaining some useful feedback as well, enter this program and specify some text file that you've written. Or, you can send in a copy of the order form located near the end of this book to obtain this program and all other QuickBASIC programs developed in this book. If your file's Fog Count is 25 or less, you've met the Air Force's specification for a readable piece of writing.

In order to run STYLE.BAS, you must open up the Run pulldown menu and select *Start*. Alternatively, you can use the Shift-F5 shortcut key. Your only required program input is the name of the file to analyze; the program prompts you for this.

QuickBASIC can produce a compiled version of any working program. See Chapter 11 for complete details on the requirements, the benefits, and the additional enhancement options.

As you'll later learn in Chapter 11, QuickBASIC also has the ability to create a compiled version of working programs. This means that you don't even have to spend the time to bring up the QuickBASIC development environment to run a program. You can do that from a DOS prompt, saving time on a regular basis. Also, this means that others can use your completed program without having to learn how to run it from within the QuickBASIC environment.

Browsing Through Your QuickBASIC Files

Historically, the keyboard has been the primary input device for entering data and controlling application programs and operating environments. Now, in the late 1980s and projected into the early 1990s, the trend is to provide more visual interfaces, such as the one you see in QuickBASIC. A mouse device now provides a more intuitively self-evident method of controlling actions that occur on the screen. In many software packages, you have the option of using keyboard or mouse inputs, or both, according to what feels comfortable to you.

For the many of you who have used keyboards in the past, it is comforting to know that there are a host of possible keystrokes available. Learning those possibilities can speed up your transition to QuickBASIC, and can make your continued use of QuickBASIC even easier. In this section, you'll learn the obvious and the not so obvious keystrokes that enable you to traverse quickly any text information displayed in your QuickBASIC windows.

The QuickBASIC editor is compatible with WordStar and Word.

This section concentrates on scrolling and cursor movement keys. This section also provides you with alternative Ctrl-key combinations to perform standard operations. These keystrokes provide compatibility with the conventions established and maintained by the popular Word-Star and Word programs. A later section titled *Editing Your Program Lines* will go further into text searching, selection, and correction.

I have spent many years using different programming languages, different word processors, and different development environments. By now, probably like yourself, I'm comfortable using the four arrow keys located in a square pattern on the right side of most keyboards. In all situations, pressing one of those keys moves the cursor up or down a line, or moves the cursor one character to the left or to the right. Mouse users can click on the single arrows located at the ends of the visible scroll bars to obtain the same effect.

For beginning users in all environments, this is enough to perform minimum movements through the text. When you start using one package more frequently, however, you want to move through the text more quickly. All of the popular software programs allow you to traverse the text in steps greater than a single character or a single line. To do so, they use the extra keys in the cursor movement keypad seen in Figure 4.4.

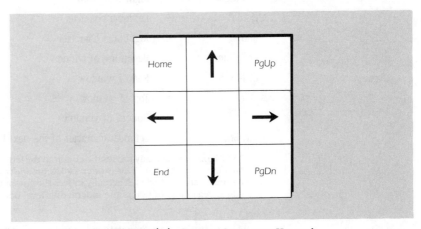

Figure 4.4 Cursor Movement Keypad

The PgUp and PgDn keys move the cursor a variable number of lines up or down in a file, according to the size of the current screen window.

Pressing the Home key immediately moves the cursor to the first character in the current line. Pressing the End key offers a logical counterbalance; it moves the cursor to the last character in the current line. The PgUp and PgDn keys offer a rapid way to move up or down in your text module or file by a windowful of lines at a time. In QuickBASIC, the number of lines controlled by these two keys varies according to the size of the current window. Remember that the Alt-Minus and Alt-Plus keys can shrink or enlarge a window by one line per press.

QuickBASIC instruction lines consist of a variety of keywords, variables, parameters, and constants, all of which are typically separated by spaces. In my experience, some of the most time saving keystroke combinations are the ones that rapidly move your cursor from one of these words to the next, either forward or backward on a line. The Ctrl-Right Arrow and Ctrl-Left Arrow keypresses do precisely this.

Speed up your editing by learning combination keystrokes.

Bring up any file now into your View window and try pressing these keys to instantly see how helpful they will be. In fact, refer to Table 4.1 and try any of the other miscellaneous key combinations available and summarized in that table. The third column presents the Word and WordStar compatible key combinations for commonplace operations.

Table 4.1 Primary Cursor Movement Key Combinations

Standard Keystroke	Effect	Alternative Keystroke
Left Arrow	Left one character	Ctrl-S
Right Arrow	Right one character	Ctrl-D
Up Arrow	Up one line	Ctrl-E
Down Arrow	Down one line	Ctrl-X
Ctrl-Left Arrow	Left one word	Ctrl-A
Ctrl-Right Arrow	Right one word	Ctrl-F
Home*	Leftmost character	Ctrl-Q-S
End	Rightmost character	Ctrl-Q-X
Ctrl-Home	Beginning of window	Ctrl-Q-R
Ctrl-End	End of window	Ctrl-Q-C
	Top of window	Ctrl-Q-E
	Bottom of window	Ctrl-Q-X
Ctrl-Enter	Leftmost character of the next line	Ctrl-J

*The Home key actually moves the cursor to the leftmost non-space or non-tab character on a line. This is often called the *indentation level*. The alternative keystroke, Ctrl-Q-S, actually moves the cursor to the first position on a line, regardless of where the indentation level begins.

After you're comfortable with moving about in your text modules and files, you can get down to the business of actually entering and editing text. QuickBASIC has a built in Smart Editor, which goes well beyond simple text insertions, deletions, and corrections. The next section will introduce you to this invaluable built-in QuickBASIC tool.

Benefiting from QuickBASIC's Smart Editor

The QuickBASIC smart editing program knows the QuickBASIC environment and understands the QuickBASIC programming language. Understanding these issues enables the editor to automatically perform a variety of tasks with each of your instruction lines. Each instruction line is processed when you complete the line. Figure 4.5 depicts the Smart Editor treating your instruction after you press either the Enter key or a cursor control key that moves the cursor to another line.

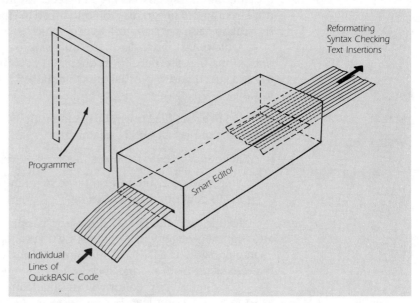

Figure 4.5 Smart Editor—Processing Lines as They Are Typed

The Smart Editor checks syntax and improves your code's appearance.

As the drawing suggests, each line is treated individually and processed in three significant ways. First, it is reformatted according to several rules of appearance. Second, the line is checked for correct syntax. And third, when necessary, extra declaration lines (see Chapter 10) are inserted into your program to allow for automatic checking of your procedure calls.

Making Your Code Easier to Read and Understand

QuickBASIC keywords such as statement or function names (see Appendix B) are capitalized by the Smart Editor. Spaces are also uniformly inserted between all operators (such as + or − or =) and operands (that is, variable names of constants). Additionally, the Smart Editor ensures consistency in capitalization of the names of variables, procedures, and symbolic constants.

Take a look at the program in Figure 4.6. This figure was captured just prior to pressing Enter on the line that reads

```
eachchar$=input$(1,#1)
```

This line was purposely entered with no spacing around the equal sign, and no spacing around the arguments to the INPUT$ function. Quick-BASIC contains many of these special built-in functions. While this chapter concentrates on the primary programming tool called a *statement*, Chapter 8 treats the topic of built-in functions in more depth. In the upcoming few chapters, you'll see a number of built-in functions used in example programs. You only need to think of them as a form of shorthand for a specially calculated value.

QuickBASIC provides these functions to take the place of complex operations that are needed frequently. For example, using `INPUT$(1, #1)` is a shorthand way of asking QuickBASIC to follow a series of built-in steps:

1. Go to a data file known by the identifier #1 (specified earlier in the program by an OPEN statement).

2. Read in one byte from the file at whatever position is current.

3. Store the determined result (the byte) in the place where the INPUT$ function happens to be.

In this case, the INPUT$ function happens to be in the middle of an assignment statement. So, in asking that *eachchar$* be assigned some character value, the INPUT$ function actually does its job and obtains that character from the file specified by the OPEN statement.

The QuickBASIC editor will automatically reformat this entire line as soon as it is complete. Because you are not required to arrange the spacing, you can type more quickly. By inserting a uniform system of

```
 File  Edit  View  Search  Run  Debug  Options                    Help
                            ┌─── STYLE.BAS ───┐
'* Main program module STYLE.BAS
'*
'* Purpose: Analyze any text file for stylistic characteristics
'*
CLS
INPUT "Please enter file to analyze: "; file$
CLS
PRINT "Style Analysis for file: "; file$
OPEN file$ FOR INPUT AS #1
  WORD% = 0
  sentence% = 0
  fog% = 0
DO
  eachchar$=input$(1,#1)
  SELECT CASE eachchar$
    CASE " ", CHR$(13)
      WORD% = WORD% + 1
      IF wordlength% > 7 THEN
───────────────────── Immediate ─────────────────────

<Shift+F1=Help> <F6=Window> <F2=Subs> <F5=Run> <F8=Step>        00014:025
```

Figure 4.6 Automatic Reformatting and Capitalizing by the Smart Editor

Smart Editor automatically inserts spaces to improve readability.

spacing (see the same line in Figure 4.7, as it was reformatted by Quick-BASIC's Smart Editor), you gain the benefit of a cleaner, more attractive, and more readable code module. And, because the Smart Editor does the work automatically, you gain this even if you are not typically inclined to write your code in this way.

In the STYLE.BAS program, notice that all QuickBASIC keywords, such as INPUT$ or PRINT or SELECT CASE, are capitalized. In fact, I typed the entire program in lower case. The capitalization and spacing were all done by the Smart Editor. Additionally, I strongly suggest using visual indentation for compound statements such as SELECT CASE and IF . . . ELSE . . . END IF. The Smart Editor will maintain the indentation level for you by moving the cursor to the latest indentation column when you press Enter. Rather than returning to column 1 each time, this feature simulates the setting of a new left margin, further enhancing the convenience of QuickBASIC's Smart Editor.

There is still one more unusual formatting feature provided by this Smart Editor. Upper and lower case of all variable names, procedure names, and symbolic constants are maintained consistently throughout your programs. In my programs, I've chosen to enter these names all in lower case. However, if I chose to switch my conventions to first-letter-uppercase (for example, *fog%* becoming *Fog%*), I would only need to change any one of the instances in the program. The Smart Editor would then immediately change all other instances of *fog%* in the program to *Fog%*.

With all of these formatting rules, the sole result is improved appearance. Consistency, organization, and visual clarity almost always contribute to program code that is easier to read, easier to debug, easier to maintain, and easier to understand. And because at least 90 percent of all program code development is consumed by these chores, you constantly benefit from the Smart Editor's automatic reformatting.

Automatic Checking for Correct Syntax

Smart Editor catches and explains syntax errors immediately.

Appearance, they say, is only skin deep. The QuickBASIC Smart Editor goes below the surface to analyze what you have actually typed as well. If the keywords, parameters, and constants are not strung together in a sensible manner, QuickBASIC is quick to tell you about it.

For example, Figure 4.7 shows a situation in which the PRINT statement was completed in the View window. A colon was erroneously typed in, instead of the intended semicolon. The Smart Editor is responsible for highlighting the probable portion of the line that contains the error. It also displays a dialog box containing an error message that explains what mistake the Smart Editor thinks it has found.

In Figure 4.7, the dialog box suggests a possible cause of the error. In this case, the editor expected a possible assignment expression after

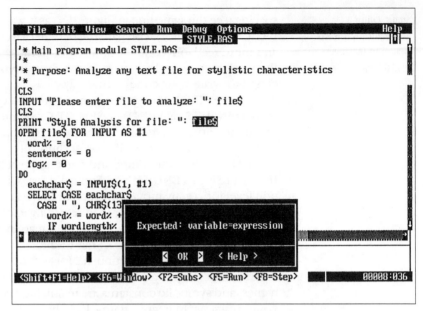

Figure 4.7 Automatic Syntax Checking by the Smart Editor

Automatic syntax
checking announces
errors as they are
discovered. But you are
not forced to fix the
erroneous statement. If
you don't correct the
error, you'll receive the
dialog box again when
you run the program.

the mistaken colon. In fact, this was not the actual problem, but the immediate feedback about a problem is enough to alert you to look closely at the line. Replacing the colon with a semicolon is easy. Many simple syntactical errors are caught in this fashion at the time you type them.

Because your mind is concentrating on each statement as you enter it, it becomes even easier to fix an error when it is discovered at that point, than to wait until your program runs later. This kind of dialog box only contains the ⟨*OK*⟩ and ⟨*Help*⟩ choices. If you perceive how to correct the error, simply choose ⟨*OK*⟩ with your mouse or the Enter key. If the error is not obvious, choose ⟨*Help*⟩ to obtain further explanations.

It is important to understand that this dialog box appears to inform you of a perceived error in the line you typed. It does not inhibit you from continuing with your work by requiring you to fix the error immediately. You can continue, and the statement in error is not checked for correct syntax again until you either run the program or work on that line again.

Distinguishing Between Syntax and Semantics

The syntax of a QuickBASIC statement or command can be specified precisely. Appendix B contains the formal syntax requirements of each QuickBASIC statement and function. This is the necessary physical layout of a command and its possible parameters. Because it is part of the grammatical rules of the language, you can know in advance whether a QuickBASIC instruction line has been constructed correctly.

Figure 4.8 contrasts the issue of *syntax* with the issue of *seman-*

Syntax refers to what you type; semantics refers to what you mean to happen when the instruction executes.

tics. Syntax refers to what you typed, how it appears, and whether it is structurally sound. Do the keywords make sense as they are combined? Are all required parameters and punctuation included? This can only go so far. Some errors, in fact, cannot be determined until you run a program. These are called semantic errors because the instruction line meets the syntactical rules but may not do what you truly intend.

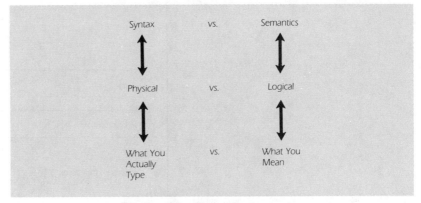

Figure 4.8 Syntax vs. Semantics

For example, you may type CHR(13) in the STYLE.BAS program, rather than CHR$(13). Syntactically, this is acceptable, because you may actually mean to refer to the thirteenth element in an array named CHR. In fact, you mean to invoke the CHR$ function to convert the decimal number 13 to an ASCII control character. Your semantics, or meaning, cannot be validated when you type the statement but only when you run the program. At that time, you will receive an appropriate dialog box announcing the error. Depending on the program context, you might receive a `Type Not Defined` or `Subscript Out Of Range` message.

Inserting Procedure and Variable Declarations

The Smart Editor occasionally inserts necessary code into your programs.

The last role played by the Smart Editor is an occasional one. Although you won't study QuickBASIC procedures (SUBs and FUNCTIONs) in depth until Chapter 10, the Smart Editor does provide some support for using procedures. As you'll learn, some blocks of code can be grouped together into an easily invoked support module called a FUNCTION or SUB, according to its role and organization.

When you incorporate such procedures into your programs, you must also DECLARE their use and appearance. Although not always necessary, the Smart Editor takes the burden off you and automatically inserts the required DECLARE statement at the beginning of your program file. It does this, however, only when you actually SAVE your file. At that point, all procedures are stored at the physical end of the program file (see Figure 4.9).

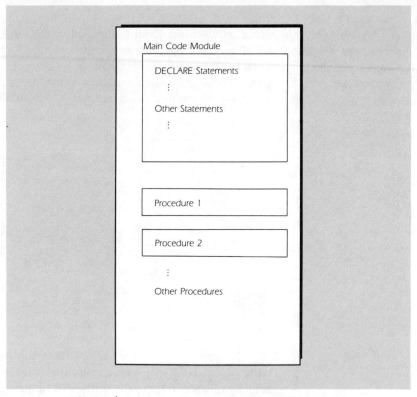

Figure 4.9 Storage Format of a Program (.BAS) File

Automatic insertion of DECLARE statements enables QuickBASIC to later verify that you have specified the proper number and type of arguments whenever you invoke a procedure.

The DECLARE statements at the beginning of the main module enable QuickBASIC to differentiate between references to procedure names and references to simple variable names. In fact, these DECLARE statements provide QuickBASIC with an additional capability. Because a DECLARE statement specifies any parameters required by the procedure, QuickBASIC can later verify that when you actually use the procedure, you correctly specify the number and type of required arguments.

Editing Your Program Lines

Now that you've learned what the Smart Editor does for you, it's time to learn what you can do for yourself. As you test a program, you discover a variety of reasons for making adjustments to your code. QuickBASIC's editor provides a host of editing tools to make this task easier. For instance, you can find specified portions of your code quickly. You can then make any desired textual corrections, deletions, or insertions.

Some editing adjustments require that you move text from one place to another in your code. To avoid retyping the desired text at the new location, QuickBASIC provides simple mechanisms for locating, selecting, deleting, copying, or moving text. This section explains how to perform these tasks using QuickBASIC's development environment.

Searching for and Replacing Specified Text

Search and replace operations make global changes easy.

As you test and work with a particular program, there are times when you wish to discover and look at each line which references a particular variable. There are other times when you may wish to do more than just look. These two situations call for the Search pulldown menu and the *Find/Change* choices.

Finding Selected Text in Your Program Files

For example, refer to the complete program listing for STYLE.BAS (see Listing 4.1). During the course of debugging, you might want to look at each line of code that references or influences the variable *word%*. To do so, you need to pull down the Search menu and select *Find*. Doing so brings up the dialog box seen in Figure 4.10

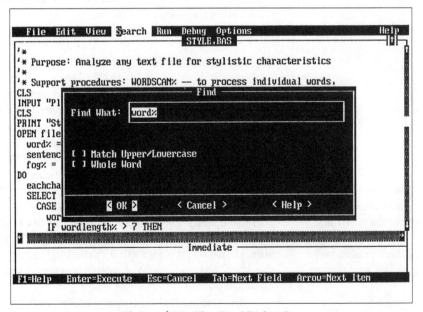

Figure 4.10 The *Find* Dialog Box

You only need to specify the desired string of characters (*word%*) and press Enter. QuickBASIC finds and highlights the characters in the next module line that contains them. In order to save you further time, QuickBASIC automatically fills in the *Find What:* text entry box. It uses whatever characters happen to have been selected on your screen prior to pulling down the Search menu. If no characters have been selected, then the keyword currently containing the cursor is used as the string to find.

After you have pulled down the menu once to find where the specified string occurs in your module, you will most likely wish to do this operation again. The Easy Search menu does not show you (although it is one of the Full menu options), but you can press function key F3 to request that the same search be performed again. In this way, you don't have to pull down the menu and enter the text string again. Pressing F3 successively takes you from one occurrence to the next throughout your entire module.

As you can see in Figure 4.10, there are two toggle switch settings that you control for the Find operation. By tabbing to either of them, or by clicking on them with a mouse, you can request that only strings that precisely match the restrictive criteria be presented to you. When you turn on either setting, an X appears between the brackets, and the restriction is enforced.

In the first case, you are shown only text strings in your module that exactly match the case of each letter in your *Find What* string. In the second setting, you see only matches that constitute complete words. If your *Find What* string happens to be embedded within a complete word (bordered by spaces or other punctuations), you are not shown this partial word match.

Pressing F3 repeats the last Find operation without requiring that you repeatedly pull down the Search menu and specify a text string to find.

Replacing Selected Text Strings

Frequently, you need to do much more than simply look at each string of characters in a program. Just as in word processing, where you may need to replace one name with another throughout your report, you may similarly want to change one variable for another throughout your program. This operation, sometimes called a *Search and Replace* operation, is obtained by choosing *Change* from the Search pulldown menu.

Some programmers adhere to the philosophy that a computer program should be self-documenting. These people choose variable names that are usually longer than average but are suggestive of the role they play in the program. For instance, in the STYLE.BAS program, the variable *word%* is an integer that counts up the number of words found in the specified text file. You might prefer to call this variable *NumberOfWords%*.

Self-documenting code often relies on very long variable names that make obvious the role those variables play within your program.

Even though the program is complete and working, you can pull down the Search menu and select *Change* to obtain the dialog box seen in Figure 4.11. You have the same two toggle switch controls in this Search and Replace operation as you previously had in the Find operation. But now, there is an additional text entry box to fill in. This allows you to specify the characters to insert after the characters to be found are first deleted. As you can see in this example, the *Find What* string is *word%* and the *Change To* string is entered as *NumberOfWords%*.

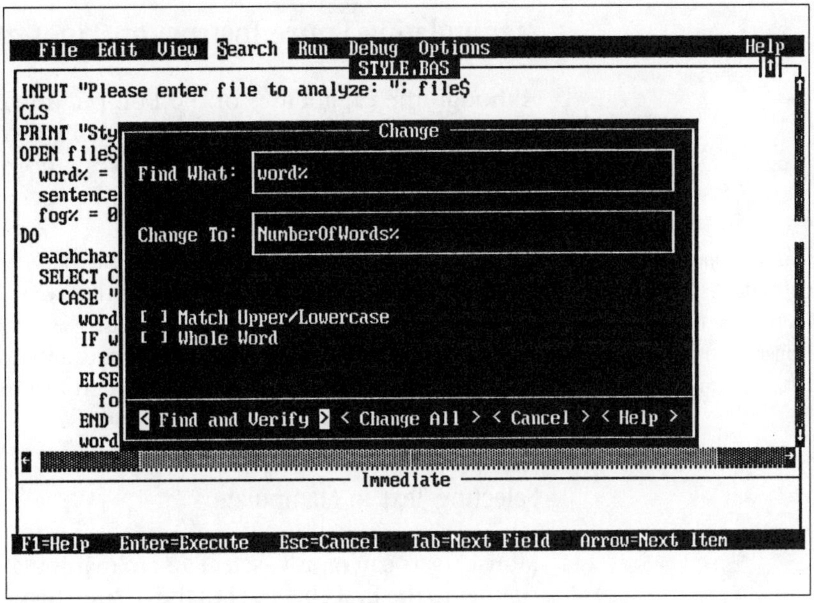

```
   File  Edit  View  Search  Run  Debug  Options                    Help
                          STYLE.BAS
 INPUT "Please enter file to analyze: "; file$
 CLS
 PRINT "Sty┌─────────────────── Change ───────────────────┐
 OPEN file$ │                                              │
   word% =  │ Find What:  ┌────────────────────────────┐   │
   sentence │             │word%                       │   │
   fog% = 0 │             └────────────────────────────┘   │
 DO         │ Change To:  ┌────────────────────────────┐   │
   eachchar │             │NumberOfWords%              │   │
   SELECT C │             └────────────────────────────┘   │
     CASE " │                                              │
       word │ [ ] Match Upper/Lowercase                    │
       IF w │ [ ] Whole Word                               │
         fo │                                              │
       ELSE │                                              │
         fo │ ◄ Find and Verify ►  < Change All >  < Cancel >  < Help > │
       END  └──────────────────────────────────────────────┘
       word
 █                                                                    →
 ├──────────────────────────── Immediate ────────────────────────────┤
 │                                                                    │
 │                                                                    │
 F1=Help   Enter=Execute   Esc=Cancel   Tab=Next Field   Arrow=Next Item
```

Figure 4.11 Search and Replace Operation

In the new variable, *NumberOfWords%*, the unique upper/lower-case capitalization is part of a self-documentating programmer's repertoire. It visually allows several words to be strung together in one variable name. The computer interprets the string as one word, but your eye clearly sees the intended three separate words.

Two important confirming options can be selected at the bottom of this dialog box. The default option, ⟨*Find and Verify*⟩, is obtained by simply pressing Enter after entering the text for the Find and Change boxes. Each successive occurrence of the *Find* string is highlighted in the View window, and you are shown a new dialog box, which asks you to either confirm the ⟨*Change*⟩ or to ⟨*Skip*⟩ this particular instance of the found text. After all occurrences of the found text are processed, a final dialog box is shown, which simply confirms that the Change process is complete.

Change All is the fastest method for searching and replacing text strings in QuickBASIC, but it is also fraught with danger for unsuspecting programmers.

The second alternative you have in the Change process is to select ⟨*Change All*⟩ at the bottom of the dialog box. This choice directs Quick-BASIC to perform the requested Search and Replace operation with no verification. Each discovered instance of the *Find What* string is replaced automatically with the *Change To* string.

Selecting the ⟨*Change All*⟩ option is usually not advisable, even for experienced programmers. The selected string often can be found lurking within another word, or in an unexpected context; automatic changes give you no chance to see unintended results before it is too late. Don't use this method unless you become 100 percent confident of the results, and even then, think twice about it.

Manipulating Entire Instruction Lines at a Time

Although the capabilities of the Edit pulldown menu can be used for any string of characters or words in your text, this is a programming environment and editing often involves whole lines of code. All of the techniques shown in this section can be used, however, to manipulate strings smaller than entire lines.

All text operations require that you first select the text to be operated on.

All text manipulation can be seen as a two-step operation: first you select some text, then you operate on that text. The operations typically take one of two forms. You may move the text from one place to another in your file, or even to another file located in another QuickBASIC window. Or, you may make a copy of the text in a new place, and then make desired adjustments in one of the copies.

Selecting Text to Manipulate

Mouse users can rapidly select text to manipulate by bringing the mouse pointer to the first character of the desired text, then holding button one down while moving the mouse pointer to the last character in the desired text. The selected text is highlighted as you move the mouse. Keyboard users have a battery of possible key combinations with which to select blocks of text. Table 4.2 summarizes the possibilities.

Table 4.2 Key Combinations Used to Select Text

Standard Keystroke	Text Selected
Shift-Left Arrow	Character to left of cursor
Shift-Right Arrow	Character to right of cursor
Shift-Ctrl-Left Arrow	Word to left of cursor
Shift-Ctrl-Right Arrow	Word to right of cursor
Shift-Down Arrow	Current line
Shift-Up Arrow	Line above cursor
Shift-PgUp	Screenful above cursor
Shift-PgDn	Screenful below cursor
Shift-Ctrl-Home	Characters from cursor to beginning of window
Shift-Ctrl-End	Characters from cursor to end of window

All of these keystrokes share one thing in common: the Shift key is held down while a cursor movement key is pressed. Doing this allows you to extend the selection cursor (the reverse video highlighting), which indicates the text that has been selected.

A common use of this multi-line selection method can be seen during new programming. The QuickBASIC hypertext help system contains a great many examples of code, which perform various tasks. Once you've looked up the Help text that explains how to write a particular type of code, you can select a block of statements from the Help window, then use *Copy* and *Paste* methods (see the following section) to incorporate those lines directly into the program you are writing in a View window.

Cutting, Copying, and Pasting Text

The Insert key toggles between insertion and overtyping modes.

Simple editing of text requires only that you position the cursor correctly, then do one of two things. Either you press the Delete key to remove individual characters, or you simply type the new characters you wish to insert at the point of the cursor. Existing characters are retained and are moved to the right to make space for the new characters. In QuickBASIC, the Insert key also works as a toggle switch if you wish to overtype characters at the point of the cursor.

There are many key combinations in QuickBASIC that enable you to manipulate groups of characters at one time. Table 4.3 summarizes them all; in this section, we'll discuss the principal ones.

Table 4.3 Key Combinations Used to Delete, Copy, or Insert

Standard Keystroke	Effect	Alternative Keystroke
Del	Deletes character at cursor, or any selected text	Ctrl-G
Backspace	Deletes character to left	Ctrl-H
	Deletes rest of word	Ctrl-T
Shift-Tab	Deletes leading spaces on a line	
Ins	Toggles insert mode	Ctrl-V
Shift-Ins	Inserts contents of clipboard	
Ctrl-Ins	Copies selected text to the clipboard, retaining it in original location	
Shift-Del	Copies selected text to the clipboard, deleting it from its original location	
	Copies current line to the clipboard, then deletes the line	Ctrl-Y
	Copies to the clipboard from cursor to end of line, then deletes original text	Ctrl-Q-Y

Copying Example Code from Help Screens to Your Program

When you are developing computer programs, you often need to deal with blocks of code involving more than just a few characters. For example, you may wish to call up a Help screen and look at one of the extensive examples of programming code. If the example shown is similar to the code you eventually must write yourself, then why not just copy the example from the Help window to the View window you are using? Then you can modify the code to fit your needs without having to type in all of the instructions from scratch.

Save time by copying example code from Help hypertext screens and then modifying it.

The steps necessary to pluck code from the Help hypertext and to place it into your program are as follows:

1. Call up the appropriate hypertext screen. Pressing F1 when the cursor is located on a keyword is the easiest way.

2. Use selection techniques as discussed earlier in this chapter to highlight the desired lines of code.

3. Use the Edit menu and select the *Copy* operation. Or use the shortcut key Ctrl-Ins. See below for an explanation of how this Copy mechanism actually works.

4. Press F6 at least once to switch the active window from Help to the View window you are using to write your program.

5. Press Ctrl-F10, or click on the title bar's Up Arrow in order to expand the window to full screen size.

6. Move the cursor to the intended location for the new instruction lines to be inserted.

7. Use the Edit menu and select the *Paste* operation. Or use the Shift-Ins shortcut key to insert the copied program lines.

8. Make any additions or adjustments to the code and continue writing and testing your program.

Using these large scale text manipulation techniques, however, is not limited to copying between windows. You may often wish to reorganize existing lines within one program, or even to copy and reconstruct certain instructions multiple times within a single program.

Moving Instructions Around Within Your Program

Clipboard is simply a vivid analogy for a temporary text holding area in memory.

The method of copying code seen in the last section is based on the use of a mechanism known as the *clipboard*. QuickBASIC reserves a portion of memory for temporary storage of text. Any selected text that is to be moved from one location to another in one or more QuickBASIC windows is placed in this temporary holding area of memory. The three operations that use this holding area are called *Cutting, Copying,* and *Pasting*.

These are the three choices available to you (with their shortcut keystrokes) when you pull down the Edit menu. Figures 4.12, 4.13, and 4.14 depict how each of these three methods employs the artifice known as the clipboard.

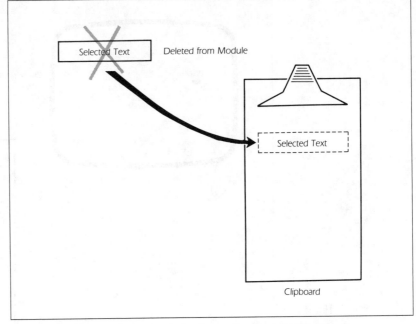

Figure 4.12 Cutting—Removing Text and Placing It
on the Clipboard

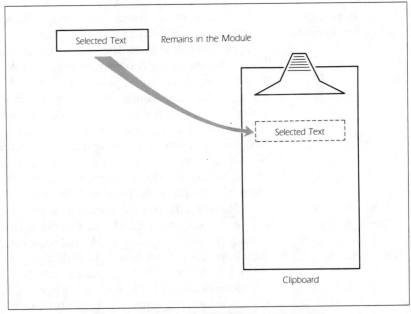

Figure 4.13 Copying—Replicating Selected Text
on the Clipboard

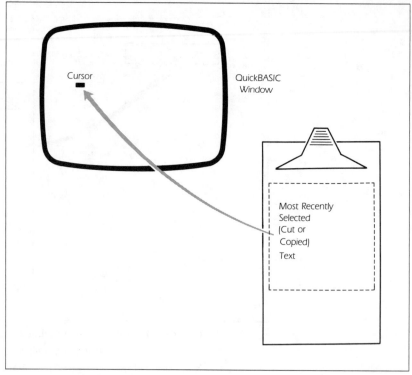

Figure 4.14 Pasting—Inserting Clipboard Contents into the File

You must first select text before you can use the Cut or Copy operations.

As Figure 4.12 depicts, the operation of Cutting removes any selected text from the window in which it appears. The removed text is then moved to the holding area of memory called the clipboard. This text remains available for later insertion into another location in one of your code modules. It only remains available, however, until the next Cut or Copy operation is performed. Only the most recent text that is cut or copied is retained on the clipboard; this new text completely overwrites any earlier information stored there.

Figure 4.13 depicts the operation of Copying. Unlike cutting, which removes the selected text from the window, copying leaves the original text intact. Like cutting, it does place a replica of the text onto the clipboard. So, after copying the text, it is then available for insertion elsewhere by using the third technique called Pasting.

You must have placed text onto the clipboard before you can use the Paste operation.

Pasting is the reverse operation, seen in Figure 4.14. Text that exists on the clipboard is placed into the file at the current location of the cursor. It remains on the clipboard so it can be inserted into several locations easily. You use a combination of *Cut* and *Paste* to effectively move selected text from one place to another. You use a *Copy* and *Paste* combination to replicate text one or more times in your file.

For example, suppose you wanted to display the progress of the STYLE.BAS program as it scans your text. A common programming technique for letting a user know that a program is working is to display progress information on the screen. In STYLE.BAS, you could select (and *copy* to the clipboard) the two PRINT statements located at the end of the program that output the number of words and sentences. Then you could insert those two statements (by *pasting* from the clipboard) within the main program loop.

Use the LOCATE statement to achieve a rolling odometer effect in your program output.

An appropriate place to insert the new display statements is just above the LOOP UNTIL EOF(1) line, as seen in Figure 4.15. Adding a LOCATE statement just before the PRINT lines assures that you obtain a rolling odometer effect rather than having two separate lines printed for each word counted. Try this adjustment now if you've typed STYLE.BAS into your computer.

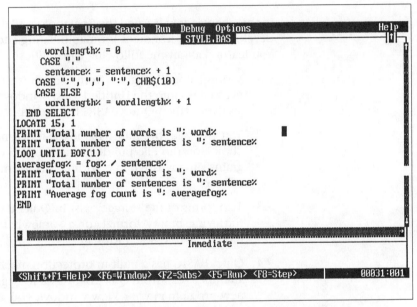

Figure 4.15 Using *Copy* and *Paste* to Enhance Your Program

Any time you have to recreate code that is similar to existing code, you should think in terms of the Copy and Paste techniques shown here. And any time you reorganize the flow of logic in a program, you should first attempt to use Cut and Paste techniques to move existing code from one place to another. Avoid extra typing whenever possible. Fast programmers are often fast typists, but they are also often the most facile users of programming editors such as QuickBASIC's Smart Editor.

Undoing a Mistake

Some editors, like QuickBASIC's Smart Editor, allow you to easily correct mistaken deletions or insertions. If you realize your error immediately, you can press the special Alt-Backspace key combination. This restores text that has just been deleted, or removes text that has just been inserted.

Use Alt-Backspace to undo an edit while the cursor is still on the same line.

However, this option is only available immediately after you insert or delete text. After you use one of the cursor control keys to move elsewhere, the *Undo* option is no longer available. This special key combination is accessible at all times, although it is not shown on the Edit menu unless you have turned on the Full Menus option for your development environment.

Review

In this chapter, you learned the final tools available in your QuickBASIC development environment for manipulating and editing program files. You learned about the following capabilities:

1. Writing a new program from scratch is as simple as typing command lines into the Untitled View window, which is immediately available when QuickBASIC first begins.

2. You give your program a name the first time you make the Save As choice on the File pulldown menu. You can store files and programs on any drive in any directory from the dialog box which appears.

3. Two forms of file storage exist in QuickBASIC: a fast loading and retrieving binary format, or a somewhat slower but eminently more readable ASCII format.

4. QuickBASIC has a built-in protection mechanism. Whenever you attempt to exit from QuickBASIC, or to begin writing or opening a new program in your View window, you are advised if any memory modules have not yet been stored. You can then ask Quick-BASIC to immediately store them all with a single keypress.

5. A host of cursor movement keys are recognized in QuickBASIC to complement mouse operations. Many of these standard keystrokes have alternative Ctrl key combinations that are compatible with the popular WordStar and Word programs.

6. QuickBASIC's editor does more than simple text manipulation. Because it understands the QuickBASIC programming language as well, it performs a number of more intelligent operations. Consequently, it is known as a Smart Editor because it:

    • Performs automatic syntax checking of each line as you enter it.

    • Reformats each line to make it easier to read by placing consistent spaces between operators and operands, and by capitalizing all QuickBASIC keywords. It also assures that all variable names, procedure names, and symbolic constants receive uniform capitalization throughout your program.

- Automatically inserts necessary declarations for procedures that you write and reference in your programs.

7. When your program runs, QuickBASIC performs a variety of validity checks on your code. Each error pauses the program and displays a dialog box explaining the perceived error, and highlighting the probable error in the line at fault. The Smart Editor stands by for your corrections.

8. The Search menu provides two easy mechanisms for finding any string of characters. A Search and Replace mechanism, called *Change*, is also available for finding and changing any string throughout your programs. The changes can be done swiftly and automatically, or can be subjected to individual verification.

9. Large blocks of text can be manipulated at once using the three options available on the Edit menu. You can *Cut* text to remove selected text from your file. You can later *Paste* text to insert it back into your file, or any other module, at the point of the cursor. Or you can *Copy* text, which leaves the original text intact, but makes another copy available for pasting or inserting. All three of these techniques make use of a special memory area called the clipboard. This area is used for the temporary holding of text that is to be cut, copied, or pasted.

Quiz for Chapter 4

1. You can begin writing a new QuickBASIC program at any time by making which choice on the File menu?

   a. Start program
   b. Begin program
   c. New program
   d. Open program

2. Which of the following is commonly known as the Development phase of a computer program's life cycle?

   a. Create-Edit-Run
   b. Edit-Test-Debug
   c. Create-Debug-Run
   d. Edit-Debug-Create

3. You should send a backup copy of your program to disk as you develop it. You can do this every 15 minutes or so with which command?

   a. Backup
   b. Store
   c. Save As
   d. Write

4. You move the cursor through your text one word at a time with which key combinations?

   a. Ctrl-Right Arrow, Ctrl-Left Arrow
   b. Shift-Right Arrow, Shift-Left Arrow
   c. Alt-Right Arrow, Alt-Left Arrow
   d. Right Arrow, Left Arrow

5. The PgUp and PgDn keys move the cursor how many lines at a time?

   a. Twenty-four lines
   b. Sixteen lines
   c. Size of the window
   d. Size of the scroll bar

6. The Smart Editor inserts spaces between:

   a. Keywords and parameters
   b. Function names and parentheses
   c. Operators and operands
   d. Capitalized and non-capitalized words

7. Which of the following are automatically capitalized by Quick-BASIC's Smart Editor?

    a. Function names
    b. Procedure names
    c. Keywords
    d. All of the above

8. When automatic syntax checking uncovers an error, which of the following does the Smart Editor not do?

    a. Display a dialog box
    b. Highlight the probable error in your program
    c. Allow you to correct the error on the spot
    d. Force you to correct the error immediately

9. Syntax refers to the actual structure and arrangement of the instructions that you type. What refers to the intended meaning and programmed result of those instructions?

    a. Suggestions
    b. Semantics
    c. Output
    d. Procedure

10. The Smart Editor occasionally inserts which of the following QuickBASIC statements into your program?

    a. FUNCTION statements
    b. SUB statements
    c. DECLARE statements
    d. CALL statements

11. The Search menu offers the ability to find strings of characters. This is often called a Search capability. This same menu offers a Search and Replace capability called:

    a. Search and Replace
    b. Find and Replace
    c. Replace
    d. Change

12. Which function key repeats the most recent Find operation?

    a. F2
    b. F3
    c. F4
    d. F5

13. You can replicate code from the Help hypertext files with which QuickBASIC sequence, available from the Edit menu?

    a. Cut and Copy
    b. Copy and Paste
    c. Clip and Copy
    d. Clip and Paste

14. The temporary memory area reserved to hold text that has been selected, then cut or copied, is called:

    a. Scissors
    b. Jar of Paste
    c. Clipboard
    d. Memory Pad

15. What keystroke can restore text that has been cut, or remove text that has been pasted?

    a. Alt-Del
    b. Alt-Backspace
    c. Alt-Ins
    d. Alt-Enter

2 | Understanding the Programming Language

Part 1 introduced the many development tools available in the Quick-BASIC environment. Because the ultimate goal of QuickBASIC is to enable you to develop application programs, this part concentrates on the fundamental nature of the built-in programming language.

Chapters 5, 6, and 7 are absolutely essential for all programmers. The fundamentals of QuickBASIC are presented in Chapter 5. Syntax, data types, and programming conventions are explained and demonstrated. All beginners should study this chapter carefully.

Chapter 6 focuses on the more complex QuickBASIC statements that facilitate decision making and repetitive looping. Experienced programmers will recognize these constructions; they constitute the flow of control in a program. Nearly every program requires one or more of these techniques, so pay careful attention to the possibilities.

Chapter 7 takes a close look at the different types of data files that can be created and manipulated from within QuickBASIC. Programs work with data, and data resides in separate files. You will learn here what the possibilities are for data storage and retrieval.

Chapters 8 and 9 take you into the more advanced ground of string manipulation and graphic management. QuickBASIC offers extensive command possibilities for managing string data and displaying your numerical data graphically. These two chapters take you beyond beginning skills into the intermediate class of user. Part 3 then presents methodology and techniques that can make an advanced user out of you.

5 | Learning the Basics

In previous chapters, you learned the basics of the QuickBASIC development environment. In this chapter, you will learn the fundamentals of the QuickBASIC programming language. You will learn what programs are and how they are constructed. You will also learn how to use them to process data of your own choosing.

Most computer programs follow the same three-part formula.

Figure 5.1 depicts the design of a typical computer program. Functionally, every computer program must first obtain data to work with, must then process that data, and must finally output the results in some usable form.

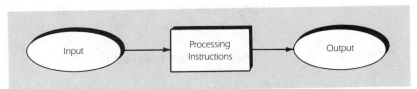

Figure 5.1 Design of a Typical Computer Program

QuickBASIC provides a variety of commands that can facilitate inputting data into a program. This chapter concentrates on the two most common commands, INPUT and READ. Others will be briefly discussed so you can decide if their capabilities merit further investigation.

QuickBASIC also offers a number of commands that control output from your program. The PRINT command is by far the most important; this chapter concentrates on it and on a variation of it called PRINT USING for formatted output.

In regard to the actual processing itself, your program is constructed of a number of parts. Figure 5.2 depicts these parts. The most important elements of each program are discussed in turn in this chapter. While each element in Figure 5.2 is not always present in every program, these aspects do represent the most typical and the most important components. You must understand what is required, as well as what is possible, in order to begin to construct your own useful and successful QuickBASIC programs.

QuickBASIC itself and good programming techniques demand a certain order to the construction of statements.

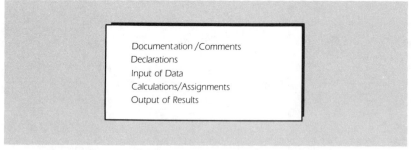

Documentation /Comments
Declarations
Input of Data
Calculations/Assignments
Output of Results

Figure 5.2 Structure of a QuickBASIC Program

Incorporating Documentation and Comments into Your Programs

Always include explanatory comments in your program code.

The simplest QuickBASIC statement is also one of the most underutilized. You can include in your programs as much explanation and program documentation as you like. Simply place an apostrophe on a statement line preceding your notation. The first few lines of the STYLE.BAS program in the preceding chapter were of this sort.

```
'* Main program module STYLE.BAS
'*
'* Purpose: Analyze any text file for stylistic
      characteristics
'*
```

Whenever you write a new program, it is a good idea to begin the program with several lines of documentation explaining the name, purpose, and any special aspects of the program. If the program includes procedures (see Chapter 10), your introductory remarks should include a brief explanation of the required parameters.

Throughout your program, add comment lines to explain any instruction lines that are not immediately obvious to a reader of your code. For example, if your variable names are not meaningful, add comments explaining how you are using the different variables. If you have any complex expressions, add a note explaining how you constructed them.

Incorporating these types of explanatory comments into your programs is easy as you write the programs, and much harder to add into your code after you've written it. The comments will make it much easier to pick up the code weeks or months later and continue to work with it. Develop the habit now and you won't regret it later.

Inputting Data into Your Program

All programs require input for processing.

Nearly all programs require some information in order to perform useful tasks. The INPUT statement enables you both to prompt a user for input data and to control where to store the user's typed responses. INPUT is at the heart of an interactive program, and as such, is at the heart of this section.

Using Different Variable Types

When data is entered or created in a program, that data must be stored in some memory area so that the program can reference the value of the data during its processing steps. In order to facilitate internal consistency in both the storage and handling of the data, QuickBASIC must know the *type* of data. For example, 67 could be a number, for use in multiplication. Or, it could be the beginning characters in the string "67 Lancaster Drive"; in this second case, 67 represents a character string.

Consequently, QuickBASIC has two primary classifications of data that can be manipulated by your programs. These categories are numbers and strings. Since computation is usually the hallmark of any computer program, QuickBASIC always assumes that your data is numerical, unless otherwise specified.

Forgetting to attach a type-declaring suffix to a variable name results in QuickBASIC's assuming that the variable is a simple integer type.

In fact, specifying the type of the data is up to you and can be done in several ways. The easiest way is to name the location where Quick-BASIC will store the data, and to append a special suffix character to the name, which defines the data type. When you name the data, you are naming the *variable* storage location that actually stores the data. When you store data in that location, you are said to be assigning a *value* to the variable. Figure 5.3 demonstrates this correspondence, and also shows examples of different types of QuickBASIC data.

As the figure suggests, a variable name (such as *AGE%*) that ends in a percent sign (%) is used to store simple integers. This is QuickBASIC's default type; this means that if you forget to append a suffix character at

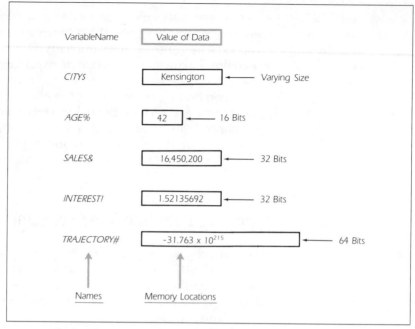

Figure 5.3 Distinguishing between a Variable and Its Value

all to the variable name, QuickBASIC will act as if you added a %, effectively treating the storage location as a simple integer. Hence, variables such as *RESULT, A,* and *ANSWER* are assumed to store simple integer values.

A simple integer can be any number between −32,768 and +32,767. These whole numbers can be stored in 16 bits, the number of memory bits used to store a simple integer variable. Whole numbers that exceed these maximum values must use a different suffix. QuickBASIC allocates twice as many storage bits for a variable name that ends with an ampersand (&), and calls such a variable a *long integer*. When using 32 bits, a variable such as *SALES&* can store numbers ranging from +2 million to −2 million. Table 5.1 displays the precise limits of data stored in QuickBASIC's different data types.

Table 5.1 Limitations of QuickBASIC's Data Values

Type of Data	Minimum Value	Maximum Value
Simple integer	−32,768	+32,767
Long integer	−2,147,483,648	+2,147,483,647
Single precision	−3.402823 E+38	+3.402823 E + 38
Double precision	−1.797693134862315 D +308	1.797693134862315 D + 308
String	0 characters	32,767 characters

Floating point numbers consist of an integer and a fractional part.

The remaining two types of numerical data are both called floating point numbers. Essentially, they differ from integers because they have a fractional part. For example, 3.2567 or 241.33 would require one of the two floating point variables, suffixed with either an exclamation point (!) or a pound sign (#). Ending a variable with ! directs QuickBASIC to use the same 32 bits of memory storage, but in a different algebraic manner.

Data stored in such a floating point variable (like *INTEREST!* in Figure 5.3) can range from approximately −3.4 times 10 to the 38th power, to +3.4 times 10 to the 38th power. Such a number is termed *single precision* in QuickBASIC, and can be indicated during either input or output by the letter E, as in Table 5.1.

Numbers requiring even greater magnitude or range can be stored in variables like *TRAJECTORY#*. The # suffix forces QuickBASIC to allocate 64 bits for each data item stored. Such a number is called *double precision* in QuickBASIC; the letter D can be used during both input and output to indicate this data type. The extra bits enable QuickBASIC to manage numbers that can exceed plus or minus 10 to the 308th power.

Store character strings in string variables.

Last of all, strings of characters are often used by programs in formatted output, in labels, and in simple text data that is stored, searched, and manipulated in various ways. Character strings must be stored in *string variables*, denoted by a dollar sign ($) suffixed to the variable name. The variable named *CITY$* in Figure 5.3 contains the 10-character value "Kensington". By convention, the most common use of a string variable requires as many bytes (8 bits each) as there are characters stored in the string.

You have now learned how to name a variable properly in order to prepare for the type of data to be stored in it. Until you actually place a data value into a variable's memory location, QuickBASIC makes one of two assumptions. If it is a numerical type of data, the variable's value is 0 until set to some other value. If it is a string type, its value is set to null (0 length). This means that its name is known, but no memory space is consumed until some characters are stored in the variable's assigned location.

Last, you can create variable names with any sequence of up to 40 characters. Although a typical name contains letters and a single suffix character, such as can be seen in Figure 5.3, you can be somewhat creative. As mentioned in Chapter 4, some programmers believe that variable names should themselves convey meaning. Although the simple names in Figure 5.3 are meaningful, sometimes you may feel the need to make longer names, such as *NumberOfWords%*.

The first character of any variable name must be a letter (A to Z). Variable names cannot exceed 40 characters in length.

Self-documenting variable names are a good idea. They do make your program easier to read and debug later. The only downside to this type of naming convention is that the longer names take longer to type and can slow down your overall programming effort. You can include any letter, number, suffix character, or the decimal point in the 40 character limit; however, the very first character must be a letter.

Obtaining Variable Values from the User

The INPUT statement can prompt for input, and then accept and store a user's entry.

The INPUT statement is QuickBASIC's principal way of obtaining values to store in variable locations. Its syntax allows for a prompting message to be displayed to the user. Variable names for which the user is expected to enter data follow the prompting message in the INPUT statement. For instance, in the STYLE.BAS program seen in the previous chapter, one of the first lines in the program was

```
INPUT "Please enter file to analyze: "; file$
```

This statement is asking for the user to enter the filename that is to be scanned and analyzed by the remainder of this program. The message in quotation marks is displayed to the user on the output screen, followed by a question mark.

```
Please enter file to analyze:?
```

The question mark is generated by QuickBASIC because of the semicolon, located just after the prompting message, in the INPUT statement. Replacing the semicolon with a comma would eliminate the question mark in the output message. The user is being told what to enter: a filename. What is actually typed is stored in the string variable *file$* and is used by the remainder of the STYLE.BAS program.

Multiple data items can be input with one INPUT statement, but the entries must agree in number and type with the variable names listed in the INPUT statement itself.

If you want the user to enter several values on the same line, you can prompt for them, listing the variable names on the INPUT line. For instance, if your program contains this statement:

```
INPUT "Please enter Employee ID and hours worked: ", ID%,
    HRS%
```

then QuickBASIC expects the user to enter two numbers separated by a comma. In response to any such INPUT statement, a user must enter a sequence of data items that correspond in both number and type to the variable names found in the statement. If this is not the case, Quick-BASIC displays the message

```
Redo from start
```

Separate several input items by commas.

and prompts the user once again for the same expected input.

So if you write the INPUT statement to expect four variable values, the program will not continue until four values have been entered, separated by commas. In addition, if the third variable in the INPUT statement is a string variable, then the third data value entered must be a string of characters.

Exploring Other Input Mechanisms

Other techniques exist for obtaining values for QuickBASIC variables. If any of these alternative methods seem appropriate to your programming needs, refer to your QuickBASIC documentation or to the on-line hypertext files for further details.

Initializing Symbolic Constants

Some data information may take the form of a known series of data values that can be preset into a program. The values can then be used in turn. QuickBASIC includes DATA statements that allow known values to be written into a program in advance. Each value can be read successively with one or more QuickBASIC READ statements, and then can be used for ongoing processing.

For example, your program may calculate payroll for a group of employees. While you may use the INPUT statement to obtain the employee's ID and the hours worked, you may also have a fixed set of wage scales for different employee grades. In this case, you could use the DATA and READ statements to initialize several variables such as *grade1!, grade2!,* and *grade3!* with the appropriate pay rates.

DATA statements may be entered anywhere in your program, although the clearest place to enter them is just before the READ statement(s) that will extract values from them. The following code segment prepares the three data values:

```
DATA 4.00, 4.50, 5.00
```

The corresponding READ statement might be

```
READ grade1!, grade2!, grade3!
```

Symbolic constants are a special kind of variable that facilitates easy updating of your program when certain data changes must occasionally occur.

This technique allows your program to refer to named variables at various places throughout the module, rather than to the constant numbers 4.00, 4.50, or 5.00. Presumably, these hourly wage rates will be changed in the future. Using the DATA/READ statement pair means that when pay scales change, only the one DATA statement must be changed in your program. These particular variables are called *symbolic constants*, since they symbolize or stand for an actual constant value. The value won't change during the execution of the program, but the program is more easily changed between runs by simply adjusting the numbers on the DATA statement.

Using Groups of Variables, or Arrays

Your company, however, may have more than three pay grades; it may have twenty grades and pay scales. And you may wish to write one set of in-

Use numberic *subscripts* to refer to individual variables in a group of similar values stored as an *array*.

structions that do the same job for each grade. If you have twenty symbolic constants named *grade1!* through *grade20!*, your program will surely be larger than necessary. Chapter 6 will demonstrate why this is so.

An *array* is simply a group of variables, all used for the same purpose and all receiving the same variable name. Each separate variable is identified uniquely by a position number in the group known as a *subscript*. In this payroll example, you would tell QuickBASIC that you wish to use such an array variable by including a special declaration statement. This statement must appear on some line in the program earlier than the first time the array is referenced.

To create the *grade!* array with sufficient unique memory areas for twenty pay rates, you need to include the following DIMension statement in your program:

```
DIM grade!(20)
```

Figure 5.4 illustrates how the twenty possible pay rates are stored in the variables known now as *grade!(1)*, *grade!(2)*, *grade!(3) . . . grade!(20)*. QuickBASIC uses the parenthesis and the subscript value to find a unique array element. Hence, your program might include multiple DATA statements that look like

```
DATA 4.0, 4.5, 5.0, 5.5, 6.25, 6.75, 7.25, 7.50, 7.65, 7.95
DATA 8.10, 8.25, 8.55, 8.7, 8.85, 8.9, 9.15, 9.2, 9.3, 9.6
```

VariableName	Value of Data
grade ! (1)	4.0
grade ! (2)	4.5
grade ! (3)	5.0
grade ! (4)	5.5
grade ! (5)	6.25
grade ! (6)	6.75
grade ! (7)	7.25
grade ! (8)	7.50
grade ! (9)	7.65
grade ! (10)	7.95
grade ! (11)	8.10
grade ! (12)	8.25
grade ! (13)	8.55
grade ! (14)	8.7
grade ! (15)	8.85
grade ! (16)	8.9
grade ! (17)	9.15
grade ! (18)	9.2
grade ! (19)	9.3
grade ! (20)	9.6

Figure 5.4 Arrays of Variables Using Subscripts for Uniqueness

Chapter 6 will present the possible looping constructions that can READ into the *grade!* array each of the twenty values available in the DATA statements. When multiple DATA statements exist, the values on them are read in order by successive READ statements.

Reading Whole Lines, or Individual Characters

Read an entire line of data at once with the LINE INPUT statement.

Another input mechanism is the LINE INPUT statement. Some users wish to accept an entire line of input characters from a user, with no regard to the meaning or placement of commas or blank spaces. This technique names a string variable to receive all of a user's typed characters up until the Enter key is pressed.

For example, suppose that your program were designed to construct a crossword puzzle using a group of words entered by the user. Since the words vary in length, your request might appear as

```
LINE INPUT "Enter the vertical words, separated by spaces:
    ", W$
```

As you begin to program more frequently, you'll soon learn that there is no one solution for programming needs. Every example you see can be programmed in another, sometimes better, way. In this crossword example, your program would have to scan through the W$ variable and extract the words separated by spaces.

Read a single character at a time with the INPUT$ function.

Alternatively, the INPUT$ function can be used with a looping construction to repetitively read one character at a time from the keyboard. The STYLE.BAS program in the previous chapter used just such a mechanism to read one character at a time from the specified text file. The instruction line seen there was

```
eachchar$ = INPUT$(1, #1)
```

This form of the INPUT$ function reads a single character from the file opened as device #1 (see Chapter 7 for more details about file and device input/output). A simpler form of keyboard input can specify exactly how many characters to read at a time. To read precisely 5 characters from the keyboard into a *PASSWORD$* variable, your program might include the following line:

```
password$ = INPUT$(5)
```

Processing Your Variables with QuickBASIC Instructions

This section deals with the possibilities and mechanisms for processing variables and values in your QuickBASIC programs. Primarily, you will learn here about the two types of expressions in QuickBASIC: numerical and logical. You will learn how to directly assign values to variables, and how to construct complex expressions consisting of a wide range of QuickBASIC operators, constants, variables, and functions. Building expressions in your programs is your principal means of taking data in one form, applying some logic or processing intelligence to it, and producing meaningful output.

Calculating and Assigning Numerical Values

Use an *operator* to perform some action on an *operand*.

An *operator* is a symbol that stands for some action you are asking QuickBASIC to perform. For example, multiplication is an action, and the QuickBASIC operator for it is an asterisk (*). Placing the * between two variable names identifies those variables as the *operands* in the expression. An *expression* is simply a collection of operators and operands that produces a single resulting value. For example, the following are simple expressions:

```
A = 2
result& = 5 * A + 67
numbermonths% = 12 * (years2 - years1)
halfremaining& = FRE(-1) / 2
```

These are numerical expressions, because they result in a single numerical value. In the first expression, the variable *A* is assigned the value 2. Hence, this type of statement is called an *assignment* statement. In the second expression, the variable *result&* is assigned the final value obtained by multiplying 5 times the value stored in *A* (which is 2) and adding 67. Hence, *result&* is assigned the value 77 (5 * 2 + 67).

The third expression demonstrates the use of parentheses to group and arrange the order, or *precedence*, of calculation. The subexpression *years2 − years1* is calculated first, then multiplied by 12 to obtain a value to store in the variable *numbermonths%*.

The last expression demonstrates that functions offer another way to generate values for variables, and that they can be combined with other numerical operands as well. The FRE function obtains the maximum available space for dimensioning a non-string array. Dividing it in two ensures that the *halfremaining&* variable can control the usage of half of that free space.

QuickBASIC offers seven different operators.

The possibilities for numerical operators include the obvious signs for addition (+), subtraction or negation (−), multiplication (*), division (/), and exponentiation (^). Also available for more complex expressions are the special QuickBASIC symbol for integer division (\), and the modulo operator (MOD).

The following are examples of these operators in action:

```
years = numdays& \ 365
months = (numdays& - 365 * years) \ 12
days = numdays& MOD 30
```

When the special integer division operator is used, each operand is rounded to an integer. When the result is obtained, it is truncated to another integer before finalizing the value of the expression.

QuickBASIC evaluates expressions according to the rules of operator precedence, or hierarchy.

When an expression becomes complicated and includes several operators, the order of execution of the operations becomes very important. Without an understanding of implied order (sometimes called the *hierarchy* or *precedence* of the operators), you cannot always be sure of the results. For example, what will be the value in *answer&* after the following expression is evaluated?

```
answer& = 5 * 6 + 2 ^ 3
```

There are a great many possible answers, but QuickBASIC would calculate an answer of 38. Properly placed parentheses always direct Quick-BASIC to calculate the sub-expressions within the parentheses first. With no guidance from you in the form of parentheses, QuickBASIC uses the operator precedence shown in Table 5.2. The order of operations is done from top to bottom in this hierarchical list of arithmetic operators.

Table 5.2 Hierarchical Order of Arithmetic Operator Precedence

Arithmetic Operator	Task Performed
( )	Grouping
^	Exponentiation
−	Negation
* or /	Multiplication or division
\	Integer division
MOD	Modulo calculation
+ or −	Addition or subtraction

Consequently, in the example above, the final value of 38 is obtained because the exponentiation is performed first ($2^3 = 8$), the multiplication is performed next ($5 * 6 = 30$), and the addition is performed last ($30 + 8 = 38$). If that default order of operation is not what you intend, you must place parentheses appropriately to influence the computational order.

Using Logical Expressions

Flow of control refers to the order in which QuickBASIC executes statements.

As you will see in Chapter 6, your QuickBASIC programs do not always execute each statement successively. When the execution of instructions is not sequential, then there is usually some logical expression that influences the *flow of control*. You must understand how to write an expression that uses logical and relational operators. Only then can you write code that manages decision making, looping, and multiple choice program actions, such as selection of menu alternatives.

Whereas an arithmetic expression evaluates to a number, a *logical expression* is one that evaluates to a TRUE or FALSE value. In this way, you can control program actions by making them dependent on whether a logical expression (that is, a *condition*) is TRUE or not. For example, you might want to display an error message on the screen if the supposed hours worked by an employee in one week, and entered by the user into variable *HRS%*, exceeded 60. The logical expression you would use would be

```
HRS% > 60
```

This expression evaluates to either TRUE (if *HRS%* is greater than 60) or FALSE (if *HRS%* is less than or even equal to 60). Although each of the operands in this expression is numerical, the net effect is a logical value. This occurs because the arithmetic operands are connected by a *relational operator*. Such an operator allows you to relate two variables or values, or to compare one to another. Table 5.3 lists the possible relational operators in QuickBASIC.

Table 5.3 QuickBASIC's Relational Operators

Operator Symbol	Action Performed
=	Equality
>	Greater than
<	Less than
< >	Inequality
>=	Greater than or equality
<=	Less than or equality

In any complex expression, arithmetic sub-expressions are always evaluated first, before any relational operations are completed.

All relational operators are below all arithmetic operators in hierarchical precedence. Hence, in any complex expression, all arithmetic computations are performed first. Then, relational operators are used to compare the arithmetic values. The result is a logical value typically used to control the next steps that the program takes.

It is best to think of logical expressions as having the logical value of TRUE or FALSE. However, that is for your benefit only, as it makes your QuickBASIC code easier to read, write, and understand. In fact, QuickBASIC assumes a value of 0 when a logical expression is FALSE, and a value of −1 when a value is TRUE. This only encourages some tricky and poor programming practices, so continue to think of logical expressions as having values of TRUE or FALSE.

Logical expressions are either TRUE or FALSE.

As Figure 5.5 depicts, there are two kinds of logical expressions that evaluate to TRUE or FALSE. In Case 1, two or more arithmetic operands can be connected by relational operators to result in a logical expression. In Case 2, multiple logical operands or expressions can be connected by logical operators to form a more complex logical expression, which itself results in a TRUE or FALSE value.

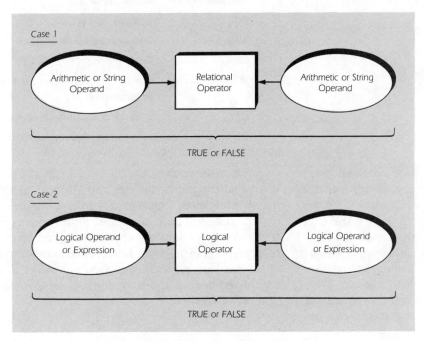

Figure 5.5 Types of Logical Expressions

For example, you might want to write a paycheck for an employee, subject to two conditions. First, the *HRS%* the employee worked must be reasonable (HRS% <= 60). Second, the employee's ID must be valid. Your program code might include a FUNCTION procedure (see Chapter 10) called VALID(id), which returns TRUE if the entered ID exists in the Personnel database file, and FALSE otherwise. You can combine these two logical expressions with the AND logical operator to obtain

```
HRS% <= 60  AND  VALID(id)
```

The AND operator makes the entire complex expression equal to TRUE only if both operands are true at the same time. In other words, the hours must not exceed 60, *and* the VALID function must return a TRUE value for the particular employee ID entered.

There are several logical operators used in QuickBASIC, and each has its own role and its own position in the hierarchical precedence ordering. All logical operations are performed after all relational operations. This makes sense. Relational operators are responsible for combining various operands into logical expressions. And a logical operator, such as the ones shown in Table 5.4, can only operate on a logical expression.

Table 5.4 Logical Operators in Precedence Order

Operator Symbol	Action Performed
NOT	Reverses the operand.
AND	Both operands must be TRUE.
OR	Either operand can be TRUE.
XOR	One or the other operand is TRUE, but not both simultaneously.
EQV	Both operands must have same value.
IMP	First operand implies the second.

Use parentheses freely in constructing complex expressions. If you don't do this, QuickBASIC uses its internal rules of precedence to perform arithmetic operations first, relational operations second, and logical expressions last.

The AND and OR operators are by far the most common ones used in typical programs. Throughout the rest of this book, you will see many examples of logical expressions using these two operators to control the program execution flow. Simply remember to use parentheses freely to group your sub-expressions when you want to assure the order of expression evaluation. And also remember that whenever operators of varying sorts are included in an expression, arithmetic operations are completed first, relational operations are done next, and logical operations are done last.

Formatting Your Screen and Printed Output

The most powerful and common output statement in QuickBASIC is the PRINT command. It can be used to direct your output to the screen, to a printer, to a file, or even to a special communications device if your computer is equipped with one. Chapter 7 concentrates on file and device input/output. Here, you will learn the mechanics of the PRINT command itself, and will concentrate on screen output.

Displaying Any Variables for Output

The PRINT command only requires that you identify the names of the variables that contain the values you want to display. PRINT displays those variable values on the next available screen line. Usually, it is a good idea to first clear the screen, using a CLS statement just prior to the PRINT command. The output then appears on successive screen lines beginning with the first.

For example, to print the values stored in the *AGE%* and *SALES&* variables, you only need to enter

```
PRINT age%, sales&
```

QuickBASIC outputs each value separated by commas in a 14-column area on your screen. So the result is

```
42            16450200
```

Had you wanted to display these numbers without the default number of separation spaces, you could have separated the variable names with semicolons instead. In this case, QuickBASIC only places a leading and trailing space before and after each variable's value when it outputs it.

```
42  16450200
```

PRINT USING offers a series of special symbols that enable you to control the detailed output display or print format of individual variables.

Naturally, you might like the 16 million dollar sales figure to be displayed with a leading dollar sign and embedded commas. In order to do this, you must use a variation on the PRINT command. The PRINT USING version allows you to specify formatting directions as part of the statement itself.

You can simply incorporate the formatting characters in quotation marks as part of the statement. For example, if you wanted to display this sales figure more attractively, you could enter

```
PRINT USING "Sales for 1988 were: $$########,"; sales&
```

The results would be

```
Sales for 1988 were: $16,450,200
```

Learn formatting symbols to control the appearance of your output.

Table 5.5 summarizes the various special formatting symbols available to you when using the PRINT USING statement. These formatting characters probably represent more potential variations in output layout than you will ever use. Because QuickBASIC produces a default layout for all conceivable output values, you only need to use the PRINT USING formatting symbols if you are not satisfied with the default appearance.

Table 5.5 Formatting Symbols for the PRINT USING Statement

Symbol	Explanation
	Outputting Numerical Values
#	A numerical digit
.	A decimal point
+	The sign of the number
−	Trailing minus sign for negative numbers
**	Asterisks in leading spaces
$$	Leading dollar sign
**$	Leading dollar sign to left of leading spaces
^^^^	Exponential format
_	Next character in format is a literal
%	Excessive numerical magnitude indicator
	Outputting String Values
!	Only the first character in the string
\ \	Outputs x + 2 characters from the string; x = number of spaces between the backslashes
&	Variable length string field; output completely

Listing 5.1 shows the CH5DEMO.BAS program and Figure 5.6 displays the output screen after running this program. The lines are numbered for convenient referencing in this section; it is not necessary to number lines in QuickBASIC.

Listing 5.1 CH5DEMO.BAS Output Demonstration Program

```
' CH5DEMO.BAS
' Demonstration program for output control
'
1 CLS
2 DATA 4.00,4.50,5.00,5.50,6.25
3 READ grade!(1), grade!(2), grade!(3), grade!(4), grade!(5)
4 PRINT "These two items use the default 14 positions each:"
5 PRINT grade!(1), grade!(3)
6 PRINT "One leading and one trailing space:"
7 PRINT grade!(3); grade!(4)
8 PRINT "This item is on the same line as the message:";
9 PRINT grade!(5)
10 DATA 375,"Joseph Dubinett"
11 DATA 995,"Sandra Mulhaney"
```

```
12 READ id1, name1$, id2, name2$
13 WAGES = 40 * grade!(1)
14 PRINT USING "Employee No 1's paycheck should be:
      $$##.##"; WAGES
15 PRINT "The following line should be completely blank:"
16 PRINT
17 PRINT "EMPLOYEE ID"; TAB(15); "NAME"; TAB(35); "WAGES"
18 PRINT id1; TAB(15); name1$;
19 PRINT USING "$$##.##"; TAB(35); 40 * grade!(1)
20 PRINT id2; TAB(15); name2$;
21 PRINT USING "$$##.##"; TAB(35); 40 * grade!(2)
```

```
These two items use the default 14 positions each:
 4              5
One leading and one trailing space:
 5 5.5
This item is on the same line as the message: 6.25
Employee No 1's paycheck should be: $160.00
The following line should be completely blank:

EMPLOYEE ID  NAME              WAGES
  375        Joseph Dubinett   $160.00
  995        Sandra Mulhaney   $180.00




Press any key to continue
```

Figure 5.6 Output Results from Running CH5DEMO.BAS

Take a moment to look through the sample lines in this program. You'll recognize many of the techniques already explained in this chapter. Line 16 is new and shows you how to produce a blank line on your output screen. Lines 17 to 21 demonstrate how to take values in your program and format an organized output table. The TAB function has the sole job of moving the print head or cursor to the column number specified in parentheses. Succeeding data to be output will appear beginning in that column.

Use LOCATE for precise row and column controls.

A typical text screen is organized into 25 rows and 80 columns. Figure 5.7 indicates that these rows are numbered from top to bottom on the screen, while the columns are numbered from left to right. The TAB function helps you to specify columnar position for output, but the LOCATE statement gives you precise row and column position control. Use this statement to position the cursor at a specific place on the screen; the next PRINT statement of any kind begins its output at that position.

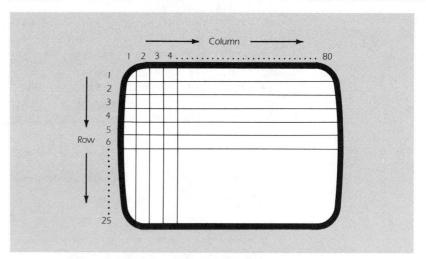

Figure 5.7 Numbering Conventions for Screen Rows
and Columns

LOCATE's rolling
odometer effect can
display progress
information for a long
running program.

You saw this LOCATE statement used in the last chapter (see Figure 4.15) to ensure that output information is always placed in the same screen position. In this way, a repeated output statement or group of statements can create a rolling odometer effect, enabling you to keep track of the progress of a program.

Review

This chapter introduced you to the fundamental aspects of programming with QuickBASIC. You learned the following facts:

1. A typical computer program consists of some means of inputting data, a series of instructions to process the data, and some final instructions for outputting the results.

2. Documentation and comments can be incorporated easily into a QuickBASIC program by beginning your remarks with an apostrophe.

3. A variable is a named memory location for your data. A value is the actual data that is stored at that location.

4. QuickBASIC allows you to specify the type of data you are using. Simply suffixing the proper symbol to your variable's name tells

QuickBASIC the type of data, and indicates how large the storage area must be.

5. Data type suffixes are available for strings ($), simple integers (%), long integers (&), single precision floating point numbers (!), and double precision floating point numbers (#).

6. The INPUT command enables you to prompt the user for input data, and then to direct the typed information to be stored into one or more variables.

7. The DATA and READ statements allow you to preset a number of fixed values for consecutive use by your program. This makes it easy to later change the values in the DATA statement with no adjustments to your program's processing lines.

8. An array of variables is a special mechanism that allows you to use one variable name for a group of similar variables, uniquely identifying each one by a different number, called the *subscript*.

9. Whole lines of data can be read at a time with the LINE INPUT statement, and individual characters can be read one at a time with the INPUT$ function.

10. Operators are symbols that indicate what action is to be performed. Operands are the variables, constants, or expressions upon which action is to be performed. An expression is simply a legal combination of operators and operands.

11. Three types of operators exist in QuickBASIC: arithmetic, relational, and logical. In any complex expression, all arithmetic operations are performed first. Relational comparison operations are performed next, resulting in logical values of TRUE or FALSE. And remaining logical operations are done last. Parentheses can be, and should be, used to group operations. Operations within parentheses are performed prior to any other steps.

12. When more than one arithmetic operator appears in an expression, a hierarchy of operation called *precedence* rules determines the order in which each operator is evaluated. A similar precedence order exists for logical operators.

13. The PRINT command is the simplest statement for outputting program results. The PRINT USING variation is often used to apply special formatting and layout rules to data output.

Quiz for Chapter 5

1. Which of the following always appears in a computer program?

   a. Input
   b. Processing
   c. Output
   d. All of the above

2. Notes or comments in your QuickBASIC programs begin with which symbol on a line?

   a. Semicolon
   b. Apostrophe
   c. Colon
   d. Asterisk

3. Individual variables can be read into your program from the keyboard with which statement?

   a. READ
   b. DATA
   c. INPUT
   d. LINE INPUT

4. If no data type suffix is affixed to a variable name, what type of data does QuickBASIC assume?

   a. Single precision floating point
   b. Simple integer
   c. Long integer
   d. String

5. Which of the following is not a data type suffix?

   a. #
   b. !
   c. @
   d. &

6. How does the range of possible values of a double precision number compare with the range of a single precision number?

   a. Four times as much
   b. Twice as much
   c. Ten times as much
   d. A billion times as much

7. Variable names must begin with a letter and are limited to how many characters?

    a. 8
    b. 12
    c. 25
    d. 40

8. Preset constant values can be stored in symbolic constants in your program with what pair of QuickBASIC statements?

    a. READ-STORE
    b. INPUT-STORE
    c. INPUT-DATA
    d. DATA-READ

9. A group of variables, all of the same type, and all using the same name, is called:

    a. A Group
    b. A Subscript
    c. An Array
    d. A Type

10. Values can be given to variables with which type of QuickBASIC statement?

    a. Declaration
    b. Comment
    c. Assignment
    d. Operation

11. The set of hierarchical rules used to determine the order of computation in an expression is called:

    a. Ordering
    b. Precedence
    c. Levels
    d. Stepping

12. A numerical expression evaluates to a number. A logical expression evaluates to:

    a. TRUE or FALSE
    b. 1 or 0
    c. 1 or −1
    d. 1 or 2

13. Which of the following is the lowest in the hierarchy of operators?

    a. Numerical operators
    b. Parentheses
    c. Logical operators
    d. Relational operators

14. Which of the following is used to generate formatted output with special format symbols?

   a. OUTPUT
   b. PRINT
   c. DISPLAY USING
   d. PRINT USING

15. The TAB function aligns your output in a particular column. What QuickBASIC statement can position output at a specific row and column?

   a. WRITE
   b. POSITION
   c. LOCATE
   d. PRINT TO

Chapter

6 | Managing the Flow of Control

In Chapter 5, you learned how to input data into your program and how to display your program's results. You also learned about assigning values to variables and constructing complex expressions using these variables. In this chapter, you will extend your understanding of QuickBASIC. You will take those arithmetic, relational, and logical expressions and begin to develop sophisticated combinations of statements.

A typical computer program does not actually follow a rigid series of steps. It is not executed precisely the same way each time the program is run. And it does not consist of simple, sequential one-line statements executed in order from top to bottom in your program text.

Compound statements require more than one program line.

A non-trivial program includes special statements that facilitate unattended decision making and repetition. All of the statements you've seen so far have fit on one line in your programs. This chapter concentrates on statements that take up multiple lines in your program. They are called *compound statements*.

There are many compound statements in QuickBASIC. Some exist for compatibility with earlier versions of BASIC; others exist for historical reasons of competition with other computer languages. All of them are variations on the two simple themes of *decision making* and *repetition*. Both types of statements rely on a logical condition, and control the execution flow in your program based on the value of that logical expression.

127

Examples of decision making statements in QuickBASIC are the IF
. . . ENDIF and the CASE SELECT statements. They enable your program to decide which of several groups of statements, called *statement
blocks*, to execute. These are the two most popular and commonly used
statements. You will learn how and when to effectively use these con-
structs within your QuickBASIC programs.

Repetition statements include the DO . . . LOOP, the WHILE . . .
WEND, and the old style FOR . . . NEXT statements. Since all three represent only minor variations on the same theme—to repeat a block of
QuickBASIC statements—you'll focus on what I consider to be the best
of the three, the DO . . . LOOP statement.

> The IF and the DO
> statements can meet all
> your flow of control
> needs. However, the
> CASE statement is worth
> adding to your repertoire
> simply for the more
> readable code that it
> allows you to write.

Based on my experience of over twenty years of programming, I
suggest that you learn three specific QuickBASIC compound statements. Figure 6.1 summarizes these three statements and suggests when
you should consider using them. The remainder of this chapter provides explanations and examples for each of them.

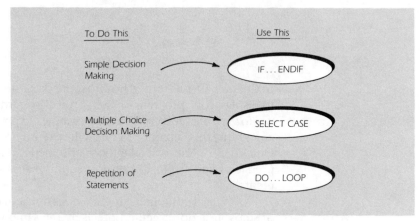

Figure 6.1 Compound Statements That Control the Flow
of Execution

Making Decisions Automatically

In a typical program, each statement is left justified, and each is executed when the preceding statement completes. The IF . . . ENDIF
compound statement enables you to change this default sequencing. It
allows you to execute a different and non-sequential group of statements, based on the value of a logical expression.

Handling Either-Or Situations

The general form of this statement is as follows:

IF *condition* THEN

> StatementBlock1

ELSE

> StatementBlock2

END IF

This control statement first evaluates the conditional expression, *condition*, and decides whether to execute StatementBlock1 or StatementBlock2. If *condition* is TRUE, then StatementBlock1 is executed; if *condition* is FALSE, StatementBlock2 is executed. Each statement block stands for one or more individual QuickBASIC statements, as you'll see in the example programs in this chapter.

The IF . . . THEN statement controls a two-way branch.

Figure 6.2 depicts this concept of logical execution flow, using the analogy of traffic flow. When an IF statement is encountered, the program must branch one way or the other. The flow moves to either the statements located in the THEN clause (StatementBlock1) or to the statements located in the ELSE clause (StatementBlock2).

When either statement block completes, control passes immediately to the program statement following the END IF line. The major purpose of an END IF line is to indicate to QuickBASIC where to pass the flow of execution control after the proper statement block has completed its execution.

In the STYLE.BAS program seen in Chapter 5, a portion of the logic for determining the Fog Count was

```
word% = word% + 1
IF wordlength% > 7 THEN
  fog% = fog% + 3
ELSE
  fog% = fog% + 1
END IF
wordlength% = 0
```

In this example, the *condition* is `wordlength% > 7` and the THEN clause consists of one statement that increments the *fog%* variable by 3.

```
fog% = fog% + 3
```

The ELSE clause also consists of a single statement, which only increments the *fog%* variable by 1.

```
fog% = fog% + 1
```

The processing logic here is based on the assumption that a word

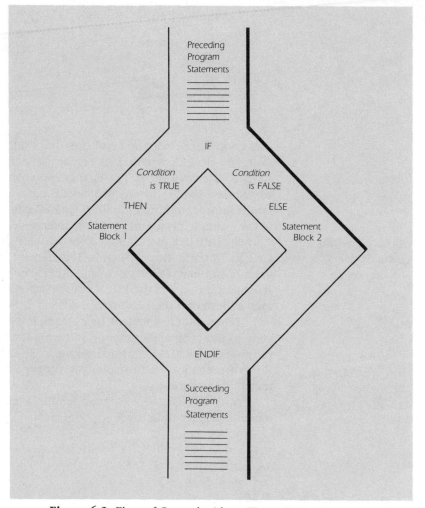

Figure 6.2 Flow of Control with an IF . . . ENDIF Statement

whose length exceeds seven characters becomes "foggier" and more difficult to understand for an average reader.

The flow of execution in this program segment is as follows:

1. Preceding statement(s):

```
word% = word% + 1
```

2. Decision making statement:

```
fog% = fog% + 3 , if wordlength% > 7
```

or

```
fog% = fog% + 1 , if wordlength% <= 7
```

3. Succeeding statement(s):

```
wordlength% = 0
```

Indenting statement blocks within compound statements is not required but is strongly advised for ease of reading and debugging your code. The flow of non-sequential control becomes instantly more visible.

The indentation of the statement blocks within the IF . . . ELSE . . . ENDIF structure is purposeful. Although not required by Quick-BASIC, it is good programming practice because it calls attention to the changing flow of control. As you can see, the indentation makes it easier to perceive the compound statement, because the keywords visually appear one above the other.

In addition, indentation makes it easier to determine what statements belong to each statement block. This becomes even more important when blocks contain multiple statements, as well as when multiple compound statements appear within one another (see the section below on *Nesting Compound Statements*).

As it turns out, this code can be rewritten (all code can be rewritten!) to highlight another aspect of the IF . . . ENDIF statement.

```
word% = word% + 1
fog% = fog% + 1
IF wordlength% > 7 THEN
  fog% = fog% + 2
END IF
wordlength% = 0
```

Read this variation and you will see that the same results occur; the logic is just different. Previously, *fog%* was incremented by either 3 or 1, depending on whether it was a big word or not. In this variation, every word contributes a fog value of 1, but big words add 2 more, making a total of 3. Doing it this way demonstrates that the ELSE clause of an IF . . . ENDIF is optional.

If you have no ELSE clause and the condition happens to be false, then control transfers directly to the END IF statement and no intervening statements are executed. The right branch in Figure 6.2 is empty, but the flow proceeds down that path just the same.

Handling Complex Conditional Situations

More complex sets of conditions can be imposed on your program's execution flow. For example, your program could be analyzing patient data in a hospital environment. Whether the patient is a male or a female will dictate which of two different test regimens should be imposed. Furthermore, if the patient is female, there may be additional tests to perform and analyze. An additional clause, the ELSEIF clause, can be used to assist in more complex situations.

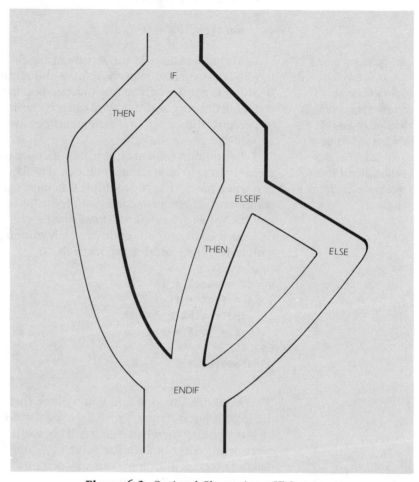

Figure 6.3 Optional Clauses in an IF Statement

Take a look at the following code segment:

```
IF sex$ = "M" THEN
  CALL pressure
  CALL heartlungs
  CALL gastro
ELSEIF sex$ = "F" THEN
  CALL bloodtest
  CALL hearttest
  CALL lungtest
  CALL breasttest
ELSE
```

```
PRINT "Sex value not indicated. Please correct!"
ENDIF
```

In this example, a second condition is now considered. The first condition is `sex$="M"`; if that is found to be TRUE, then the Statement-Block1 is executed. This statement block consists of three successive CALL statements. If the first condition is not found to be true, then the next optional block (ELSEIF) is considered.

Add ELSEIF clauses for additional logical branches.

Besides a possible ELSE clause, you can have as many ELSEIF clauses as you like. This provides you with the ability to test any number of additional conditions. This example has only one additional condition, `sex$="F"`. This second condition is tested whenever the first condition is determined not to be TRUE; if the ELSEIF condition is true, THEN the StatementBlock2 consisting of four CALL statements is executed.

Only if all of the preceding conditions are found to be FALSE does the ELSE clause ever get executed. In fact, it is only there to handle the error case where neither expected value (`sex$="M"` or `F`) is found. Figure 6.3 depicts how you can expand an IF statement to manage the flow of control through one or more ELSEIF clauses.

Controlling Multi-Way Decision Making

All decision making can be handled with the block IF statement discussed in the last section. However, you will discover a number of advantages to a SELECT CASE statement.

The CASE statement is easier to read than a complex IF.

This compound statement can also handle multiple choice situations, but it has more constraints than an IF . . . ELSEIF . . . ELSE . . . ENDIF statement. Consequently, it can be constructed more simply and read more easily.

The general structure of the SELECT CASE statement is

SELECT CASE *expression*

    CASE *ValueList1*

        StatementBlock1

    CASE *ValueList2*

        StatementBlock2

        .
        .

    CASE ELSE

        StatementBlockn

END SELECT

Use a CASE statement to control branching based on different values of one variable.

An IF statement can control branching to multiple blocks of statements, based on multiple conditions. The CASE statement is more appropriate for situations where only one condition exists, and that condition is used to test for multiple values.

For instance, a common use of the CASE statement is in coding a menu program such as MENU.BAS seen in Listing 6.1. First, a series of choices is displayed on the screen. Then, the user is prompted to make one of the choices. The CASE statement is used to pass the flow of execution to one of several procedures written to handle the chores presented on the menu. The expected output screen produced by MENU.BAS can be seen in Figure 6.4.

Listing 6.1 Use of a SELECT CASE for Menu Management

```
DECLARE SUB employee ()
DECLARE SUB payroll ()
DECLARE SUB payables ()
DECLARE SUB receivables ()
DECLARE SUB ledger ()
' Program MENU.BAS
' Demonstrates CASE and DO compound statements
' Displays menu, accepts user choice, passes control to
      procedures
'
CONST FALSE = 0, TRUE = NOT FALSE
CLS
FINISHED = FALSE
standard$ = "Your selection, please?"
message$ = standard$
DO WHILE NOT FINISHED
  CLS
  PRINT TAB(25); "Main Administrative System"
  LOCATE 5, 15
  PRINT TAB(15); "1   Employee Management", CHR$(10)
  PRINT TAB(15); "2   Payroll Processing", CHR$(10)
  PRINT TAB(15); "3   Receivables", CHR$(10)
  PRINT TAB(15); "4   Payables", CHR$(10)
  PRINT TAB(15); "5   General Ledger", CHR$(10), CHR$(10)
  PRINT TAB(15); "Q   Quit", CHR$(10)
  LOCATE 20, 1
  PRINT message$
  message$ = standard$
  choice$ = INPUT$(1)
  SELECT CASE choice$
    CASE "1"
      CALL employee
```

```
      CASE "2"
        CALL payroll
      CASE "3"
        CALL receivables
      CASE "4"
        CALL payables
      CASE "5"
        CALL ledger
      CASE "Q"
        FINISHED = TRUE
      CASE ELSE
        LOCATE 18, 1
        message$ = "Invalid Choice! Please Select Again."
    END SELECT
LOOP
```

```
                    Main Administrative System


          1   Employee Management

          2   Payroll Processing

          3   Receivables

          4   Payables

          5   General Ledger


          Q   Quit


      Your selection, please?
```

Figure 6.4 Output of the MENU.BAS Program

You can readily modify the MENU.BAS code by substituting your own menu choices in the PRINT statements, and substituting your own procedure names in the CALL statements. Writing procedures to do these kinds of tasks is the subject of Chapter 10. The DO . . . LOOP appearing in this program is discussed in a later section of this chapter.

CASE handles parallel situations. IF handles overlapping situations.

Whereas you can construct overlapping conditions with an IF statement, the CASE statement scrupulously enforces the situation depicted in Figure 6.5. The IF statement checks each new condition before deciding whether to branch to the appropriate statement block or to evaluate a new condition. The CASE statement, on the other hand, evaluates only one expression; it can then quickly branch to the appropriate statement block.

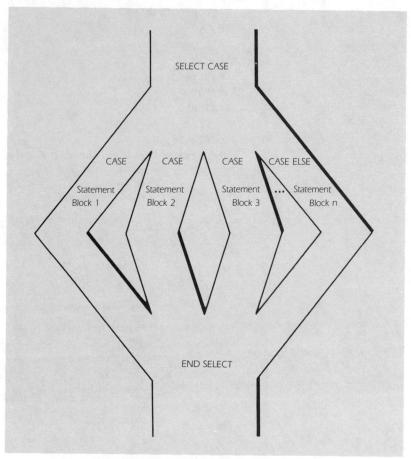

Figure 6.5 CASE Statements Presenting Multiple
Choice Control

Suppose you want to enhance the Fog Count algorithm above. Perhaps you wish to distinguish between simply long words (which receive a fog value of 3) and really long, complex words. A word that exceeds 11 characters should add 5 to the Fog Count rather than 3. You can use a CASE statement for just such a purpose.

```
SELECT CASE wordlength%
   CASE IS > 10
      fog% = fog% + 5
   CASE 8, 9, 10
      fog% = fog% + 3
   CASE 1 TO 7
      fog% = fog% + 1
```

```
CASE ELSE
   PRINT "Something is wrong with the word length
     algorithm!"
END SELECT
```

Always include a CASE ELSE clause in the SELECT CASE statement; this will handle unexpected situations in a concrete manner.

Once again, a CASE ELSE clause is added to handle the unexpected situation. Always write such a clause, even when you are sure that your various CASE clauses cover all possibilities. There is always something that may cause the logic to fail; your program should handle such eventualities.

Notice the various possibilities demonstrated here. The CASE expression is simply the variable containing the length of the word (*word-length%*). Your list of possible values can be presented as an expression to be evaluated, such as the first CASE clause. If the word length is any number greater than 10, the first statement block is executed, and the value of *fog%* is incremented by 5. The flow of control then passes to the statement after END SELECT.

If the word length is not greater than 10, the second possible set of values is checked. It is expressed in the second CASE clause as an explicit list of values, either 8, 9, or 10. If the word length is one of these, then *fog%* is incremented by 3.

Last, if the word length is any number from 1 to 7, the third CASE statement handles it, using the special keyword TO for specifying an inclusive value range to consider.

If you do not include a CASE ELSE clause and the value of your CASE expression cannot be found in any of your specified value lists, then none of the CASE statement blocks are executed . . . and you won't know that has happened. That's why a CASE ELSE clause is so important. Because nothing executes but the succeeding program statements, it may hurt nothing. On the other hand, your program may not perform properly, because it may rely on at least one of the CASE statement blocks having executed.

Do not allow overlapping values in different CASE value lists.

You should also note that the order of your CASE clauses is important. A CASE statement stops checking its value lists when the expression value is found, therefore only the statement block in the first successful CASE is executed. If your expression's value can be found in two or more value lists, only the first statement block will be executed. So, plan to make your value lists unique, or *mutually exclusive*. The same value should not be able to be found in the value lists from two separate CASE clauses.

Another example of a CASE statement was seen earlier in the STYLE.BAS program. Its CASE looked like this:

```
eachchar$ = INPUT$(1, #1)
SELECT CASE eachchar$
  CASE " ", CHR$(13)
    word% = word% + 1
    IF wordlength% > 7 THEN
```

```
      fog% = fog% + 3
    ELSE
      fog% = fog% + 1
    END IF
    wordlength% = 0
  CASE "."
    sentence% = sentence% + 1
  CASE ";", ",", ":", CHR$(10)
  CASE ELSE
    wordlength% = wordlength% + 1
END SELECT
```

The CASE expression here is a single character that is retrieved from a file with the INPUT$ function. The first CASE clause tests for two special file characters: a space and a carriage return. Each is interpreted as following a complete word in the file. The second CASE statement explicitly skips over frequent file punctuation symbols such as the semicolon, the comma, the colon, and the line feed character. When these characters are scanned, they are skipped because they should not contribute to the word length.

All other characters are assumed to be part of a word; if this is not so in your text files, simply add any other characters to be skipped to the second CASE clause.

Repeating Blocks of Code

Repeat a group of instructions with a DO statement.

Sometimes, it becomes distracting to provide too many alternatives. QuickBASIC has several constructions that enable you to repeat blocks of instructions. Each is cosmetically different, but functionally the same. Learning the most flexible DO . . . LOOP statement is my advice. You can develop all necessary kinds of repetition with the variations available on this command alone.

In this section, you'll learn the three most common applications of a repetition loop. First, you'll see examples of how to construct a loop that repeats a block of statements a known number of times. Second, you'll learn how QuickBASIC allows you to access data in a file and perform a block of instructions a varying number of times, depending on the size of the file. Third, you'll learn the most general case, in which a loop is also performed a varying number of times, but the number of times is based on any logical expression becoming true.

Repeating a Loop a Fixed Number of Times

The DO . . . LOOP construction in QuickBASIC is extremely powerful and, at the same time, extremely flexible. One of its possible uses is to control the repetition of a block of statements a fixed number of times. The general syntax of one form of the DO . . . LOOP statement is

DO WHILE *condition*

StatementBlock

LOOP

or

DO UNTIL *condition*

StatementBlock

LOOP

In the DO WHILE variation, the statement block is repeatedly executed as long as the *condition* remains TRUE. In the DO UNTIL variation, the statement block is repeatedly executed only until the *condition* becomes TRUE. Either mechanism can be adjusted to create a similar end result; each has its place depending on the logic of your program.

A construction such as DO WHILE or DO UNTIL may not execute a group of statements at all. This occurs if the loop's condition is not TRUE when the DO statement is first reached.

It is important to realize that, with either the DO WHILE or the DO UNTIL construction, the *condition* is evaluated first. Only then is the decision made as to whether or not the statement block is executed. Therefore, it is possible that the statement block will not even be executed once. If it is possible that the group of statements you are dealing with may not need to be executed even once, you must use this construction of the DO . . . LOOP statement. Figure 6.6 depicts this situation, which has the loop test occurring at its beginning.

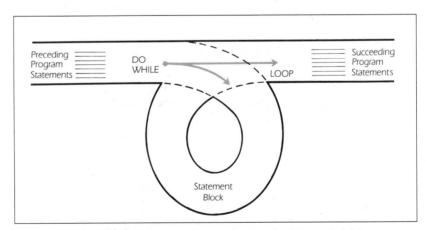

Figure 6.6 Testing at the Beginning of a DO . . . LOOP

As a first example of this type of DO . . . LOOP, take a look at program HYPNO1.BAS in Listing 6.2. Five statements make up the statement block controlled by the `counter > 0` condition. Go ahead and enter this short program into your QuickBASIC system and try it out. You'll make several adjustments to it in the course of the next several pages of this chapter.

Listing 6.2 Example of a Counting Loop

```
' HYPNO1.BAS demonstrates a counting loop
'
counter = 75
CLS
message$ = "You are getting sleepy..."
DO WHILE counter > 0
  LOCATE 5, counter - LEN(message$)
  PRINT message$; counter
  PRINT STRING$(counter, "!") + STRING$(80 - counter, " ")
  SLEEP (2)
  counter = counter - 1

LOOP
```

You must adjust the loop counter somewhere within a counting loop. Otherwise, you will inadvertently discover what is meant by an infinite loop!

The *counter* variable is called the loop counter, since it is not only part of the condition, but it is varied within the loop itself. In fact, a counting loop such as this must adjust the value of the loop counter each time the loop is executed. Otherwise, the loop's *condition* may never become TRUE and the statement block will repeat without end. This happens frequently when programs are developed; you then have programmed what is called an *infinite loop*. If you do this, simply press Ctrl-Break to stop the program and correct your coding.

Nesting Compound Statements

Program HYPNO1.BAS works primarily because the *counter* variable is initialized to 75 prior to the DO WHILE statement, and is then decremented by 1 each time through the loop with the statement

```
counter = counter - 1
```

When you write repeating loops, you can decrement or increment the counter, and you can do so by any amount (not simply the common amount of 1). The LOCATE statement positions the message at a variable column location on row 5. This column value is dependent on both the LEN function, which computes the length of the message, and the decrementing counter itself. The SLEEP function is unique to QuickBASIC and allows you to pause your program a fixed number of seconds during each pass through the loop. This one's fun; try it on your computer.

In fact, if you run this program, you'll discover that it works all right up to a point. The message is first displayed at column 50, because the LOCATE statement calculates the column as

```
counter - LEN(message$)
```

and the message in this program is 25 characters long (counter begins with a value of 75). The message is supposed to move to the left on the screen, as the 75 exclamation points are removed one by one. However, when the counter is reduced from 75 to 25 (50 repetitions of the loop), the column value becomes 0. At this point, the program stops, and QuickBASIC highlights the LOCATE line and displays a dialog box proclaiming `Illegal function call`.

Develop more sophisticated applications by including, or *nesting*, compound statements within one another.

The solution to this program problem is to nest an IF statement within the DO . . . LOOP. Your program can then test for the point at which the column value drops to an illegal value (no longer on the screen). Listing 6.3 demonstrates this solution; the HYPNO2.BAS program makes the test and performs the single chore of setting *column* to 1 if its calculated value drops below 1. Try this adjustment on your system. The message stops moving at the leftmost column on your screen, but the counter continues to decrement properly.

Listing 6.3 Nesting Compound Statements

```
' HYPNO2.BAS demonstrates a counting loop
'
counter = 75
CLS
message$ = "You are getting sleepy..."
DO WHILE counter > 0
  column = counter - LEN(message$)
  IF column < 1 THEN
    column = 1
  END IF
  LOCATE 5, column
  PRINT message$; counter
  PRINT STRING$(counter, "!") + STRING$(80 - counter, " ")
  SLEEP (2)
  counter = counter - 1

LOOP
```

Program HYPNO3.BAS takes this evolution one step further. As a developing programmer, you may ask yourself how to adjust the program so the message continues to move to the left even when the left side of the screen is reached. In other words, what is the logic used by scrolling programs? The nested IF statement in Listing 6.4 holds the answer.

Listing 6.4 Scrolling off the Left Side of the Screen

```
' HYPNO3.BAS demonstrates a counting loop
'
counter = 30
CLS
message$ = "You are getting sleepy..."
length = LEN(message$)
NumChars = length
DO WHILE counter > 0
  column = counter - length
  IF column < 1 THEN
    NumChars = length + column - 1
    column = 1
  END IF
  LOCATE 5, column
  PRINT RIGHT$(message$, NumChars); counter; " "
  PRINT STRING$(counter, "!") + STRING$(80 - counter, " ")
  SLEEP (2)
  counter = counter - 1

LOOP
CLS
```

In this solution, the *message$* is no longer printed in its entirety. In its place, the RIGHT$ function is used, which extracts a certain number of characters from the right side of the *message$* string. The number of characters printed (*NumChars*) equals the actual message length until column 1 is reached. From that point on, the IF statement block adjusts the *NumChars* variable to appropriately cut the string down before it is printed. It's a nice visual effect.

Notice that the IF . . . END IF statements are both entirely contained within the DO WHILE . . . LOOP statements. Whenever one compound statement appears within another, you must be careful that the enclosed statement's beginning and end are completely nested within the other enclosing statement. Many errors occur when complicated nestings are not done carefully.

Nested statements must be entirely contained within one another. The beginning of one must not be placed before the end of another.

Repeating Code a Varying Number of Times

Two common situations exist in which blocks of QuickBASIC statements are repeated a varying number of times. You'll learn how to deal with both in this section. You need the first case when you process an unknown amount of data from a file. And you need the second case for virtually all other general situations in which you must repeat code an unknown number of times. The most common situation for this is a menu program, which must continually repeat the menu of choices until a user chooses to *Quit* the program.

Processing an Entire File's Worth of Data

When the WHILE or UNTIL clause follows the loop, the enclosed statements are always executed at least once.

The STYLE.BAS program seen earlier demonstrated the second major form of the DO . . . LOOP statement. Programs that use this second general form test for the loop's condition at the end of at least one pass through the loop. This general form is

DO

StatementBlock

LOOP UNTIL *condition*

or

DO

StatementBlock

LOOP WHILE *condition*

Because the condition is not even tested until the end of the loop, the statement block is always executed at least once. Figure 6.7 depicts this variation on Figure 6.6.

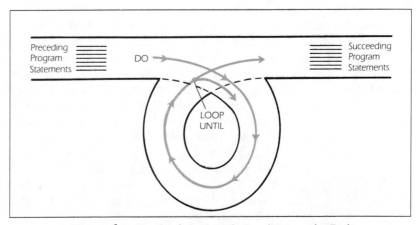

Figure 6.7 Testing for a Loop's Condition at the End

The STYLE.BAS program enclosed a group of statements within the following DO . . . LOOP statement:

DO

```
StatementBlock
LOOP UNTIL EOF(1)
```

The statement block itself includes a SELECT CASE statement, which itself includes an IF statement. Figure 6.8 revisits the issue of nested statements, as seen in the STYLE.BAS program. Notice how this visual alignment method quickly confirms the correct nesting of each statement. Using this visual technique can just as easily discover a bug in your nesting if your program doesn't work correctly.

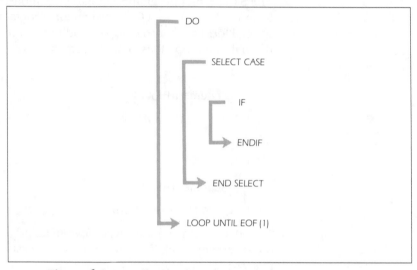

Figure 6.8 Visually Checking for Proper Compound Nesting

Failing to adjust the file position pointer when reading data from a file can give rise to a second form of infinite loop!

The way to terminate the scanning of an entire file is simply to use the EOF or end-of-file function in the loop's *condition*. It returns a TRUE value when all of the file's data has been read. In the STYLE.BAS program, the INPUT$ function was used to read one character at a time from the file. It is important that this INPUT$ function appear within the loop.

A *file traversal loop* is one that performs some operation or procedure for every record in a file. Just as a counting loop requires that the counter be adjusted within the loop to avoid the unfortunate situation of an infinite loop, so does a file traversal loop require that the file position pointer be adjusted by reading the data from the file. Each Quick-BASIC statement that reads data from a file automatically adjusts the file position pointer, bringing you that much closer to the end of the file (when EOF( ) will be TRUE).

Repeating Statements Based on Any General Condition

Either of the two forms of the DO . . . LOOP can be used with any condition at all. The condition is neither limited to a counting loop nor to a file traversal loop. Those are simply two of the most common types of programming situations.

For example, your program may be designed to handle the printing of a company's payroll. In a small company, you may design an interactive program that prompts for an employee ID, then prints the paycheck for that employee. The following code might do this:

Interactive programs require frequent keyboard input. Batch programs require virtually no input from the keyboard, preferring to obtain their data from either preset DATA statements or previously prepared files.

```
DO
  INPUT "Please enter the employee's ID:"; ID$
  IF ID$ <> "9999" THEN
    CALL PAYCHECK
  END IF
LOOP UNTIL ID$ = "9999"
```

In this simple program segment, the PAYCHECK procedure is called to process each employee's ID and print a paycheck. The special entry of an ID equal to "9999" is a code meant to signify the end of the payroll cycle. The IF statement ensures that no paycheck is printed for this ID. The loop also ends when this employee ID is encountered.

Of course, your company may have 15,000 employees. An interactive program for payroll would be out of the question. This interactive program could be easily turned into a batch file by replacing the INPUT statement with a series of DATA statements preceding the DO statement, and a READ ID$ statement located within the loop.

Repeating Statements Until the User Decides to Stop

The MENU.BAS program seen earlier in this chapter (see Listing 6.1) enables you to select one of several menu choices. The surrounding DO . . . LOOP causes the entire loop to repeat over and over again until the user enters a **Q** to Quit the MENU program. Until this **Q** is entered, the loop ensures that the menu is displayed, the user's choice is read into the program, and one of several procedures is executed.

When **Q** is entered, the special *FINISHED* variable is set to TRUE to help control the exit from the loop. The effect is that the flow of execution moves to the statement following the LOOP statement. This generally ends the MENU program, although if you wanted to program any finalization statements, this would be the time when they would execute. You would simply write those final executable statements at the end of the program, just after the LOOP statement.

Notice the special CONST declaration statement used in this program. Although there are special internal reasons why this makes good sense, it is enough to say that this technique makes your programs much easier to read, understand, and modify. The CONST statement actually defines two variables called TRUE and FALSE, which can then be used throughout your program in logical expressions. Notice also the choice of a variable name (*FINISHED*) that has some suggestive value, in addition to working as a control variable for the loop.

Review

In this chapter, you learned the three major compound statements that control the flow of execution in QuickBASIC programs. You learned the following information:

1. All execution control that adjusts the flow of sequential statements is either based on a decision making statement or a repetition statement.

2. Multiple statements can be executed at one time, subject to flow of control mechanisms. Groups of statements executed this way are called statement blocks.

3. Programs can make decisions themselves, based on the TRUE or FALSE value of logical expressions. The IF statement controls simple and complex decision making. Execution passes to one block of instructions or another, based on whether the IF statement uses the optional ELSE or ELSEIF clauses.

4. Indenting statement blocks is not necessary, but is good programming practice. It makes your programs easier to write, debug, and maintain.

5. Multiple choice decisions can be easily handled with the convenient CASE statement. Values for the different CASE clauses can be ranges, explicit values, or even conditional expressions.

6. Blocks of code can be repeated with the DO . . . LOOP compound statement. A condition can be tested either at the beginning or at the end of the loop. The code within the loop can be repeated either WHILE the condition is TRUE, or UNTIL the condition is TRUE.

7. Loops can be programmed to repeat a fixed number of times, or until all the data from a file has been processed. Or they can repeat a varying number of times, depending on when a logical expression becomes true.

Quiz for Chapter 6

1. Executing QuickBASIC statements in an order different from the way in which they appear in the program is called:

   a. Flow of control
   b. Flow of logic
   c. Statement blocks
   d. Compound statements

2. Decision making in QuickBASIC programs depends on:

   a. Statement blocks
   b. Repetition loops
   c. Logical expressions
   d. Flow of control

3. A group of statements whose execution depends on the logic of a compound statement is called:

   a. A computer program
   b. A DO . . . LOOP
   c. An IF statement
   d. A statement block

4. Which of the following is not absolutely needed for complex programming?

   a. IF statements
   b. CASE statements
   c. DO statements
   d. Assignment statements

5. Indentation:

   a. Is optional
   b. Is good programming practice
   c. Is helpful in debugging
   d. All of the above

6. Which of the following clauses is optional?

   a. IF
   b. ELSE
   c. DO
   d. SELECT CASE

7. Which of the following evaluates a conditional expression at the end of its appropriate compound statement?

   a. IF
   b. CASE
   c. DO WHILE
   d. LOOP UNTIL

8. Although not absolutely required, good programming practice would suggest that you always include which of these clauses?

   a. ELSEIF
   b. CASE ELSE
   c. ELSE
   d. WHILE

9. What is it called when your program fails to terminate a repeating group of code?

   a. Bad
   b. An infinite loop
   c. A bomb
   d. All of the above

10. What is a loop called that repeats a group of instructions a fixed number of times?

    a. File traversal loop
    b. Menu loop
    c. Counting loop
    d. Nested loop

11. Which function enables a DO . . . LOOP to traverse the data within an entire file?

    a. READ
    b. INPUT
    c. FILE
    d. EOF

12. Which of the following is not found in a QuickBASIC loop?

    a. UNTIL
    b. WHILE
    c. REPEAT
    d. DO

13. Which QuickBASIC statement is needed to create TRUE and FALSE variables?

    a. DECLARE
    b. CONST
    c. LOGICAL
    d. ASSIGN

14. Which of the following is not a repetition statement in Quick-BASIC?

    a. DO . . . LOOP
    b. FOR . . . NEXT
    c. WHILE . . . WEND
    d. REPEAT . . . UNTIL

15. A compound statement always involves:

    a. Two lines
    b. Three lines
    c. Four lines
    d. More than one line

7 Controlling File and Device Input/Output

So far in Part 2, you've learned how to manipulate variables, assign values to those variables, and direct the flow of execution control. You've even begun to see how simple built-in functions are used in Quick-BASIC programs. Up to this point, though, your programs have been limited in the amount of data that can be processed easily. Practically speaking, the limit has been the amount of information entered from the keyboard during program operation, or the preset values stored in DATA statements. In this chapter, you'll take a giant step forward toward developing programs that use and manage the larger amounts of information stored in disk files.

Files are known by both data structure and the data access method used. They are either structured or unstructured, and they are accessed in either a sequential or random manner.

First, you'll learn about the three primary types of data files used by most programs: unstructured sequential, structured sequential, and random access. Then, you'll learn the QuickBASIC statements necessary to store data in each of these types of files, as well as to retrieve data from them.

Last, you'll study a series of example programs designed to demonstrate how to use these general techniques in specific applications. The particular applications chosen include a QuickBASIC program to access data from a file generated by LOTUS 1-2-3. The examples also include programs for retrieving data from a WordStar MailMerge file or an ASCII file generated by dBASE III Plus or dBASE IV.

Preparing Files for Input or Output Operations

Whenever QuickBASIC uses a data file of any sort, it must follow a required computer system procedure called *opening* the file. Figure 7.1 depicts the OPEN operation as being analogous to opening a box; only when the box is actually open can data be put into it or taken from it.

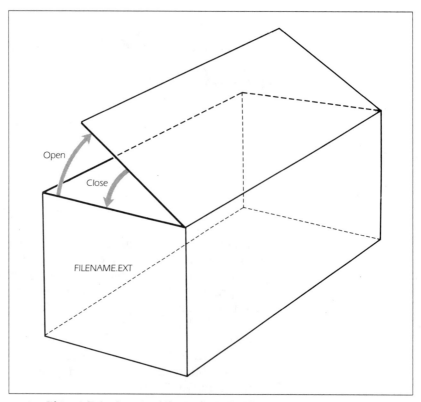

Open

Close

FILENAME.EXT

Figure 7.1 Opening/Closing a Disk File to Access its Contents

You must *open* a file before working with the data within it, and you must *close* the file afterwards.

Similarly, another computer operation is required to *close* the file and put it and its contents away on the specified disk drive. When this final operation is complete, any intermediate data still in memory is *flushed* to the disk. This means that it is copied to the more permanent contents of a disk file. Until this data is written to the disk, a power failure would cause it to be irretrievably lost. All computer languages must have operations equivalent to these QuickBASIC OPEN and CLOSE statements. However, if you forget to close the file properly, QuickBASIC will do that for you automatically when your program ends normally.

The actual command to open a file for use by a program is

```
OPEN "filename.ext" FOR OperType AS #IDNum
```

You must replace "filename.ext" with the name of the actual file you wish to read from or write to. IDNum is any number from 1 to 255 that is not currently being used to represent another file. The pound sign is a required symbol preceding the ID number.

You must also replace OperType with one of the following words: INPUT, OUTPUT, RANDOM, APPEND, or BINARY. This keyword tells QuickBASIC how you intend to use the file.

For example, you can open the MAIL.LST file for the purpose of reading its contents with this command:

```
OPEN "mail.lst" FOR INPUT AS #1
```

INPUT means you intend to read text data from the file. OUTPUT means you will be writing text data into the file. Both of these keywords indicate that your file is organized as a series of data groups that will be accessed in successive order. This is known as a *sequential* file.

A sequential file is often compared to an audio tape. There may be many individual songs on the tape, but they are recorded one after the other. To get to the seventh song, you must sequentially pass through each of the first six songs. Similarly, to get to the seventh record in a sequential file, you must first read the preceding six records.

When you open a file for OUTPUT, the tape analogy can be extended. This automatically creates the file, if it didn't exist on your disk. Or, if it did exist, it rewinds the file to the beginning storage position (like song one on the audio tape). Writing data into a file opened for OUTPUT effectively erases any former data in the file, treating it as a fresh tape or a blank slate.

Be cautious about writing data to a file. Opening the file for OUTPUT erases old data; opening the file for APPEND adds new data to the existing information.

When you want to retain old data in a file, yet add new records to it, you open the file with the OperType APPEND. This essentially fast forwards the file to the end of whatever data is there. New records are then written at the end of the existing records; they are *appended* to the existing file.

Many on-line applications require that you be able to access instantly any particular record for either reading or updating. This kind of database management task requires that you use the special OperType RANDOM. This tells QuickBASIC that you intend to use the random access mode of file access, in which both reading and writing are alternately possible. In addition, you can read or write any record in the file easily without sequentially moving through the file to the correct record number.

The last possibility for OperType is BINARY, which allows you to read or write individual bytes of the file. Unlike each of the preceding methods, used typically for text files, BINARY access mode is used for files whose data is not simply ASCII in format. Non-text files, such as executable .EXE files, are only read or modified using this final BINARY mode.

The OPEN command is required to establish a connection between your program and the actual location of the file on disk; the operating system manages the special connective process. Figure 7.2 depicts the different types of connections that can be made with this OPEN command.

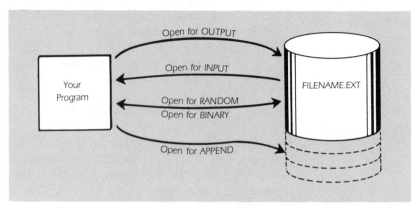

Figure 7.2 Opening a File for Different Types of Access

The reverse of opening a file is shown in the following simple statement:

```
CLOSE #IDNum
```

CLOSE a file when you are finished working with it. This helps to assure file integrity in the event of a power failure.

When you are finished accessing a file, it is best to issue this command. Use the same ID number with which you identified the file to the OPEN command. The sooner you close a file after working with it, the surer you will be that any intermediate data in memory is properly written to the file. Otherwise, a power failure may cause you to lose data that still remains in memory; your file may then experience data loss or data integrity problems.

Understanding the Three Types of Files

This chapter is itself an example of an unstructured sequential file. It consists of a series of paragraphs, each of which is ended by the conventional control characters for Carriage Return and Line Feed (CR-LF). An apparent space between paragraphs can be considered a paragraph that consists of no sentences. A title line for a section is itself another type of paragraph that consists of one sentence.

Using Unstructured Sequential Files

In Chapter 4, you first saw the STYLE.BAS program, which analyzes text files for a count of words and sentences, and also computes a Fog Count based on the readability of your writing. This program uses the INPUT$ function to read in one character at a time. It performs its primary analytical and counting tasks whenever a space character indicates the end of a word, or a Carriage Return indicates the end of a paragraph.

Any file of text can be processed in precisely this way. A programming language like QuickBASIC actually processes your program instructions in a manner similar to the STYLE.BAS program. Analyzing a file's contents one word at a time is called *parsing*. Naturally, Quick-BASIC goes well beyond STYLE.BAS. When a separation character is found, such as a space or other punctuation symbol, QuickBASIC looks at the word just defined to see if it is a keyword. If it is, then QuickBASIC knows just what action to perform. If it is not, QuickBASIC looks to see if the word represents one of your variables. And so it goes for an entire program.

A text file like the ones dealt with by QuickBASIC or by STYLE.BAS is called *free form*. Each group of characters up until the CR-LF pair is called a *record*. And each record can be any length, including zero. The blank paragraph between normal paragraphs is called an *empty string*, or a *null record*.

Delimiter characters separate *fields* and CR-LF pairs separate *records*.

Another common example of an unstructured file is the MAIL.LST file seen in Figure 7.3. This file shows a series of unstructured records, each of which contains name and address information. Since the first and last names, the street address, and the city are all of variable length, the overall width of each record is different. So this is called an unstructured file. Individual data items, or *fields*, are distinguished from one another in each record by delimiter characters. A comma delimits any one field from another, while quotation marks distinguish each string value.

```
"Krausman","Wilhelm","73 Rose St.","Bergenfield","NJ","06721"
"Scarapelle","Paul","P.O.B. 2221","New Milford","CT","06776"
"Karras","Josephine","State University","Danbury","CT","06810"
"Christiansen","T.J.","Old Ridgebury Rd.","Danbury","CT","06817"
"Cannutti","George","Old Squirrel Rd.","Ridgefield","CT","06877"
"Dutchman","Richard","110 Myrtle Av.","Westport","CT","06880"
"Baker","Carolyn","18 Queens Way","Westport","CT","06880"
"Edwards","Hamilton","27 Top Drive Rd.","Redding","CT","06896"
"Bingham","Richard","RR 2","Forestville","ON","K0K 1W0"
"Chewing","Stanford","132 West 48th Ave.","Vancouver","BC","V5X 1Z4"
```

Figure 7.3 The MAIL.LST File—Unstructured and Sequential

The INPUT$ function can be used for any text files (see STYLE.BAS in Chapter 4), but must be used for extensive text files that contain large paragraphs of text. If the line is less than 256 characters, you can use the LINE INPUT statement as an alternative to the INPUT$ function. This is preferable for short records because of significantly reduced input/output overhead. However, you will still have to scan each record received to extract individual field values.

The INPUT statement is more appropriate for simpler data files containing normal text records (such as the MAIL.LST file). The MAILPRN and MAILPRN2 programs later in this chapter will demonstrate how to manipulate files like this. INPUT allows you to specify the individual field names to read from each record. QuickBASIC's INPUT does the job of scanning for punctuation and extracting any numerical or string values from the individual line.

If you must create an unstructured sequential file from Quick-BASIC, you can use the PRINT statement. However, the file records will look like the output you see on a screen. Remember that the values are stored in zones beginning every 14 columns. This produces a neat columnar output, which may be precisely what you want. On the other hand, you may want your output to look like MAIL.LST, with commas between each field and quotation marks around each string value. To do this, simply replace PRINT with WRITE as a new output statement.

For example, the program TEST.BAS below demonstrates the difference in output format between the two statements. The first PRINT statement produces a visual column ruler. The second PRINT statement creates a typical zoned output (14 columns per output zone, with a space added after each string field). The WRITE statement outputs the same four field values but wastes no space, using commas and quotation marks to separate field values.

```
' Program TEST.DTA shows difference in PRINT and WRITE
    outputs
OPEN "test.dta" FOR OUTPUT AS #1
PRINT #1,
    "12345678901234567890123456789012345678901234567890"
PRINT #1, "String1", 76, "String2", 4
WRITE #1, "String1", 76, "String2", 4
close #1
end
```

The resulting TEST.DTA file looks like:

```
12345678901234567890123456789012345678901234567890
String1       76            String2       4
"String1",76,"String2",4
```

Use the WRITE command to produce an unstructured sequential file suitable for mail merge applications with your word processor.

The PRINT statement produces zoned output, while the WRITE statement produces records containing delimiters and appropriate punctuation. Many programs—for example, many word processing mail merge applications—require data in this latter format.

Using Structured Sequential Files

By contrast, a structured file is composed of individual fields that contain a fixed number of characters, making each complete record a consistent length. Figure 7.4 shows the DONATION.TXT file, which represents a structured sequential file.

```
    3 1ST GRADE MOMS - ROOM 8        7 MONTHS OF COOKIES      84.00
   47 ABOUT CHILDREN                 2 CHILDREN'S PUZZLES     10.00
  181 ABOUT FACE AND BODY            EYELASH TINT             12.00
   16 ACE GYMNASTICS                 ONE MONTH LESSONS        74.00
   28 ADROIT CERAMICS                QUICHE DISH              19.00
   31 ARNOLD VETERINARY CLINIC       PET EXAM                 25.00
    6 ALTA BREAST CENTER             BILATERAL MAMMOGRAPHY    95.00
   82 AMERICAN DRY CLEANERS          CLOTHING ALTERATIONS     10.00
   54 AMERICAN THEATER               2 ORCHESTRA TICKETS      50.00
   19 KINDALL CHIROPRACTIC CENTER    LUMBAR PILLOW            23.00
   76 BRAND-NEW GALLERY              FRAMED POSTER           115.00
  115 BASKIN-ROBBINS                 2 BANANA SPLITS           8.00
   57 BAY AREA WIND SYMPHONY         4 TICKETS                48.00
  132 BEARS & THINGS, INC.           BUSINESS BEAR            22.00
   95 PRESIDENTIAL BOOKS             GIFT CERTIFICATE         10.00
   64 BERKELEY ICE HOCKEY            4 PASSES                 18.00
   86 BERKELEY SHAKESPEARE           2 TICKETS                28.00
  164 BERKELEY SYMPHONY              2 TICKETS                40.00
```

Figure 7.4 The DONATION.TXT File—Structured and Sequential

Each line consists of a fixed number of characters, but each field within that line occupies a known position and has a known width. As you'll see below in the 123FILE.BAS program, the LINE INPUT command reads an entire record at a time, up to each succeeding CR-LF. Then, the MID$ function is used to extract individual fields. When a field is supposed to be numerical, but has been read with LINE INPUT, it initially appears to QuickBASIC as a string value. You'll see below how to use the VAL function to convert this string into a numerical value.

Structured files assign a fixed width to each field value, often leading to wasted space at the end of fields. Unstructured files do not waste any space.

A sequential file that has this type of consistent definition for its contents is called structured. The records, displayed as in Figure 7.4, appear as a table of information; each individual field item appears in its own column. Many relational database systems store data in just this type of format. However, a QuickBASIC sequential file, even when structured like this, can still only be read or written in sequence. As with the audio tape analogy, records can only be accessed by passing over each preceding record in the file.

Using Random Access Files

The most flexible and powerful form of file access is called *random*, because you can read or write any record in the file, and you can do so in any order. A typical file that is accessed randomly looks like the EMPLOYEE.DTA file seen in Figure 7.5. It looks just like the structured file discussed in the last section. The data seen in the box representing the file itself could conceivably be found in a sequential file. However, the information above and to the left of the visual file makes this random file different. The label at the top of each column identifies the *field name*. This is a program variable name used by your program when it references the data in that column.

Record Number	ID	First Name	Last Name	Date of Hire	Marital Status	Pay Grade	Salary
1	3421	Karen	Busman	02/15/88	M	13	2100.00
2	1121	Robert	Cantor	08/21/88	M	12	1850.00
3	2196	William	Taylor	04/15/88	S	11	1700.00
4	6172	Anne	Jones	03/12/89	S	10	1625.00

Figure 7.5 The EMPLOYEE.DTA File—Structured for Random Access

Each record is made up of a group of field values. In this example, a single record has values for the employee's ID, first and last names, date of hire, marital status, pay grade, and salary. Each employee is uniquely identified by a row in this file, and each row is assigned a number by QuickBASIC. For instance, the assigned number for William Taylor is 3, because his row is the third complete record in the file.

QuickBASIC provides a special mechanism for manipulating all the data in one of these random access file rows. It is called a *user-defined type*. Unlike simple data types such as INTEGER, LONG, STRING, SINGLE, or DOUBLE, a user-defined type is a complex grouping of these simpler types. For instance, the following TYPE command precisely defines the record seen in the EMPLOYEE.DTA file:

A user-defined type enables you to combine simple QuickBASIC data types into a more complex grouping of variables. Even other user-defined types may be combined into this new and more sophisticated data type.

```
TYPE CONTACT
   id AS LONG
   first AS STRING * 10
   last AS STRING * 15
   date AS STRING * 8
   marital AS STRING * 1
   grade AS INTEGER
   salary AS SINGLE
END TYPE
```

Column 1 of the file is hereby defined as a LONG integer. Remember from Chapter 4 that this represents a whole number up to a maximum of approximately two billion (4 storage bytes are used). This is used for a numerical ID, which may exceed a simple integer's maximum five-digit value of 32,767. Columns 2 through 5 are various strings of length 10, 15, 8, and 1 to represent the first and last names, the date of hire, and the employee's marital status.

The employee's pay grade is a simple two-digit number, so it can be stored in a simple INTEGER variable. However, the salary is a floating point number; given the probable limited dollar range, a single precision (SINGLE) floating point number is sufficient.

Use the TYPE statement to set up records in a random access file.

But this TYPE statement merely defines the nature of the group data to be stored in the random access file's record. With simple data types, you actually use variables that are constructed of a particular type of data. With complex user-defined types, you must likewise define a variable of that type. The DIM statement permits you to do this. For example,

```
DIM eachline AS contact
```

specifies that your program will use a variable named *eachline* of type *contact*. The manner of referencing the fields of this variable is somewhat new, but straightforward. You combine the variable name, a period, and the field name. For example, after reading an entire row from the file into the variable *eachline*, you can reference individual fields with these expressions:

```
eachline.id
eachline.first
eachline.last
eachline.date
eachline.marital
eachline.grade
eachline.salary
```

Figure 7.6 clarifies the situation. In this figure, the user-defined type itself represents the record's structure. The TYPE statement specifies the name CONTACT as the special keyword to later be used for defining variables of this new user-defined type. At the bottom of the figure, the CONTACT data type contains the field names themselves, as well as the width of each field. The individual variable called *eachline* contains the information that is actually manipulated in the program. It contains each record's data as it comes in from the file. For that matter, as you'll see later in this chapter, the same variable is typically used for writing a record to the file.

Programs RANDOMRD, RANDOMWR, and RANDOMCH later in this chapter all demonstrate how to use this user-defined type with a random access file. New commands for writing or reading randomly are

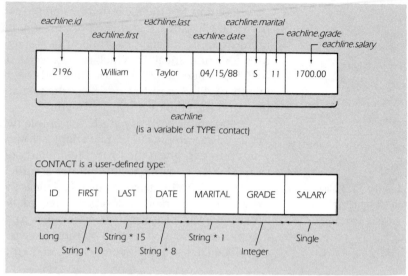

Figure 7.6 Variables of a Particular Type, as Used by Programs

the PUT and GET commands. They will be explained below along with the program files that use them.

In these application programs, you will see how to read or update existing records, as well as add new records in a random access file. These are the key tasks required by any database management system, and you can perform them now with the commands at your disposal in QuickBASIC. In Chapter 10, these independent programs will be combined with the flow of control MENU.BAS program from Chapter 6 to form a complete QuickBASIC database management application system.

In short, the random access mechanism is like the latest in compact disk technology; with a compact disk, you can select which song you want to hear. As with the random access file, selection is made by a song number. With a file created and accessed in random mode, you access any record by its relative number in the file.

Figure 7.7 contrasts random access with sequential access, using the audio recording analogy. Powerful database applications use the random access method, primarily for speed. The next section discusses this and other tradeoffs between these different types of file access.

Sequential files are like audio tapes, while random access files are better compared to compact disks.

Pros and Cons of the Various File Types

Each principal type of files (sequential and random) has its unique set of advantages and disadvantages. The nature of your application normally dictates which file type is best for you:

Use a random access technique for applications that

- Are online and require rapid access to any record in the file.

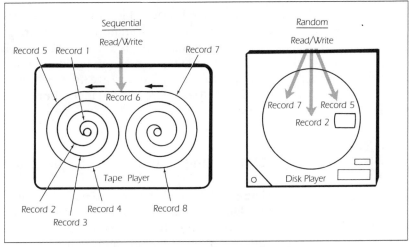

Figure 7.7 Sequential vs. Random Access

Use random access for on-line applications; use sequential access for applications that are not time demanding.

- Require frequent deletions or insertions of records. The way in which QuickBASIC reads, writes, and maintains random access files means less input/output overhead than required by a sequential file.

- Support record updating. These types of programs must have the simultaneous read and write access to the data records that the RANDOM feature provides.

- Must frequently sort the stored records.

Use a sequential access technique for applications that

- Use variable length records. This produces a much more efficient use of file space. No trailing spaces are found after any field values.

- Are historical in purpose. Such data is rarely changed and only infrequently accessed.

- Must run in systems that are short on disk space. Sequential files are able to better use the available space.

- Are "quick and dirty," requiring fast answers and not requiring frequent re-use of the program developed. Using a sequential file saves the time normally required to design and prepare the field structure of a random access file.

Practical Applications of Individual File Types

In this section, you will apply what you learned earlier in this chapter. You will study complete programs that demonstrate how to use the file types presented above. But these are not silly textbook examples. Each of them represents a common situation encountered by QuickBASIC users. Each of them can also be used as a template for modification and eventual use in your programming environment. Feel free to use any of them as you see fit. You can save time by ordering a floppy disk containing all the programs developed in this book; the order form is at the end of the book.

Manipulating a Lotus 1-2-3 Sequential File

Figure 7.4 showed the DONATION.TXT file, a structured sequential file. This file was produced by Lotus 1-2-3 as an unformatted file. In 1-2-3, you can output any spreadsheet to a structured sequential file with the /Print/File command. You only need to specify the desired range, and to indicate that the output is to be unformatted with the /Other/Unformatted command.

Use LINE INPUT to read LOTUS 1-2-3 generated files.

As discussed earlier in this chapter, one of the easiest ways of reading the data from a file like this is with QuickBASIC's LINE INPUT statement. Listing 7.1 shows the 123FILE.BAS program that does just this.

Listing 7.1 123FILE.BAS, Which Reads Lotus 1-2-3 Structured
Sequential Files

```
'123FILE.BAS demonstrates how to process unformatted Lotus
     print output files
'
CLS
OPEN "donation.txt" FOR INPUT AS #1
DO WHILE NOT EOF(1)
   LINE INPUT #1, lotusline$
   code$ = MID$(lotusline$, 1, 3)
   donor$ = MID$(lotusline$, 4, 31)
   gift$ = MID$(lotusline$, 35, 22)
   value$ = MID$(lotusline$, 57, 7)
   PRINT code$; donor$; gift$; value$
   total = total + VAL(value$)
LOOP
PRINT
PRINT USING "Total contributions: $$#######.##"; TAB(31);
     total
CLOSE #1
END
```

This program pulls together many elements of programming discussed in the last three chapters. The OPEN command links the program to the actual DONATION.TXT file on disk. It specifies that the file is to be used for INPUT only in this program, and that it will be later referred to as #1. In fact, other than closing the file at the end of the program, the LINE INPUT statement is the only command that uses this connection.

The central DO . . . LOOP in the program reads all records up until the end-of-file mark. The EOF(1) function becomes TRUE when all data in the file has been read, so the DO loop stops repeating at that time. The loop itself demonstrates several things. First, the LINE INPUT statement stores the entire structured record in a string variable called *lotusline$*. Then, the MID$ function is used to extract the known field widths from each *lotusline$*.

QuickBASIC sequential files consist of only character strings.

An important fact to understand is that all QuickBASIC sequential files interpret the contents of their records to be character strings. This is true even if the contents appear to be a number! Running the 123FILE.BAS program results in the output seen in Figure 7.8.

```
    3 1ST GRADE MOMS - ROOM 8      7 MONTHS OF COOKIES      84.00
   47 ABOUT CHILDREN                2 CHILDREN'S PUZZLES     10.00
  181 ABOUT FACE AND BODY           EYELASH TINT            12.00
   16 ACE GYMNASTICS                ONE MONTH LESSONS       74.00
   28 ADROIT CERAMICS               QUICHE DISH             19.00
   31 ARNOLD VETERINARY CLINIC      PET EXAM                25.00
    6 ALTA BREAST CENTER            BILATERAL MAMMOGRAPHY   95.00
   82 AMERICAN DRY CLEANERS         CLOTHING ALTERATIONS    10.00
   54 AMERICAN THEATER              2 ORCHESTRA TICKETS     50.00
   19 KINDALL CHIROPRACTIC CENTER   LUMBAR PILLOW           23.00
   76 BRAND-NEW GALLERY             FRAMED POSTER          115.00
  115 BASKIN-ROBBINS                2 BANANA SPLITS          8.00
   57 BAY AREA WIND SYMPHONY        4 TICKETS               48.00
  132 BEARS & THINGS, INC.          BUSINESS BEAR           22.00
   95 PRESIDENTIAL BOOKS            GIFT CERTIFICATE        10.00
   64 BERKELEY ICE HOCKEY           4 PASSES                10.00
   86 BERKELEY SHAKESPEARE          2 TICKETS               20.00
  164 BERKELEY SYMPHONY             2 TICKETS               40.00

                          Total contributions:   $691.00


Press any key to continue
```

Figure 7.8 Screen Output from 123FILE.BAS

The DONATION.TXT file contains a list of gifts donated by local merchants to a school fund-raising auction. Each donor's name and gift are assigned both a school code and an estimated value. The purpose of this program is to demonstrate how to access the data prepared by a Lotus 1-2-3 user. This program uses QuickBASIC to display the gift list and to calculate the total estimated dollar value of everything.

The MID$ function used in program 123FILE.BAS takes three parameters. Its general form is

MID$(*StringName$, Start, SubStringLength*)

When used correctly in a QuickBASIC statement, the MID$ function is replaced by the character portion of *StringName$*, which begins in position *Start*, whose length is *SubStringLength*.

Since *lotusline$* contains an entire record of characters each time through the DO loop, the ID code is extracted from it with MID$. Knowing that this code is 3 characters wide, beginning with position 1, the value returned by

```
MID$(lotusline$, 1, 3)
```

can be assigned to *code$*. Similarly, referring to the program, the donor's name is extracted to *donor$*; its length is 31 characters beginning with position 4. *Gift$* begins in position 35 and extends for 22 characters, and *value$* starts in position 57 and takes up 7 character spaces.

> Sequential files store numbers as strings of characters. You must use the VAL function before using these numbers in arithmetic calculations.

However, because sequential files store numbers as strings of characters, you must not perform any calculations with them until you convert them back to numbers. The VAL function does this. Hence, to generate a running total, the following statement uses the VAL function:

```
total = total + VAL(value$)
```

VAL converts the string of characters in *value$* to a numerical quantity, which can be added to the simple integer variable *total*. Remember that simple integer variables are limited to a maximum value of 32,767. This program assumes that the individual dollar amounts are actually whole numbers, and that their total does not exceed the maximum.

Using a dBASE or WordStar Sequential File for Mailing Labels

Figure 7.3 showed the MAIL.LST file prepared for the purpose of mail merging. Many word processors contains special features that enable you to prepare one letter to be sent to a group of people. This type of mail merge file is an unstructured sequential file containing the names and addresses of the recipients of the letter.

In fact, this type of file is often and easily prepared by a database management system, or by a programming language such as Quick-BASIC. You learned earlier how to prepare such a file with QuickBASIC. However, this particular file was prepared by my dBASE IV system from a dBASE file that contains my client list. The dBASE command to prepare such a file is:

```
COPY TO MAIL.LST DELIMITED WITH " ;
    FIELD LAST,FIRST,ADDR,CITY,STATE,ZIP
```

Because the file is unstructured and sequential, each record can be read quickly with an INPUT statement, as demonstrated in the QuickBASIC MAILPRN.BAS program seen in Listing 7.2. Each field is properly delimited with commas, so the INPUT statement specifies the individual field names to be read from the record. The result of the program is the names and addresses printed separately on 1-inch mailing labels.

Listing 7.2 MAILPRN.BAS Program, Which Outputs
to the Printer

```
'MAILPRN.BAS demonstrates how to process field-delimited
'            file such as those used in word processing
'            mail merging.
' Output prints 1" labels on the printer.
'

CLS
OPEN "mail.lst" FOR INPUT AS #1
OPEN "lpt1:" FOR OUTPUT AS #2
DO WHILE NOT EOF(1)
    INPUT #1, lastname$, first$, address$, city$, state$,
        zip$
    PRINT #2, first$; " "; lastname$
    PRINT #2, address$
    PRINT #2, city$; ", "; state$; "  "; zip$
    PRINT #2,
    PRINT #2,
    PRINT #2,
LOOP
CLOSE #1
END
```

This program is our first example of how to connect a QuickBASIC program for both input from a file and non-default output to a printer. Thus far, all output has been to the default video monitor. Here, a second OPEN statement is used to identify your LPT1: printer as the #2 "connection" in your program. This example accurately suggests that the OPEN statement enables you to connect your program to either a disk file or a separate physical piece of hardware, such as a printer.

The OPEN statement can connect a QuickBASIC program either to a file or to a separate hardware device.

Notice carefully that the first OPEN statement connects the MAIL.LST file to your program. It indicates that this file will be used for input, and can be identified as #1 in statements such as INPUT #1 seen within the DO loop. The other OPEN statement connects your program to the printer, indicating that any reference to #2 will be for output purposes only. The PRINT #2 statements within the DO loop all support this design. If it weren't for the #2 in these PRINT statements, all output would have been to the video monitor.

As it stands, the program contains six output PRINT statements. These account for six lines output to the printer. The first three contain the name, address, and city-state-zip information in the standard format seen on mailing labels. The next three account for three blank lines. Since the standard printer output is six lines to the inch, these lines account for precisely 1 inch of output per label. Using continuous feed labels, the output of MAILPRN.BAS seen in Figure 7.9 is precisely one name and complete address printed on each 1-inch label.

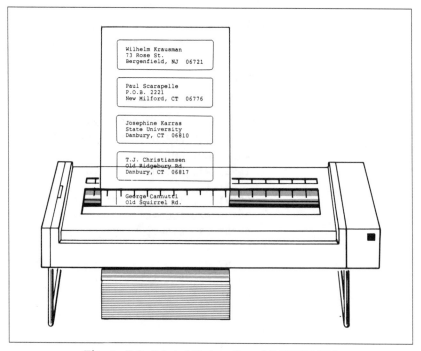

Figure 7.9 Printed Output from MAILPRN.BAS

Nest an IF within a DO to select records for processing.

Many applications do not need to process all of the records in a sequential file. Selection of only some records is a common requirement. Because the DO loop is your means of repetitively processing all records in a file, you must use an IF statement to control the selection of only some of the records. Take a look in Listing 7.3 at the modification to the mailing program.

Listing 7.3 Selection of Records Using an IF Statement

```
'MAILPRN2.BAS demonstrates how to process field-delimited
'            files such as those used in word processing
'            mail merging.
' Produces 1" mailing labels on the printer.
```

```
' Also demonstrates how to produce a selective set of
        labels.
'
CLS
OPEN "mail.lst" FOR INPUT AS #1
OPEN "lpt1:" FOR OUTPUT AS #2
DO WHILE NOT EOF(1)
  INPUT #1, lastname$, first$, address$, city$, state$, zip$
  IF zip$ >= "A" THEN
    PRINT #2, first$; " "; lastname$
    PRINT #2, address$
    PRINT #2, city$; ", "; state$; "  "; zip$
    PRINT #2,
    PRINT #2,
    PRINT #2,
  END IF
LOOP
CLOSE #1
CLOSE #2
END
```

Control the selection criteria with the IF condition.

The only difference between MAILPRN2.BAS and its predecessor is the new IF statement. By specifying a condition here, your PRINT statements will only apply to records that meet the condition. In this mailing list example, the typical selection criterion is based on zip code. So, including

```
IF zip$ >= "947" AND zip$ < "949" THEN
```

ensures that only labels for a small region of clients in Northern California are printed. Similarly, because the characters in the *zip$* field can contain letters as well as digits, you can select only Canadian or other non-US addresses with

```
IF zip$ >= "A" AND zip$ <= "Z" THEN
```

Managing Your Own Complete Database with QuickBASIC

Figure 7.5 depicted a typical database that can be maintained by your QuickBASIC system. The three most common operations required by a database management application are

1. Adding new records to the file

2. Retrieving existing records for display

3. Updating existing records with new data

The GET and PUT statements give QuickBASIC random access to data records.

This section presents three programs designed to handle these three chores. They are all based on techniques you've already seen, in tandem with the new methods for dealing with random access files. First, the GET and PUT statements are used to randomly read from or write to individual records. Second, the TYPE statement is used to create a user-defined type in the precise shape required by the design of the EMPLOYEE.DTA file shown in Figure 7.5.

Handling On-Line Record Retrievals

The first program, RANDOMRD.BAS, incorporates most of the necessary techniques for random access file manipulation. This program, seen in Listing 7.4, is used to retrieve existing record information for on-line display. Figure 7.10 shows the typical screen output from this program. A TYPE statement is used to define the new type called CONTACT, as was discussed earlier in this chapter. Then, a DIM statement specifies that the program will use a variable called *eachline* when it wants to access any particular record in the EMPLOYEE.DTA file (opened for RANDOM access).

Listing 7.4 Retrieving Records for Display with
RANDOMRD.BAS

```
' RANDOMRD.BAS demonstrates on-line record retrieval.
'
' The GET statement can randomly retrieve any complete
     record.
' A user defined type specifies the nature of a 'record'.
'
CONST FALSE = 0, TRUE = NOT FALSE
TYPE contact
   id AS LONG
   first AS STRING * 10
   last AS STRING * 15
   date AS STRING * 8
   marital AS STRING * 1
   grade AS INTEGER
   salary AS SINGLE
END TYPE
DIM eachline AS contact
CLS
OPEN "employee.dta" FOR RANDOM AS #1 LEN = LEN(eachline)
DONE = FALSE
DO
   INPUT "Enter next record number to retrieve:"; recno
   IF recno = 9999 THEN
```

```
      DONE = TRUE
   ELSE
      CLS
      GET #1, recno, eachline
      PRINT "Employee Number"; eachline.id, eachline.first;
        eachline.last
      PRINT
      PRINT "Date of Hire:"; eachline.date
      PRINT "Marital Status:"; eachline.marital
      PRINT "Pay Grade:"; eachline.grade
      PRINT USING "Salary $$####.##"; eachline.salary
      PRINT
   END IF
LOOP UNTIL DONE
CLOSE #1
END
```

```
Employee Number 987666      Sandra     Karlson

Date of Hire:12/24/86
Marital Status:M
Pay Grade: 13
Salary $2000.00

Enter next record number to retrieve:?
```

Figure 7.10 Sample Screen Output from RANDOMRD.BAS

Name your logical
variables according to
their function.

The DO loop in this program is based on a logical test using a variable called *DONE*. Once again, the choice of variable name is purposely suggestive of the task it serves in the program. The loop will repeat until the user enters a record number of 9999, indicating that the program should end. The IF test discovers this input value, then switches the value of *DONE* from FALSE to TRUE, thereby directing the LOOP UNTIL DONE statement to stop its repetitions.

The GET #1 statement specifies the record number to retrieve and the variable name (*eachline*) to receive the record information. Once

Use type name and item name to identify random access record elements.

received, the PRINT statements display the information using the methods discussed above. Remember that each element in a random access file record can be referenced by the TYPE name followed by a period and then by its item name. So, after each record is read, that record's numerical grade value can be found in the *eachline.grade* variable. The date of hire can be found in the *eachline.date* variable. And so on.

Numerical values in a random access file are actually stored in their 2, 4, or 8-byte numerical forms. So you can directly use these values in computations as soon as you've gotten (GET #1) each record into the record variable (*eachline*). For example, if you wanted to total all employees' salaries to determine the bank balance required to cover the payroll, the following line would do the job:

```
total = total + eachline.salary
```

Adding New Records to Your Database

Adding new records to an existing random access file can be handled by the RANDOMWR.BAS program seen in Listing 7.5. A typical input screen managed by this program is seen in Figure 7.11.

Listing 7.5 Adding New Records to Your Database

```
' RANDOMWR.BAS demonstrates on-line record storage.
'
' The PUT statement can randomly store any complete record.
' A user defined type specifies the nature of a 'record'.
'
CONST FALSE = 0, TRUE = NOT FALSE
TYPE contact
  id AS LONG
  first AS STRING * 10
  last AS STRING * 15
  date AS STRING * 8
  marital AS STRING * 1
  grade AS INTEGER
  salary AS SINGLE
END TYPE
DIM eachline AS contact
CLS
OPEN "employee.dta" FOR RANDOM AS #1 LEN = LEN(eachline)
lastrec = LOF(1) \ LEN(eachline)
DONE = FALSE
DO
  CLS
  INPUT " Please enter new Employee's ID"; eachline.id
```

```
    IF eachline.id = 9999 THEN
      DONE = TRUE
    ELSE
      INPUT "                    and first name"; eachline.first
      INPUT "                     and lastname"; eachline.last
      INPUT "                   and date of hire"; eachline.date
      INPUT "              and marital status";
        eachline.marital
      INPUT "                     and pay grade"; eachline.grade
      INPUT "                       and salary"; eachline.salary
      lastrec = lastrec + 1
      PUT #1, lastrec, eachline
    END IF
LOOP UNTIL DONE
CLOSE #1
END
```

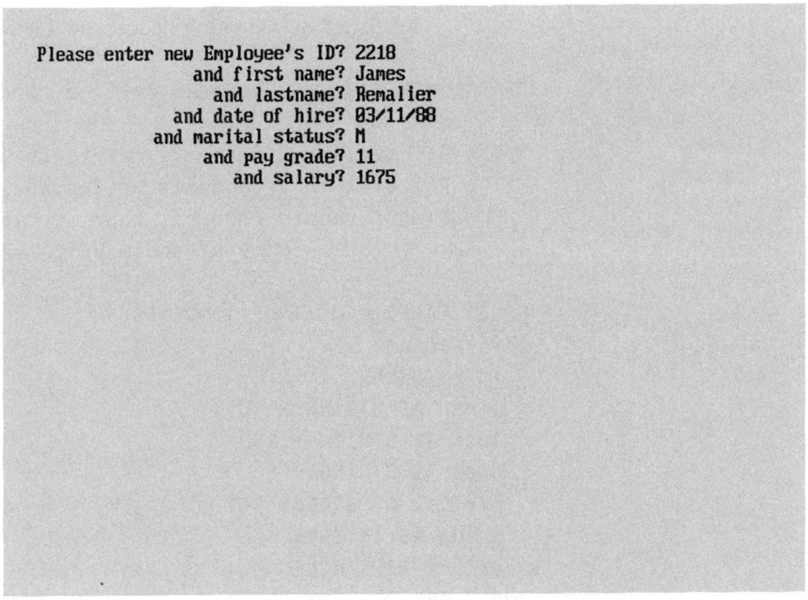

```
Please enter new Employee's ID? 2218
              and first name? James
               and lastname? Remalier
           and date of hire? 03/11/88
           and marital status? M
               and pay grade? 11
                  and salary? 1675
```

Figure 7.11 Sample Input Screen for RANDOMWR.BAS

A program that adds records must calculate each new record's number.

Because this program adds new records to the file, it must calculate a unique new number for each new record. It does this with the line:

```
lastrec = LOF(1) \ LEN(eachline)
```

This line uses the LOF function to determine the total length of the EMPLOYEE.DTA file (identified by #1). It then uses the LEN function to obtain the length of the *eachline* variable. Dividing the file length by the record length produces the number of records in the file, which is then assigned to the variable *lastrec*. Prior to storing each new record into the file, the PUT command at the end of the DO loop increments this number by 1 to produce a new unique record number, as follows:

```
lastrec = lastrec + 1
```

Use a unique code to signal the end of data entry.

Once again, the ID code of 9999 is used by the program to determine when you want to stop adding new records to the database.

Updating Existing Records in Your Database

Files opened for random access can actually be read from or written to at will. Program RANDOMCH.BAS in Listing 7.6 demonstrates how to combine GET and PUT statements to manage this process.

Listing 7.6 Updating Records in a Random Access File

```
' RANDOMCH.BAS demonstrates on-line record update.
'
' The GET statement randomly retrieves any complete record.
' The PUT statement randomly writes any complete record.
' Updating a record requires that it first be randomly read,
'           followed by a random write of the same record.
'
CONST FALSE = 0, TRUE = NOT FALSE
TYPE contact
  id AS LONG
  first AS STRING * 10
  last AS STRING * 15
  date AS STRING * 8
  marital AS STRING * 1
  grade AS INTEGER
  salary AS SINGLE
END TYPE
DIM eachline AS contact
CLS
OPEN "employee.dta" FOR RANDOM AS #1 LEN = LEN(eachline)
DONE = FALSE
DO
  INPUT "Enter next record number to update:"; recno
  IF recno = 9999 THEN
    DONE = TRUE
  ELSE
    CLS
    GET #1, recno, eachline
```

```
      PRINT "Employee Number"; eachline.id, eachline.first;
        eachline.last
      PRINT
      PRINT "Date of Hire:"; eachline.date
      PRINT "Marital Status:"; eachline.marital
      PRINT "Pay Grade:"; eachline.grade
      PRINT USING "Salary $$####.##"; eachline.salary
      PRINT
      INPUT "Please enter any changes to employee ID";
        eachline.id
      INPUT "                        and first name";
        eachline.first
      INPUT "                        and lastname";
        eachline.last
      INPUT "                      and date of hire";
        eachline.date
      INPUT "                    and marital status";
        eachline.marital
      INPUT "                        and pay grade";
        eachline.grade
      INPUT "                          and salary";
        eachline.salary
      PRINT
      PUT #1, recno, eachline
    END IF
LOOP UNTIL DONE
CLOSE #1
END
```

In order to update any particular record's field values, you must first ask the user for the record number to update. The INPUT statement handles this chore:

```
INPUT "Enter next record number to update:"; recno
```

The heart of the program is in the ELSE statement. After clearing the screen, the GET command reads the requested record number and PRINTs the currently stored field values. As Figure 7.12 shows, the program then executes a series of successive INPUT commands to obtain new values to be stored in that particular record's fields. After all of the field values are obtained with the INPUT statements, the PUT statement stores them in the file at that particular record's location.

These three programs form a mini-system for managing your own database with QuickBASIC. In designing your own programs, you need to change the TYPE statement to reflect the various field names in your database structure. You then must change any INPUT and PRINT statements that reference these names. With these adjustments, the three

Use these programs as models for your own simple QuickBASIC database system.

```
Employee Number 2196        William    Taylor

Date of Hire:04/15/88
Marital Status:S
Pay Grade: 11
Salary  $1700.00

Please enter any changes to employee ID? 2196
                      and first name? William
                       and lastname? Taylor
                   and date of hire? 04/15/88
                   and marital status? M
                      and pay grade? 12
                        and salary? 1850
```

Figure 7.12 Screen Display During Random Record Updates

sample programs in this chapter can be used virtually as they stand for your own unique database applications.

Review

This chapter concentrated on management of the large amount of data that can be stored in a disk file. You learned many things about manipulating such files:

1. Each file must be found on disk by the operating system and connected to your program. The OPEN statement does this.

2. When finished with a file's data, your program must ask the operating system to close the connection and write any remaining memory data out to the disk file. The CLOSE statement does this.

3. Files may be accessed in one of five ways, which you specify when you OPEN the file. You can open a file for INPUT, OUTPUT, RANDOM access, BINARY access, or APPEND modes. INPUT and OUTPUT are simple sequential modes of access. RANDOM permits both input and output, and allows records to be accessed at random. APPEND enables you to add new records to an existing sequential file. And BINARY permits byte-level access for both input and output.

4. An unstructured sequential file is simply a group of data items of

variable length, terminated by a carriage return and line feed pair of control characters. No spaces are wasted at the end of each field; string values are enclosed in quotation marks.

5. A structured sequential file relies on fixed widths for field values. String values are padded with spaces, and numerical fields are right justified in the portion of the record dedicated to them.

6. Numbers are stored in sequential files as strings of characters. Before using them in computations, you must convert them to numerical quantities with the VAL function.

7. INPUT and LINE INPUT are used to access data in a sequential file. WRITE and PRINT are used to store data in a sequential file.

8. GET retrieves entire records in a random access file, while PUT is used to store entire records.

9. Random access files can be used to manage your own database of records. Each record represents a complex grouping of simple data types. You define this record structure with a TYPE statement; it is called a *user-defined type*. Variables can be defined to store these record values with a DIM statement.

10. Random access files are best for on-line applications that require rapid file access, frequent deletions or insertions, or in-place record updating.

11. Sequential files are best for managing variable length record information, for working in systems that are short on disk space, or for working with infrequently accessed data.

12. QuickBASIC's file types enable you to manipulate Lotus 1-2-3, dBASE, or WordStar/WordPerfect-type files.

Quiz for Chapter 7

1. Which QuickBASIC command establishes the connection between a program and a disk file?

   a. INPUT
   b. GET
   c. READ
   d. OPEN

2. Which of the following is not a valid file operation type?

   a. INPUT
   b. PRINT
   c. APPEND
   d. BINARY

3. Which is not a valid QuickBASIC file type?

   a. Unstructured sequential
   b. Structured sequential
   c. Unstructured random
   d. Structured random

4. What QuickBASIC file operation can reduce the likelihood of data loss during a power failure?

   a. BACKUP
   b. PUT
   c. CLOSE
   d. SAVE

5. What character(s) indicate the end of a record?

   a. EOF
   b. CR-LF
   c. Esc
   d. Enter

6. Which of the following has the least overhead for reading an entire record from a sequential file?

   a. LINE INPUT
   b. INPUT
   c. READ
   d. GET

7. Which QuickBASIC command can be most easily used to produce an unstructured sequential file for mail merge purposes?

   a. PRINT
   b. WRITE
   c. PUT
   d. DO

8. Which of the following files wastes the least amount of space?

    a. Unstructured sequential
    b. Structured sequential
    c. Structured random
    d. Unstructured random

9. The LINE INPUT command is limited to records that do not exceed how many characters?

    a. 80
    b. 128
    c. 256
    d. 255

10. If the digits 765 are read from a sequential file, they are stored as:

    a. A number
    b. A character
    c. A 2, 4, or 8-byte number
    d. A string of characters

11. The columns in a random access file are known as:

    a. Records
    b. Fields
    c. Variables
    d. Values

12. Simple data types can be grouped into a more complex variable type called:

    a. Group type
    b. Complex type
    c. User-defined type
    d. Advanced type

13. Which statement defines a variable used to store record values in a random access file?

    a. TYPE
    b. DIM
    c. Assignment statement
    d. DEFINE

14. What QuickBASIC statement permits selectivity in file manipulations?

    a. SELECT
    b. IF
    c. DO
    d. FOR

15. Which statement prepares a second system printer to be used by a QuickBASIC program as output device number four?

   a. OPEN "lpt1:" FOR OUTPUT AS #4
   b. OPEN "lpt2:" FOR RANDOM AS #4
   c. OPEN "lpt4:" FOR OUTPUT AS #2
   d. OPEN "lpt1:" FOR RANDOM AS #4

8 | Processing Character Strings

In the last chapter, you learned how to manipulate files containing both strings and numbers. You've already used several string functions. In this chapter, you will revisit those few functions, and study a wide range of additional string processing capabilities in QuickBASIC.

Most QuickBASIC applications deal with character data.

Chapter 5 made it clear that data is made up of either character strings or numerical quantities. Chapter 7 demonstrated that sequential files store all data, both numbers and characters, as strings of characters. These facts make string management essential for effective computer programming.

As was true in Chapter 7, the first part of this chapter will concentrate on the fundamentals of string processing. The second part will present a series of practical programs designed to highlight the power of QuickBASIC's string capabilities. In this chapter, you will see complete programs that demonstrate how to use string functions to

1. Center titles on reports or screen output

2. Activate or deactivate any special printer features

3. Produce numerical output with leading zeros printed

4. Encrypt system or file passwords

5. Modify the upper/lower case of text strings in a file

6. Verify that dates stored in string variables are valid

Understanding Functions

Appendix B describes all of QuickBASIC's statements and built-in functions. A statement is the primary type of instruction; each QuickBASIC program line consists of a statement and any necessary support clauses or parameters. You've already seen many statements. Some are single line statements, such as assignments, while others take more than one line to be complete, such as flow of control statements.

A function is a special breed of QuickBASIC feature. It has a value, like a variable, but it represents a series of instruction steps, like a program.

A *function* is a cross between an assignment statement and an entire program of statements. QuickBASIC has a wide range of built-in functions that you can use immediately. You will learn how to build your own new functions in Chapter 10. This chapter explains functions in general and demonstrates those most useful for string manipulations.

Figure 8.1 shows how a function is like an assignment statement. As you know, a variable is simply a named place in memory for a value. The following two statements merely assign the number 45 or the string value "Berkeley" to different variables:

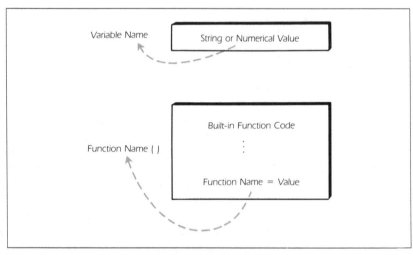

Figure 8.1 Similarity Between a Function and an Assignment Statement

```
MyInfo = 45

Street$ = "Berkeley"
```

Other variables or expressions can then use these variable names to produce more complex or useful results, such as

```
Target = .80 * HeartRate - MyInfo
```

A function is like a variable in that it has a unique name. A function is also like a variable in that it has a unique value. But it goes beyond a variable;

its value can be determined by an unlimited number of processing steps, just like a complete program. However, it is not as powerful as a complete program. A function cannot have independent file I/O and independent console (screen and keyboard) interaction with a user. A function is a mini-program whose only task is to determine a value for itself. In this respect, a function is closer to the depiction seen in Figure 8.2.

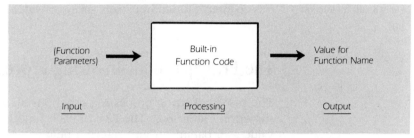

Figure 8.2 Similarity Between a Function and a Mini-Program

Functions usually require inputs. Using these inputs, they can save program development time by providing a short-hand representation for a frequent series of processing steps.

Most functions require input information; this input appears as parameters in parentheses. For instance, a function named TARGET might require two input parameters: a heart rate (HeartRate) and a person's age (Age).

Its formal syntax (required form) is

TARGET (*Parameter1, Parameter2*)

As in Figure 8.2, the function requires double parentheses around its input parameters. Most functions require at least one parameter, although some require none while others require several. Just remember that when a function appears anywhere in a QuickBASIC program, it is used as a simple variable.

A function can only run its built-in logic when the function name, along with any required parameters, appears in your program. The function is said to be *referenced* when the flow of control passes to this point in your program. Furthermore, a function is not a stand-alone program; it can only be used within a QuickBASIC expression, like a variable. So, the TARGET function might appear as

```
answer = TARGET(170,38)
```

In this example, invoking the code for the TARGET function produces a simple expression in your QuickBASIC program. You know that the answer is computed from the two input values of heart rate (170) and age (38). In many built-in functions, it is not important to you how the function operates; only the result counts. When a built-in function exists to perform a particular task, you needn't develop the program code to compute the desired result.

In the simple TARGET example, you might suspect that the internal logic is equivalent to the following simple expression:

```
TARGET = .80 * Parameter1 - Parameter2
```

The value of a function is not fixed. It is recomputed each time the function's name appears in an executing QuickBASIC instruction line.

However, unlike a simple variable, which has a simple value, a function computes a new value instantaneously, based on its input parameters. The new value is then used in place of the function, just as a stored value is used in place of a named variable in QuickBASIC expressions.

More complex examples abound. In fact, as you'll see throughout this chapter, a function usually saves considerably more than one step.

The Principal Built-In String Processing Functions

The principal string processing functions all adhere to the depiction shown in Figure 8.2. The task of each function is to take an existing value as a parameter and return a new value as the resulting output. These functions fall into three categories, summarized in Table 8.1.

Table 8.1 Categories of QuickBASIC String Processing Functions

Type Name	Definition
	Extraction
LEFT$	Returns leftmost characters
LTRIM$	Removes leading spaces
MID$	Returns a substring
RIGHT$	Returns rightmost characters
RTRIM$	Removes trailing spaces
	Conversion
LCASE$	Enforces lower case
STR$	Converts number to string
UCASE$	Enforces upper case
VAL	Converts string to number
	Miscellaneous
ASC	Returns ASCII character value
CHR$	Returns unique ASCII character
INSTR	Returns position of a substring
LEN	Obtains length of a string
SPACE$	Returns a string of spaces
STRING$	Repeats a string of characters

Although there are a few other functions, their use is confined to limited applications. This chapter concerns itself with the most popular, the most powerful, and the most commonly needed string functions. There are even some QuickBASIC statements that manipulate strings; only the MID$ statement is discussed here in conjunction with its related function. However, all functions and statements that deal with strings are presented in summary form in Appendix B.

Extracting Portions of Strings

In all of the situations you've seen to this point, string variables have only consumed as many character positions (bytes) as were necessary to store the string. This was true regardless of whether you entered the string from the keyboard or obtained the string value from a data file. In other words, a string like "COMPUTER OPTIONS" only takes up 16 bytes when assigned to a previously undefined string variable, as follows:

```
SX$ = "COMPUTER OPTIONS"
```

There are times, however, when you want a variable to contain a precise number of characters, regardless of how many characters the user may enter at the keyboard. A password may contain exactly 5 characters, or a mailing address field may allow exactly 25 characters and no more. You can do this with the now-familiar DIM statement

```
DIM SX AS STRING * 25
```

The DIM statement can fix the size of a string variable, while eliminating the need to append a $ suffix to the variable name.

A side benefit of this statement is that, in addition to defining a fixed width for the variable, the name is simultaneously defined as a string variable. The dollar sign suffix is no longer necessary throughout your program. You can simply type SX without having to constantly remember to add the $ suffix. Many of the programs shown in this text would be easier to type in if you used DIM statements rather than typing all the suffixes. However, the variable use would not be as obvious, and the intention of this book is to be clear, simple, and direct.

Assume that *SX* has been defined, and that its value (see Figure 8.3) has been entered from the keyboard. This figure summarizes the results discussed in this section. Each extraction function produces a different result, depending on the particular portion of the subject string *SX* that you want to extract.

The five functions that extract portions of an existing string provide the flexibility of obtaining substrings from the left, the middle, or the right side of a string.

The LEFT$ function enables you to create a new substring consisting of the leftmost *n* characters from a subject string. The syntax is

LEFT$(*SubjectString, n*)

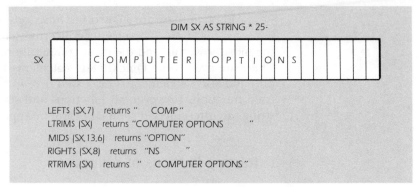

Figure 8.3 Example of Extraction Functions

As Figure 8.3 indicates, the *SubjectString* in each example is *SX*, which contains 25 characters. The first 3 characters are spaces, followed by "COMPUTER OPTIONS", followed again by 6 trailing spaces. If you specify a new string, such as *NewString$*, to receive the result of the example in Figure 8.3,

```
NewString$ = LEFT$(SX,7)
```

then NewString$ will contain a 7-character string consisting of 3 spaces followed by "COMP"; these are the first 7 characters in the subject string *SX*.

The reverse of the LEFT$ function is the RIGHT$ function; the syntax is similar. Assigning the rightmost 8 characters of *SX* to New-String$

```
NewString$ = RIGHT$(SX,8)
```

results in a *NewString$* variable that contains the letters "NS", followed by 6 spaces; these are the rightmost 8 characters in the *SX* string.

Often, however, you are not interested in leading or trailing blank spaces. The LTRIM$ function strips any leading spaces from a string. In this example,

```
NewString$ = LTRIM$(SX)
```

the result is that *NewString$* contains a 22-character string consisting of the 16 characters "COMPUTER OPTIONS" followed by the 6 trailing spaces from *SX*.

The reverse of this is to strip off trailing blank spaces. The RTRIM$ function does this. For example,

Use RTRIM$ plus a space character to combine fields with variable contents, like first and last names.

```
NewString$ = RTRIM$(SX)
```

produces a *NewString$* that contains the 3 leading spaces from *SX*, followed by "COMPUTER OPTIONS". To be absolutely sure of stripping off both leading and trailing blank spaces, you must use both functions.

```
NewString$ = RTRIM$ (LTRIM$(SX) )
```

Nesting RTRIM$ and LTRIM$ functions can guarantee that no trailing or leading blank spaces remain in the resulting string.

The result now is "COMPUTER OPTIONS" with all trailing and leading blank spaces stripped away. This accurately suggests that functions can be nested within one another. You can use a function (which represents a value) as easily as you can use a variable (which represents a value). In this example, the variable *SX* is used as the parameter for the LTRIM$ function. The string function LTRIM$(SX) is used as the parameter for the RTRIM$ function.

Converting String Information

Strings can be changed in two principal ways. First, the case of the string can be changed: from upper to lower or from lower to upper. Second, a string containing digits can be converted to a numerical quantity for possible computation, or a numerical quantity can be converted to a string for easier output manipulations.

Changing the Case of a String

Converting a string such as "COMPUTER OPTIONS" to lower case is as simple as making it the parameter in the LCASE$ function. For example,

```
NewString$ = LCASE$ ("COMPUTER OPTIONS")
```

results in a *NewString$* that contains "COMPUTER OPTIONS". The reverse function is straightforward. UCASE$ converts all characters in the subject string to upper case. For example,

```
NewString$ = UCASE$ ("SAN FRANCISCO CHRONICLE")
```

results in a *NewString$* that contains "SAN FRANCISCO CHRONICLE". Program REVISE.BAS, shown later in this chapter, demonstrates how to combine functions to produce a string whose first letter is capitalized and whose remaining characters are in lower case.

Changing Data Types

A common area of misunderstanding is the handling of digits by a computer language. What looks like a number to you or me is sometimes seen by the language as a string of digits. A string is different from a

Digits are stored differently by QuickBASIC according to whether they are to be treated as numerical or as string values.

number. A string consists of a series of one-byte ASCII codes, while a number (which may visually look just the same) is stored in a 2, 4, or even 8-byte mathematical format. These different formats (for integer and floating point types) require different treatment.

QuickBASIC provides two functions for converting between these types. It is up to you to use them as necessary, converting strings to integers prior to computation, or converting integers to strings prior to concatenation. *Concatenation* is the combination of two or more string values into one longer string. For instance, if the variables *FIRST$* and *LAST$* respectively contain the strings "Judd" and "Robbins", then you can concatenate them together by using the plus (+) operator.

```
RESULT$ = FIRST$ + LAST$
```

The *RESULT$* variable will contain "JuddRobbins" when this operation completes. During typical output, you probably would concatenate a space in between these two names.

```
RESULT$ = FIRST$ + " " + LAST$
```

In this case, the *RESULT$* variable holds the more readable "Judd Robbins".

Use character conversions to replace leading zeros with leading spaces.

As you'll see later in programs LEADZERO.BAS and VALI-DATE.BAS, there are situations when you must convert between these two data types. For example, program LEADZERO.BAS takes a seven-digit number (like 1,000,345) and first converts it to a string of characters (1000345).

```
converted$ = STR$(1000345)
```

Then, the RIGHT$ function is used to return all of the characters except the leading 1.

```
result$ = RIGHT$(converted$, 6)
```

This enables you to display or print a number with leading zeros (for example, 000345), a necessity in some inventory management applications.

The counterpoint situation occurs when data appears in string format, such as the *year$* variable in program VALIDATE.BAS. In this program, a two-digit year value must undergo some computations to determine if the year in question is a leap year. Since *year$* is a string quantity that contains two digits, the VAL function is used to convert it to a numerical quantity.

*Year$* is a 2-character string, while VAL(year$) is a 2-byte integer. A year is a leap year if it is evenly divisible by 4.

```
IF VAL(year$) = (INT(VAL(year$) / 4) * 4) THEN
```

```
      leapyear = TRUE
END IF
```

Other Useful String Processing Functions

The remaining string functions remind me of a magician's hat (see Figure 8.4). Each one represents a different trick with a special purpose or nature to it. You only rarely need to pull any one of these out of the hat, but knowing how and when to do so can add magic to the programs you write.

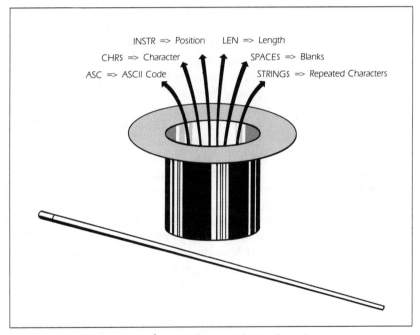

Figure 8.4 Miscellaneous String Functions

Converting Between ASCII Codes and Character Strings

ASC and CHR$ provide rapid conversion between ASCII codes and character strings.

The ASC function returns the ASCII code for a single character. If you provide a parameter that contains more than one character, you'll get back as the value of this function the ASCII code for the first character in the string. For instance, if you enter

PRINT ASC("b")

or

PRINT ASC("brain food")

you'll receive the number 98 printed on your video monitor; 98 is the ASCII code that represents a lower-case "b". Program PASSWORD.BAS uses the ASC function to encrypt a password before storing it in a file. In this way, even if others access the file, they will see only a misleading sequence of characters. Each password entry is later processed with the same algorithm to determine its validity. Only if the password entered produces the same algorithmic result is it considered a correct password.

As you would expect, the reverse function (CHR$) takes any ASCII code and returns the character associated with that code. For example, if you enter

```
PRINT CHR$(98)
```

you'll receive the letter "b" displayed on your monitor. The CHR$ function only produces the one letter that corresponds to the number entered in the parentheses. Although the ASCII codes in the range 1 to 128 are fairly fixed, the numbers in the range 129 to 256 do vary quite a bit. This high range is called the extended ASCII set. You could easily write a program to display the characters in your system's extended range. Simply use a DO loop and a counting variable. You can then print the CHR$ function value for the counter variable itself.

Obtain compressed print with *control characters*.

Try this on your system. Remember to try it for both video output and printer output, because many characters print differently than they display on the screen. You will also discover if you do this that some ASCII numbers do not result in a visible character at all. These numbers are called *control characters*. The ASCII character related to each numerical code entered acts to control the video or printer device. For example, program PRINTER.BAS uses this technique to switch a printer between compressed and normal pitch.

Determining the Length of a String

The LEN function is frequently used to determine how many characters are stored in a string variable. You've seen it in earlier characters and you'll see it later in CENTER.BAS. This program demonstrates how to center a title or any other text string prior to video or printer output.

LEN returns a number that represents the stored length of a string. So if *string1$* contains "SepAprJunNov", then

```
PRINT LEN(string1$)
```

will output a value of 12. This numerical value can be used in later computations or expressions, as you'll see in both the CENTER.BAS program and the REVISE.BAS program.

Searching for One String Inside Another

The INSTR function enables you to discover the character position of a smaller string within another larger one. Its syntax requires two parameters. If the second string value can be found anywhere inside the first string, then INSTR returns a number equal to the beginning position where the string equivalence was found. For example, INSTR can be used to determine that the substring "Apr" exists within string1$ beginning at position 4.

Suppose you were using a variable called *month$* and you wanted to determine if a particular *month$* contained thirty days or not. You could use the 12-character string1$, defined above, to contain the four 3-character months that contain thirty days each. Then, you could use the INSTR function in the actual test, as follows:

```
IF INSTR(string1$, month$) <> 0 THEN
   PRINT month$; " has thirty days"
END IF
```

INSTR returns a value of 0 if the second string cannot be found inside the first string.

This expression works because INSTR returns a value of 0 if the second string cannot be found in the first one. So, if *month$* contains "Apr", then the value of INSTR is 4; if *month$* contains "Aug", then the value of INSTR is 0.

Repeating String Characters

The remaining two functions come in handy when you format your output. You've already seen how to use the TAB function to move the cursor or print head to a specific column. You can also use the SPACE$ function to output a fixed number of spaces between any two strings. This function takes one parameter, which indicates how many spaces to output.

For example, to separate 3 columns on output by exactly 10 spaces, you can print a header line as follows:

```
PRINT "COLUMN1"; SPACE$(10);"COLUMN2"; SPACE$(10);"COLUMN3"
```

The result will be

```
COLUMN1          COLUMN2          COLUMN3
```

When you later output information to appear in each column, you can similarly print SPACE$(10) between each columnar variable.

The STRING$ function is similar to SPACE$. However, instead of simply outputting a number of space characters, you can specify a different character as well as the number of times to repeat that character.

For instance, if you wanted to repeat the asterisk character 15 times on each side of a report title, you could write an instruction such as

```
PRINT STRING$(15,"*");" Report Title Goes Here ";STRING$(15,
    "*")
```

which would produce the following output:

```
*************** Report Title Goes Here ***************
```

This particular function is most commonly used for dressing up a text output with special characters such as lines, asterisks, dashes, or equal signs. Extended ASCII characters can be used; the second parameter can simply be the ASCII code for such a character. For instance,

```
PRINT STRING$(15,221)
```

would output a string of 15 characters on your system, each of which would have the ASCII code 221. Typically, this code represents a thin but solid vertical bar.

Practical Applications of String Processing Functions

Use these programs as they stand, or build them into your programming system.

The following six programs demonstrate nearly all of the string functions discussed in the preceding sections. Each program represents a useful application technique. You can use any of these programs as they stand, or you can modify them and include the adjusted instructions in programs that you write. All of these programs are included on the program disk that can be ordered (see the order form at the end of this book).

Centering Strings for Reports or Video Output

Program CENTER.BAS is shown in Listing 8.1, and its example output can be seen in Figure 8.5.

Listing 8.1 CENTER.BAS—Centering Any String for Output

```
' CENTER.BAS
' Prepares any string to be centered on a report or screen
    output.
' Variable SIZE controls the horizontal size of the paper or
    screen.
```

```
' Three example title lines are centered and output for
    demonstration.
'
size = 80
title1$ = "Computer Options FY 89 Preliminary Report"
title2$ = "Company Confidential"
title3$ = "Education Division"
CLS
len1 = LEN(title1$)
len2 = LEN(title2$)
len3 = LEN(title3$)
column1 = (size - len1) / 2
column2 = (size - len2) / 2
column3 = (size - len3) / 2
LOCATE 1, column1
PRINT title1$
LOCATE 3, column2
PRINT title2$
LOCATE 5, column3
PRINT title3$
END
```

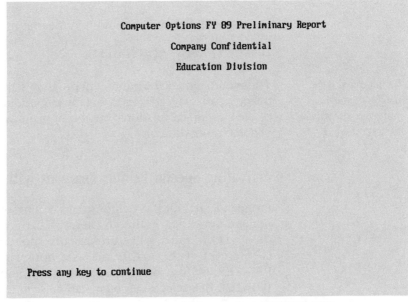

Figure 8.5 Sample Output from CENTER.BAS

In this and the following example programs, several program steps are written as separate steps when they could actually be combined. This is done to make the program clearer and easier to read. For instance, the first title line to be centered is stored in variable *title1$* with this statement:

```
title1$ = "Computer Options FY 89 Preliminary Report"
```

The LEN function is used to store the numerical length of this title in variable *len1*.

```
len1 = LEN(title1$)
```

    The column in which the title should be output is calculated by subtracting the title's length from the size of the output report or screen (stored in variable *size*). This gives the number of positions left on the line. Halving this number gives the number of spaces to skip before printing the title itself.

```
column1 = (size - len1) / 2
```

    After locating the cursor at this column and on the proper row, the title can be printed and it will appear centered:

```
LOCATE 1, column1
PRINT title1$
```

For example, the cursor could have been moved with this statement:

```
LOCATE 1, (80 - LEN(title1$) / 2
```

Do not embed fixed numbers throughout your code; use variable names instead.

This would reduce the number of program statements, but would make the program less readable. In fact, by embedding the number 80 in each of the column calculations, the job of maintaining the program would become more difficult.

Activating Special Printer Features with Control Codes

Program PRINTER.BAS demonstrates the important CHR$ function. As pointed out earlier in this chapter, you can input a numerical code to this function, and it will return the corresponding ASCII character. This is true even if the ASCII code is a non-printing control character. PRINTER.BAS can be seen in Listing 8.2, and its screen output, the PRINTER.BAS selection screen, can be seen in Figure 8.6.

Listing 8.2 PRINTER.BAS—Activating a Printer's
Special Features

```
' PRINTER.BAS demonstrates how to use string functions
'           to control special printer features.
```

```
'
CLS
OPEN "lpt1:" FOR OUTPUT AS #9
EpsonCompress$ = CHR$(15)
EpsonExpand$ = CHR$(18)
HPLaserCompress$ = CHR$(27) + "&k2S"
HPLaserExpand$ = CHR$(27) + "&k0S"
PRINT TAB(25); "Printer Control Program"
PRINT
PRINT "1  Compressed mode on IBM/Epson"
PRINT "2  Compressed mode on HP LaserJet"
PRINT
PRINT "3  Normal 10 pitch mode on IBM/Epson"
PRINT "4  Normal 10 pitch mode on HP LaserJet"
PRINT
INPUT "Select one, please: ", choice
SELECT CASE choice
  CASE 1
    PRINT #9, EpsonCompress$
    PRINT "OK. Epson printer now in compressed mode."
  CASE 2
    PRINT #9, HPLaserCompress$
    PRINT "OK. HP LaserJet now in compressed mode."
  CASE 3
    PRINT #9, EpsonExpand$
    PRINT "OK. Epson printer now in normal 10 pitch mode."
  CASE 4
    PRINT #9, HPLaserExpand$
    PRINT "OK. HP LaserJet now in normal 10 pitch mode."
  CASE ELSE
    PRINT "Invalid choice. No control code sent to printer."
END SELECT
CLOSE #9
END
```

Control sequences are not printed. They typically consist of at least one non-printable ASCII code. Codes submitted this way are treated by the printer as control instructions, rather than printing requests.

Every printer includes documentation explaining its special features. These features are available by sending special control codes to the printer. Rather than printing these codes, the printer accepts them as instructions to activate or deactivate the special feature(s). This submission of control characters is called a *control sequence*, and can consist of one or more ASCII characters.

For demonstration purposes, PRINTER.BAS shows how to use the CHR$ function to turn compressed printing mode on or off. The program also offers the choice of doing this on either a standard Epson/IBM dot matrix printer or on the increasingly popular Hewlett-Packard LaserJet printer.

The program uses standard instructions to display a menu

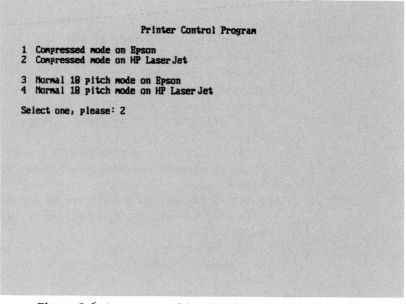

Figure 8.6 Appearance of the PRINTER.BAS Selection Screen

(PRINT), to accept a user's choice (INPUT), and to control the flow of execution (SELECT CASE). The heart of this program lies in the initial assignment of the necessary control sequences to four special variables.

```
EpsonCompress$ = CHR$(15)
EpsonExpand$ = CHR$(18)
HPLaserCompress$ = CHR$(27) + "&k2S"
HPLaserExpand$ = CHR$(27) + "&k0S"
```

The two variables, *EpsonCompress$* and *EpsonExpand$*, are assigned the single control characters necessary to activate or deactivate compressed mode on many IBM and Epson printers. For a Hewlett Packard LaserJet, the activation sequence is more complex. It requires 5 characters. The first character is the non-printing ESC character whose ASCII code is decimal 27. The CHR$ function is used to concatenate that character to the next 4 printable characters.

An *escape sequence* always begins with the Escape control character, CHR$(27).

Both *HPLaserCompress$* and *HPLaserExpand$* similarly contain the *escape sequences* necessary to activate or deactivate standard compressed mode on this printer. The PRINT #9, *ControlVariable* statement ensures that the control sequence is actually transmitted to the printer.

This type of program is often used to print wide spreadsheets or database files that exceed the width of the output device. For example, on typical 8.5-inch by 11-inch paper, using standard 10-pitch output, my CLIENTS file appears as you see in Figure 8.7. After running PRINTER.BAS, and selecting the appropriate compressed mode choice, the now compressed output appears as in Figure 8.8. When output

First, assuming the desired column width is six digits, the seven-digit number 1000000 is added to the *testvalue*.

```
enlarged = 1000000 + testvalue
```

Then, the STR$ function converts this seven-digit number to a seven-digit string.

```
converted$ = STR$(enlarged)
```

The final *result$* is merely the rightmost 6 characters of *converted$*. These characters exclude the character "1" but leave the leading zeros and the string equivalent of the original number.

```
result$ = RIGHT$(converted$, 6)
```

Encrypting a Password

Simple encryption is usually enough to protect your data.

Password protection could easily be the subject of an entire book. In the program PASSWORD.BAS, seen in Listing 8.4, four different string functions are used to provide a measure of password protection.

Listing 8.4 PASSWORD.BAS—Using Encryption Techniques

```
' PASSWORD.BAS demonstrates encryption technique for
     passwords
'
DIM pass AS STRING * 5
DIM StoredValue AS STRING * 5
OPEN "password.dta" FOR OUTPUT AS #1
INPUT "Enter new password, please"; pass
letter1$ = LEFT$(pass, 1)
letter2$ = MID$(pass, 2, 1)
letter3$ = MID$(pass, 3, 1)
letter4$ = MID$(pass, 4, 1)
letter5$ = RIGHT$(pass, 1)
asc1 = ASC(letter1$)
asc2 = ASC(letter2$)
asc3 = ASC(letter3$)
asc4 = ASC(letter4$)
asc5 = ASC(letter5$)
encrypt = asc1 * asc2 * asc3 + asc4 - asc5
'The following would actually appear in the system Password/
     Access file.
StoredValue = LTRIM$(STR$(encrypt))
PRINT #1, StoredValue
END
```

The "PASSWORD.DTA" file is designed to store a 5-character password. This password can presumably be used by a variety of other programs to validate a user's authority to make a choice, use a program, run a routine, and so forth. This program offers the mechanism whereby the password is stored into the PASSWORD.DTA file. Those other programs must use the same algorithm as this program to reconstruct the stored password.

If the password entered into the variable *pass* were stored exactly as it was entered, then any system user could simply view the contents of the PASSWORD.DTA file to learn the password. This program uses the LEFT$, MID$, and RIGHT$ functions to generate a misleading new string to actually store in the password file. First, the individual characters of the password are extracted.

```
letter1$ = LEFT$(pass, 1)
letter2$ = MID$(pass, 2, 1)
letter3$ = MID$(pass, 3, 1)
letter4$ = MID$(pass, 4, 1)
letter5$ = RIGHT$(pass, 1)
```

Then, the ASC function obtains the numerical ASCII code for each character, and these five numbers are combined together to produce an encryption value.

```
asc1 = ASC(letter1$)
asc2 = ASC(letter2$)
asc3 = ASC(letter3$)
asc4 = ASC(letter4$)
asc5 = ASC(letter5$)
encrypt = asc1 * asc2 * asc3 + asc4 - asc5
```

A positive number, when converted to a string, always has at least one leading space. This is due to the position reserved for the number's arithmetic sign.

Reconverting this value back to a string, the result is then trimmed of its leftmost spaces with LTRIM. Last, this character string is stored in a variable previously defined as having a fixed width of 5 bytes.

```
DIM StoredValue AS STRING * 5
StoredValue = LTRIM$(STR$(encrypt))
PRINT #1, StoredValue
```

PRINT outputs a 5-byte character string to the PASSWORD.DTA file. However, the password that is stored is nothing like the actual password required by a system user. For example, this complicated algorithm would take an input value for *pass* of "JUDD" and store a value in the PASSWORD.DTA file of "42775". A user who later entered "42775" would be disappointed because that is not the true password. An attempt to enter "42775" would merely cause the verification algorithm to process each of those characters, producing a completely different and invalid string.

Fixing the Upper/Lower Case of a Data File

Complex programs are often built upon simpler, existing programs.

Program REVISE.BAS looks much more imposing than it actually is. As seen in Listing 8.5, it is really a modest variation on the RAND-OMCH.BAS program seen in Chapter 7. Its only chore is to read through all of the records in the EMPLOYEE.DTA file and to fix up the entries for first and last name.

Listing 8.5 REVISE.BAS—Ensuring First Letter Capitalization

```
' REVISE.BAS demonstrates string manipulations.
'
' Retrieve each record with GET.
' Revise each first and last name field values:
' Capitalize the first letter only; lower case the remaining
        letters
' Rewrite each revised field with PUT.
'
CONST FALSE = 0, TRUE = NOT FALSE
TYPE contact
  id AS LONG
  first AS STRING * 10
  last AS STRING * 15
  date AS STRING * 8
  marital AS STRING * 1
  grade AS INTEGER
  salary AS SINGLE
END TYPE
DIM eachline AS contact
OPEN "employee.dta" FOR RANDOM AS #1 LEN = LEN(eachline)
DONE = FALSE
recno = 1
CLS
PRINT "ORIGINAL STRINGS IN DATA BASE"; TAB(43); "REVISED
        STRINGS"
PRINT
maxrecs = LOF(1) \ LEN(eachline)
DO UNTIL recno > maxrecs
    GET #1, recno, eachline
'   First, fix up the FIRST name.
    former$ = eachline.first
    length = LEN(former$)
    position1$ = LEFT$(former$, 1)
```

```
        remainder$ = MID$(former$, 2, length - 1)
        newfirst$ = UCASE$(position1$) + LCASE$(remainder$)
'
'
'       Then, do the same to the LAST name.
        former$ = eachline.last
        length = LEN(former$)
        position1$ = LEFT$(former$, 1)
        remainder$ = MID$(former$, 2, length - 1)
        newlast$ = UCASE$(position1$) + LCASE$(remainder$)

        PRINT eachline.first, eachline.last, newfirst$, newlast$

        eachline.first = newfirst$
        eachline.last = newlast$
        PUT #1, recno, eachline
        recno = recno + 1
LOOP
CLOSE #1
END
```

Use character conversion functions to make the data in a file consistent.

Sometimes, text entries are made in upper case only. And sometimes, another person may enter names in lower case only. Then again, a third person may enter names in a more conventional first-letter-capitalized fashion. In order to make the database consistent, this program rewrites all first and last names in the first-letter-capitalized manner. Figure 8.10 demonstrates the result.

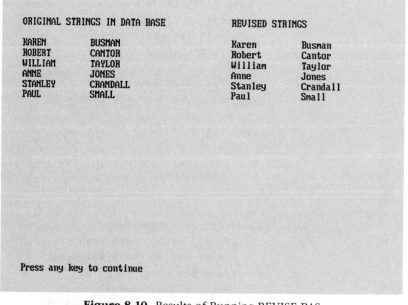

```
ORIGINAL STRINGS IN DATA BASE          REVISED STRINGS

KAREN          BUSMAN                  Karen          Busman
ROBERT         CANTOR                  Robert         Cantor
WILLIAM        TAYLOR                  William        Taylor
ANNE           JONES                   Anne           Jones
STANLEY        CRANDALL                Stanley        Crandall
PAUL           SMALL                   Paul           Small




Press any key to continue
```

Figure 8.10 Results of Running REVISE.BAS

REVISE.BAS shows how to automatically process all records in a random access file.

This program can be used as a template for any logic that must successively process all of the records in a random access file. The string manipulations that are critical here can be seen in these five lines:

```
former$ = eachline.first
length = LEN(former$)
position1$ = LEFT$(former$, 1)
remainder$ = MID$(former$, 2, length - 1)
newfirst$ = UCASE$(position1$) + LCASE$(remainder$)
```

First, the name is obtained from the database and stored into the *former$* variable. Then, its length is determined by the LEN function. After extracting the first character and storing it in *position1$*, the length is used to compute the number of characters remaining in the name (length − 1).

The MID$ function stores these remaining characters in the *remainder$* variable. The new name, with first letter capitalized, is obtained by concatenating the upper-case value of the first character with the lower-case value of the remaining characters. A PUT statement then updates the file with these adjusted values. Because functions can be nested, you can of course combine all five lines into one. However, no one would enjoy reading such a line.

A MID$ statement exists in QuickBASIC also. Unlike the function that extracts a substring from a larger string, the MID$ statement can assign a new substring value to a portion of a larger string. For example, if *SR$* contains "About time!", then

```
MID$(SR$, 7) = "town!"
```

replaces "time!" with "town!" beginning in position 7.

Ensuring that a String of Characters Represents a Valid Date

The final program to study here is VALIDATE.BAS, seen in Listing 8.6. Its only chore is to demonstrate the algorithm that validates a date. Two string processing tricks are used to make this test logic work. You can incorporate this code into any of your programs that must validate date values.

Listing 8.6 VALIDATE.BAS—Validating Dates in QuickBASIC

```
' VALIDATE.BAS demonstrates string conversion and date
    validation methods.
'
CONST FALSE = 0, TRUE = NOT FALSE
```

```
DIM testdate AS STRING * 8
CLS
INPUT "Please enter a date to be validated (mm/dd/yy):",
    testdate
year$ = MID$(testdate, 7, 2)
IF VAL(year$) = (INT(VAL(year$) / 4) * 4) THEN
   leapyear = TRUE
ELSE
   leapyear = FALSE
END IF
month$ = MID$(testdate, 1, 2)
day$ = MID$(testdate, 4, 2)
valid = TRUE
IF year$ < "00" OR year$ > "99" THEN
  valid = FALSE
  PRINT "Year is invalid"
ELSE
  IF month$ >= "01" AND month$ <= "12" THEN
    possible$ = MID$("3129313031303131303131", 2 *
      VAL(month$) - 1, 2)
    IF day$ < "01" OR day$ > possible$ THEN
      valid = FALSE
      PRINT "Day is invalid"
      'Check for possible leap year
    ELSEIF month$ = "02" AND day$ = "29" AND NOT leapyear
      THEN
      valid = FALSE
      PRINT "There was no Feb. 29 in 19"; year$
    END IF
  ELSE
    valid = FALSE
    PRINT "Month is invalid"
  END IF
END IF
IF valid THEN
  ' Date is good. Program can continue with it."
  PRINT "Date is OK."
ELSE
  ' Date is bad. User should be alerted, and reentry
      solicited here.
END IF
END
```

Remember to check for leap year when performing date calculations.

First, as pointed out earlier in this chapter when discussing the VAL function, a leap year can be defined as any year that is divisible by 4. Since *year$* is a character variable, it must be converted to a number for the necessary computation. This VAL(*year$*) is first divided by 4, then truncated to an integer, then multiplied by 4. The result will only equal the original number if that number were divisible by 4 to begin with. In this case, the program sets the variable *leapyear* equal to TRUE.

The second trick used by this program appears in the test for a valid day entry. A variable named *possible$* is created by extracting the number of days in a particular month from the long string "312931303130313130313031". Since this string is exactly 24 characters long, and valid month values range from 1 to 12, the expression

```
2 * VAL(month$) - 1
```

represents the starting position in this long string of the number of days in that month. The MID$ function extracts exactly 2 characters beginning at this position and stores them in the variable *possible$*. This value is then used as the maximum number of days for that month.

Review

This chapter focused on the many string processing functions built into your QuickBASIC programming language. You learned many things about these functions:

1. A function is a cross between an assignment statement and a mini-program, and has many of the best features of each. A function can be thought of as a short-hand notation for a single value, obtained after a series of processing steps.

2. The principal functions available in QuickBASIC fall into three categories: extraction of substrings from larger strings, conversions of both case and type, and miscellaneous functions that deal with length, position, and ASCII values.

3. The LEFT$ and LTRIM$ functions return string characters obtained from the left side of a string. You can either specify a fixed number of characters (LEFT$) or ask for leading spaces to be suppressed (LTRIM$).

4. The same capabilities are available for obtaining string values from the right side of a string with the RIGHT$ and RTRIM$ functions.

5. MID$ enables you to obtain a substring of any length from within a string.

6. A string's case can be changed from upper to lower with the LCASE$ function, or from lower to upper with the UCASE$ function.

7. A string containing digits can be converted to a number, suitable

for computational expressions, with the VAL function. The reverse can be done, converting a number to a string, with the STR$ function.

8. Miscellaneous functions are available to convert an ASCII code to a character (CHR$) or a character to an ASCII code (ASC). Also, the INSTR function searches within one string for the occurrence of another, the LEN function returns the length of a string, the SPACE$ function returns a specified number of space characters, and the STRING$ function returns a specified number of any designated character.

Complete programs are included in this chapter to demonstrate how to use string functions to center titles, control special printer features, generate leading zeros on a printout, encrypt a password, revise character fields in a database, and validate date fields.

Quiz for Chapter 8

1. The final result of a function is a:

   a. String
   b. Number
   c. Value
   d. Field

2. The value of a function is computed:

   a. When referenced
   b. When written
   c. When defined
   d. When initialized

3. Which function strips off leading spaces?

   a. LEFT$
   b. LTRIM$
   c. STRIP$
   d. TRIM$

4. Which function extracts a substring from a string?

   a. SUB$
   b. SUBSTR$
   c. MID$
   d. STR$

5. Which function returns a character corresponding to an ASCII code?

   a. ASC
   b. CHR$
   c. ASCII$
   d. VAL

6. Which function converts a string to a number?

   a. STR$
   b. CHR$
   c. ASC
   d. VAL

7. Which function converts a number to a string?

   a. STR$
   b. CHR$
   c. ASC
   d. VAL

8. Which reference produces "************"?

   a. STRING$(10,"*")

    b. SPACE$(10,"*")

    c. CHR$(12,"*")

    d. STRING$(12,"*")

9. What is equivalent to `INSTR("abcdefg","def")`?

    a. 7

    b. 3

    c. 0

    d. 4

10. What is equivalent to `MID$("NovFebMar", 3, 3)`?

    a. Nov

    b. Feb

    c. Mar

    d. vFe

11. What suffix is necessary to ensure that `DIM S AS STRING * 3` defines S as a string variable?

    a. $

    b. %

    c. &

    d. None of the above

12. What is equivalent to `UCASE$(LCASE$(LTRIM$("abc")))`?

    a. abc

    b. ABC

    c. Abc

    d. A

13. What is the process of combining strings together called?

    a. Stringing

    b. Adding

    c. Tacking

    d. Concatenating

14. What function is used to activate a printer's special features?

    a. PRINT

    b. CHR$

    c. ASC

    d. ESC

15. A string variable is defined with a `DIM SR AS STRING * 10` statement. It then is assigned a value with the statement `SR="BMT"`. What is the result of `LEN(SR)`?

    a. 3

    b. BMT

    c. 10

    d. "BMT   "

Chapter 9 | Developing Graphics Programs

In Part 2, you've now learned the principal elements of any programming language. QuickBASIC shares with other languages the fundamentals of variables, types, assignment statements, flow of control statements, file and device I/O, and built-in functions. Chapter 8 taught you the extensive set of string manipulation features found in Quick-BASIC. Most programming languages do not provide so rich an array of string functions.

This chapter breaks new ground by introducing you to Quick-BASIC's graphic capabilities. Most computer languages offer no graphic commands whatsoever; however, QuickBASIC offers a broad range of special graphic commands. You will learn the most useful individual commands with which to dress up your program's output.

In general, graphic output control is another way to display the same output information formerly shown with a PRINT statement. Commands exist to draw individual points on the screen, as well as to animate figures for game playing. This chapter, however, focuses on the most common business and scientific applications, those requiring graphic output of lines, rectangles (bars), and circles.

The chapter first presents each of the QuickBASIC commands that can generate these types of graphic output. Then, complete sample programs demonstrate how to create your own line figures or graphs, as well as your own rectangular or circular screen output windows. These are the fundamental tools of the graphic designer; they will allow you to be as creative as you like with your own output.

This chapter also includes and explains complete programs that demonstrate how to create pie charts or bar charts with QuickBASIC. No longer will you have to think in terms of a separate graphics program to present data that your programming language generates or accesses.

Understanding the Individual Graphics Commands

Up until now, your programming output has been limited to a video display that shows 25 lines of information; each line holds at most 80 characters. Graphic output is much more precise than this. A graphic image uses all of the possible individual dots on your screen. Each dot of light is called a picture element, or *pixel*. Any unique graphic shape is created by turning on or off a different set of these pixels. As you'll see, the commands used to do this often have a color associated with them. You can control the color of your graphic images as well as their shape.

The Graphic Screen System

The SCREEN command tells QuickBASIC what combination of monitor and graphic adapter your system is using.

The number of pixels on each screen differs. It depends on both the type of monitor you have and the type of video adapter that is installed in your computer. Before executing any graphic instructions, you must tell QuickBASIC which combination of monitor/adapter you have. This is done with the SCREEN command

SCREEN *mode*

The *mode* parameter specifies one of several adapter/monitor alternatives. Mode 0, which is the default, only supports text output; therefore, none of the graphic commands presented in this chapter will work without a preceding SCREEN statement. Table 9.1 summarizes the more commonly used modes available to you.

Screen mode 2 is probably the most commonly used, because it simultaneously supports both the 80 × 25 text format and the conventional 640 × 200 graphic layout. Virtually all programs that provide any graphic output at all support these formats. The programs in this chapter use SCREEN 2 commands. If your hardware supports higher resolution, one of the other screen modes can be used to generate crisper and more detailed graphic results.

Graphic coordinates are precisely the reverse of the text coordinate system you've seen so far in this book.

The commands seen below all use a coordinate grid concept for generating graphic output. Just like the (row, column) approach for text output, points on a graphic screen are located by a pair of values. The (x, y) pair, however, is reversed from what you learned with text output. As Figure 9.1 indicates, the first value in the pair of numbers indicates the distance to travel across the screen, whereas the second value specifies how far down to travel.

Table 9.1 Display Alternatives in QuickBASIC

Screen Mode	Description
0	The default. Text mode only. {40 or 80} × {25 or 43 or 50} text. Minimum monochrome monitor required.
1	320 × 200 medium resolution graphics. 40 × 25 text. 4 foreground colors, 16 background colors. Minimum CGA required.
2	640 × 200 high resolution graphics. 80 × 25 text. 1 foreground color, 1 background color. Minimum CGA required.
9	640 × 350 enhanced resolution graphics. 80 × {25 or 43} text. Minimum EGA required.
11	640 × 480 very high resolution graphics. 80 × {30 or 60} text. Minimum VGA required.

For example, the point (500, 150) shown in Figure 9.1 is reached by moving to the right 500 pixels, and down 150 pixels. In the conventional grid layout, the starting location for this count-off is (0, 0), the upper left corner of the screen. These *absolute coordinates* depend on which screen mode you specify.

Figure 9.1 depicts SCREEN 2. There is no valid (500, 150) in mode 1 (the limit is 320 × 200), while the location of (500, 150) in mode 9 is actually positioned higher on the screen. This is because the vertical range of pixels in mode 9 goes from 0 to 349, rather than the more limited 0 to 199 of screen mode 2. So a number of 150 does not move you down from the top row of the screen as much in mode 9 as it does in mode 2.

Drawing Lines, Boxes, and Windows

Lines are just a series of illuminated pixels between any two screen points.

Line graphs, stick figures, check marks, and, ultimately, any graphic image can be created with a set of line segments. The LINE command in QuickBASIC enables you to easily and quickly draw a line between any two points on your screen. The simplest form of the command is

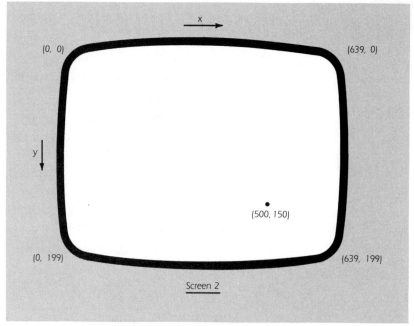

Figure 9.1 Graphic Coordinate Grid

LINE (*x1, y1*) − (*x2, y2*)

The (x1, y1) pair of values represents the grid position of the starting point of the line segment, while the (x2, y2) pair of values represents the ending point of the line segment. For example, the following LINE command draws a line on the screen from point (0, 50) on the left border to point (35, 65) located just to the right and down from the starting point, as shown in Figure 9.2.

```
LINE (0, 50) - (35, 65)
```

Most graphic figures can be drawn with a series of LINE statements.

Drawing a continuous sequence of lines requires multiple LINE statements. In each one, the starting (x, y) coordinate pair should be the same as the ending (x, y) pair of the preceding line segment. For example, to take the line just drawn and make it into a check mark, you can issue the following LINE statement:

```
LINE (35, 65) - (135, 0)
```

Notice how this second line segment begins at point (35, 65), which is precisely where the preceding line segment ended. Figure 9.3 depicts how this check mark appears in the upper left corner of a 640 x 200 video image.

Other graphic output appears in this figure as well. Program GRAPHICS.BAS (see Listing 9.1) contains the demonstration statements necessary to generate the images seen in Figure 9.3.

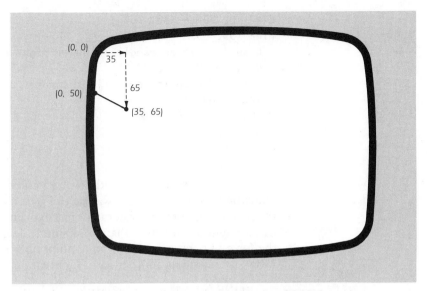

Figure 9.2 Line Drawing in QuickBASIC

Remember to set the screen mode before executing any graphics commands.

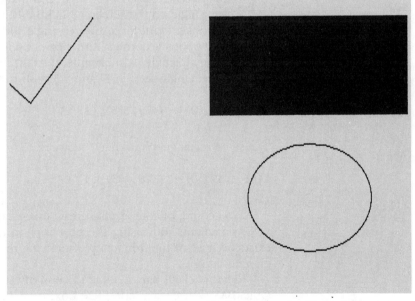

Figure 9.3 Drawing Lines, Boxes, and Circles (Output of GRAPHICS.BAS)

Listing 9.1 GRAPHICS.BAS—Fundamental Graphic Commands

```
' GRAPHICS.BAS
'
SCREEN 2
' Draw a check mark on left side of screen
```

```
LINE (0, 50) - (35, 65)
LINE (35, 65) - (135, 0)
' Draw a solid rectangle in upper right corner
LINE (320, 0) - (639, 75), 3, BF
' Draw a circle in lower right corner
CIRCLE (480, 140), 100
DO UNTIL INKEY$ <> ""
LOOP
END
```

As you can see, the SCREEN 2 statement appears first and tells QuickBASIC the type of hardware in use. The check mark is drawn with the two successive LINE statements just explained. But a LINE statement can do significantly more than draw simple lines. Because rectangles in the form of bars or windows are commonplace in graphic output, the LINE statement has another form for creating these figures:

LINE (*x1, y1*) − (*x2, y2*), *color*, [B ¦ BF], *style*

A special version of the LINE command creates filled or unfilled screen windows. You can control both the color of the window and the style of the lines making up the window.

This special version of the LINE command directs QuickBASIC to create a rectangle on the screen. QuickBASIC uses the two coordinate pairs as opposite corners of the rectangle. Because any rectangle has two pairs of opposite corners, either pair of points can be used to generate the same rectangle. For example, the GRAPHICS.BAS program generates the rectangle seen in Figure 9.3 with the statement

```
LINE (320, 0) - (639, 75), 3, BF
```

The same rectangle could have been created with the statement

```
LINE (639, 0) - (320, 75), 3, BF
```

You could, of course, also create this rectangle with four separate LINE statements. But using the new version of LINE is easier, and it exists because of the frequency of drawing rectangles in conventional graphic output.

The special B parameter at the end of this LINE statement directs QuickBASIC to draw a complete box, or window, consisting of four connected lines. If you specify BF, then you are asking QuickBASIC to fill the box in with the *color* specified by the preceding parameter. In this example, color 3 was selected. Unfortunately, screen mode 2 only offers one foreground color and one background color. So the *color* parameter here makes no difference in the output.

On your system, in a different screen mode, you can control different colors for your boxes. As you'll see below, you can output text as well as graphic images on these screens. Drawing a box with a different color than the rest of the screen is a good way to highlight this new screen "window" prior to putting information (graphic or text) into the box.

The final parameter to the LINE command, the *style* parameter, allows you to draw dashed lines. You can define the style of the dash with any hexadecimal integer. For example,

```
style = &HFF00
```

A hexadecimal integer contains 16 bits. Each line consists of a series of bits, either turned on or off. The LINE command uses your value for *style* and turns on or off the successive pixels in the line according to the bit pattern in your hexadecimal number. For instance, the pattern you will use most commonly is a hexadecimal FF00. This means 8 bits that are on, followed by 8 bits that are off. A hexadecimal 8A2C corresponds to the on/off bit pattern of 1000101000101100; this creates a more broken pattern for the dashes.

Missing parameters, when not included in a command, must be replaced by a place-holding comma.

If you do not use the B or BF parameters, you can still use this *style* parameter to draw individual lines consisting of dashes. If you do use the B or BF parameter, the lines of the box itself will be dashed. Because all of these additional parameters (color, box, and style) are optional, you must include a comma for any parameter not included in your LINE statement.

For example, to draw a dashed line without specifying colors, you could enter

```
LINE (35, 65) - (135, 0), , , &HFF00
```

To draw a dashed box without specifying a color, you could enter

```
LINE (35, 65) - (135, 0), , BF, &HFF00
```

Drawing Circles in QuickBASIC

Although lines and rectangles are common, circles are also seen quite often in graphic output. This section discusses how to generate the most common types of complete circle. Program PIE.BAS later in this chapter takes these techniques and discusses how to represent your data in a typical pie chart form.

Before using the CIRCLE command, you must understand several fundamental characteristics of a circle. Figure 9.4 highlights these important areas.

Every circle must have its center located within the coordinate grid, according to the screen mode. The circle itself is sized around that center by its radius. This radius represents the fixed distance from the center to any point on the drawn circle.

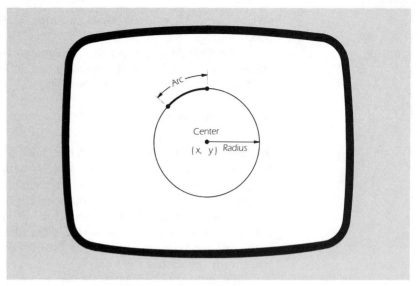

Figure 9.4 Fundamental Characteristics of Circles

The simplest form of the CIRCLE command needs only these commands to draw a circle anywhere on your screen. The required syntax specifies a center at (x, y) and a value for the radius.

CIRCLE (*x, y*), *radius*

As seen in the GRAPHICS.BAS program and in the program's output (see Figure 9.3), you can draw a circle using this statement:

```
CIRCLE (480, 140), 100
```

First, this statement centers the circle in the lower right portion of the screen at position (480, 140). Next, it draws a uniform circle of points located at 100 units (the radius) around this center.

The final statement in program GRAPHICS.BAS is a DO command.

You must pause the graphic output of a compiled program so it can be seen.

```
DO UNTIL INKEY$ <> ""
LOOP
```

This command is not necessary if you run your program from the QuickBASIC development environment. When executed there, the output screen is produced, followed by the message

```
Press any key to continue
```

Even after returning to the development environment, you can switch back to the graphic output screen by pressing F4. However, because of the screen mode switch in the program, there is a problem when running an executable version (.EXE) of your program. Chapter 11 discusses how to create such a program, which can be run from a DOS command prompt, not requiring the QuickBASIC development environment at all.

When running an .EXE version of graphic programs, remember to include a special loop at the end of the program. This ensures that the graphic output remains displayed until a key is pressed.

When you run the executable .EXE versions of the graphic programs seen in this chapter, the output is sent to the screen as expected. However, when the program ends, the screen is instantly erased by DOS, which returns the display to text mode to display its command prompt. You must ensure that the display lingers as long as necessary before this happens.

The DO loop handles this problem. It loops continuously until the user presses a key (any key) on the keyboard. The special INKEY$ function checks the keyboard buffer for such a keypress. As long as no key is pressed, the INKEY$ function returns a null value (" "). This special construction guarantees that the user can look at the program output as long as he or she likes, then return to the DOS prompt by pressing a key. This causes the DO loop and then the program to end.

Developing Useful Graphic Application Programs

You've now learned the two primary commands in QuickBASIC for generating a host of unique graphic outputs. In this section, you'll learn some advanced techniques for using these commands to produce the common business graphs called pie charts and bar charts.

Understanding Arcs, Radians, and Degrees

An arc is merely a portion of a circle. As shown in Figure 9.5, an arc requires you to specify the center and radius of the circle on which it is located. It can then be uniquely defined by a starting and ending angle. Figure 9.5 depicts this situation.

Understanding arcs becomes important when you wish to represent data as pie slices in a pie chart. A pie slice, or wedge, is visually quite obvious; graphically, it consists of the cross-hatched area in Figure 9.5 bordered by two radius lines and the arc connecting them. These two radius lines are drawn from the circle's center to the beginning and ending points of the arc.

The CIRCLE command discussed earlier actually can accept additional parameters. You can specify color for the circle, and you can limit what is drawn to an arc rather than a whole circle. As shown below, you can even cause the lines forming a pie slice to be drawn at the same time as the arc. The required syntax for drawing arcs is

CIRCLE (*x, y*), *radius*, [*color*], *start, end*

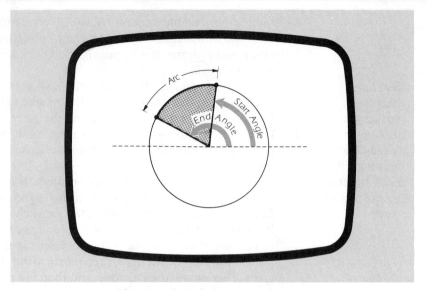

Figure 9.5 Defining a Circular Arc

The color parameter is optional. In the examples below, it is not used. The commas must remain, however; only the parameter value itself is missing. The *start* and *end* angle values must be *radians*. If you are more comfortable with the idea of a circle containing 360 degrees, you need to learn that the same circle contains 2 PI (2π) radians. PI is a mathematical constant (3.14159265359); in QuickBASIC, our examples treat it as a double precision constant (# suffix). Figure 9.6 depicts this correspondence between radians and degrees.

Drawing Arcs and Pie Slices

Placing a negative sign before a start or end angle for a circular arc causes a radius to be drawn from the circle's center to that start or end point. Negating both start and end variables generates a visual pie slice.

A unique feature of the CIRCLE command, when drawing arcs, is that you can simultaneously draw a line from the center of the circle to either the start or end point of the arc. To do this, you only need to put a negative sign in front of the start or end angle value.

Suppose you wanted to draw a complete pie slice from point A to point B in Figure 9.6 (the cross-hatched area). This represents 90 degrees, or PI/2 radians. Your CIRCLE command would look like this:

```
PI = 3.14159265359#
CIRCLE (x, y), radius, , -0.00001, -PI / 2
```

You specify whatever center location and whatever size you want (the radius); a quarter circle will be drawn, as in the A-B pie slice of Figure 9.6. Since −0 and +0 are mathematically indistinguishable, you must

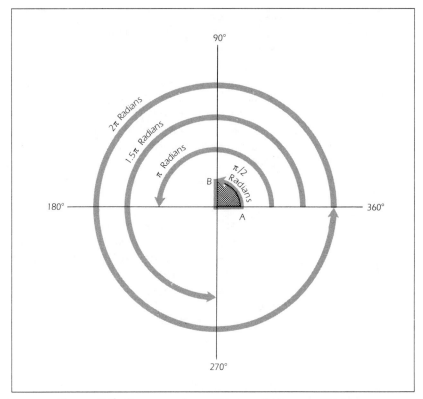

Figure 9.6 Correspondence Between Radians and Degrees

actually start the first angle as a very small non-zero number. Otherwise, the side of the pie slice on the zero line will not be drawn.

A pie chart consists of a series of separately drawn pie slices.

This slice technique is crucial to the drawing of a pie chart, as seen in program PIE.BAS (Listing 9.2). Figure 9.7 shows the result of running the PIE.BAS program. This program can be used as it stands in your application. To adjust the final pie chart to your data, you must adjust these two initial statements:

```
DATA 3,4,6,8,13
HowMany = 5
```

The sample data is brought into the program with this DATA statement and the READ statement found inside the first DO loop. The *HowMany* variable tells the program how many data items are to be graphed.

Listing 9.2 PIE.BAS—Generating a Business Pie Chart

```
' PIE.BAS
'
SCREEN 2
DATA 3,4,6,8,13
```

```
HowMany = 5
TwoPi# = 2 * 3.14159265359#
DIM slice(HowMany)
counter = 1
'   Read slice values and obtain a total
DO UNTIL counter > HowMany
   READ slice(counter)
   total = total + slice(counter)
   counter = counter + 1
LOOP
'   Draw wedges for each slice value
counter = 1
start! = 0
DO UNTIL counter > HowMany
   finish! = start! + TwoPi# * (slice(counter) / total)
   CIRCLE (480, 140), 100, , -start!, -finish!
   start! = finish!
   counter = counter + 1
LOOP
'   Label the slices with text
LOCATE 17, 67
PRINT "Apples"
LOCATE 15, 64
PRINT "Pears"
LOCATE 15, 55
PRINT "Peaches"
LOCATE 18, 50
PRINT "Cherries"
LOCATE 20, 60
PRINT "Bananas"
DO UNTIL INKEY$ <> ""
LOOP
END
```

The same circle seen in the GRAPHICS.BAS program is redrawn in this program. The same center and radius is used, although you can easily change the CIRCLE statement to place or size it differently.

The first loop is used to read all of the data items into the *slice* array, which is dimensioned to hold *HowMany* elements. In addition, the individual values of the data items are summed up to produce a *total*.

```
DIM slice(HowMany)
counter = 1
'   Read slice values and obtain a total
DO UNTIL counter > HowMany
   READ slice(counter)
   total = total + slice(counter)
```

```
    counter = counter + 1
LOOP
```

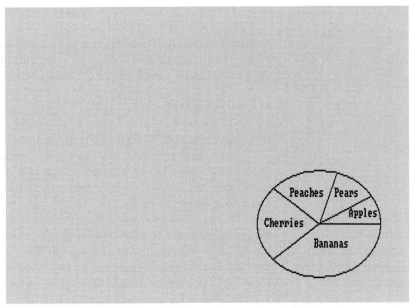

Figure 9.7 Output Pie Chart from Running PIE.BAS

The second DO loop contains the actual CIRCLE command. On each iteration through the loop, one pie slice is drawn. Note that to draw the arc and both radii to the start and end points, the *start!* and *finish!* variables are both negated.

The starting angle for each pie slice must equal the ending angle for the preceding pie slice.

Earlier, you learned that you can draw a continuous series of line segments by making the start point for each segment equal to the end point of the preceding segment. A similar possibility exists here. Making the *start!* angle of each pie slice equal to the *finish!* angle of the preceding pie slice can generate a series of pie slices. One radial side of each pie slice actually draws over the radial side of the preceding pie slice.

The key instruction to look at is in the second DO loop, just before the CIRCLE instruction.

```
finish! = start! + TwoPi# * (slice(counter) / total)
CIRCLE (480, 140), 100, , -start!, -finish!
```

Each *finish!* value equals the sum of the start angle plus the proper amount of angle attributable to the data item. Since the data item value was READ into *slice(counter)*, its portion of the total pie equals.

```
slice (counter) / total
```

The program defines a variable *TwoPi#* as equal to the 2*PI radians contained in any circle. Multiplying *TwoPi#* by each item's portion of the total

```
TwoPi# * (slice(counter) / total)
```

results in the amount of circular angle appropriate to represent the data. Adding this amount to the pie slice's beginning angle (*start!*) produces the proper *finish!* angle. After drawing each slice, the statement

```
start! = finish!
```

resets the next slice's *start!* angle to the last slice's *finish!* angle.

After all of the slices are drawn, the remaining statements in the program label each slice. A combination LOCATE and PRINT statement can effectively label each slice because SCREEN mode 2 allows both text and graphics to easily co-exist.

> Chapter 12 explains how to run programs one step at a time. This is commonly used during debugging.

One last thing to notice about this program is that the initial value for *start!* is 0, not −0.00001. Although a zero value would work, the last pie slice drawn is really the one responsible for drawing the zero angle line. If you ran this program very slowly, you would see that the first pie slice does not draw both radii. The last slice takes care of the situation. It actually draws a radial line for the 2 * PI angle. You will learn how to run programs one instruction at a time in Chapter 12.

Creating Bar Charts with Your Data

> A bar chart consists of a series of rectangles.

Bar charts, or bar graphs, are basically nothing more than a series of rectangles; therefore, you can use a series of LINE statements to produce such a chart. The B (box) parameter is used to make each box, and the F parameter is used to fill each rectangle with a color.

Several techniques can be seen in program BAR.BAS (see Listing 9.3). The output from BAR.BAS is shown in Figure 9.8. Basically, the structure of the program is the same as PIE.BAS above. The data items are stored in the *slice* array. The first DO loop stores each item value from the DATA statement into the slice array, and a total is computed.

Listing 9.3 BAR.BAS—Producing a Vertical Bar Chart

```
' BAR.BAS
'
SCREEN 2
DATA 3,4,6,8,13
HowMany = 5
DIM slice(HowMany)
counter = 1
'   Read slice values and obtain a total
```

```
DO UNTIL counter > HowMany
   READ slice(counter)
   total = total + slice(counter)
   counter = counter + 1
LOOP
'  Draw vertical filled rectangles for each slice value
counter = 1
start1 = 0
start2 = 180
DO UNTIL counter > HowMany
   percent = slice(counter) / total
   wide = 640 \ (HowMany + 1)
   high = INT(180 * percent)
   LINE (start1, start2) - STEP(wide, -high), 3, BF
   counter = counter + 1
   start1 = start1 + INT(640 / HowMany)
LOOP
'  Label the bars with text
LOCATE 24, 1
PRINT "Apples"; TAB(17); "Pears"; TAB(33); "Peaches";
     TAB(49); "Cherries";
LOCATE 24, 65
PRINT "Bananas"
DO UNTIL INKEY$ <> ""
LOOP
END
```

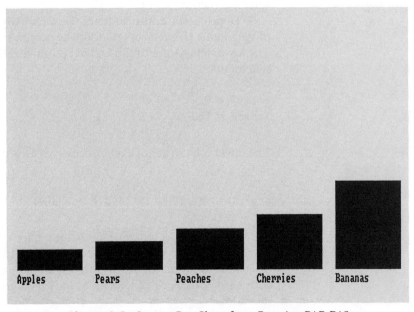

Figure 9.8 Output Bar Chart from Running BAR.BAS

Leave space in a bar chart for the axes and the axis labels.

The second loop generates as many vertical bars as there are data items (that is, variable *HowMany*). First, the height of each bar is determined as an appropriate percentage of the total value. The *total* value is arbitrarily assigned 180 pixels; this leaves 20 pixels free at the bottom of the screen for bar labels. Each bar's percentage of the total is stored in variable *percent*.

```
percent = slice(counter) / total
```

The height of each bar is based on the data value's percent of the total 180 pixels.

```
high = INT(180 * percent)
```

Naturally, you can change this range if you like. Some users prefer the maximum bar height to equal the maximum data item value, rather than the total value of all items. This is a personal preference. Generating bar graphs can become very sophisticated. You can adjust both maximum and minimum range values, the width of the bars, and even whether the bars appear vertically or horizontally. Program BAR.BAS provides the basic function; you can make your own adjustments to make it appear exactly as you want.

The key LINE drawing loop here requires some further explanation. The bar's direction on the screen is up, and this runs against the normal coordinate direction seen in Figure 9.1. Putting a negative sign in front of the *high* value causes the rectangle to extend in the negative screen direction, or up.

Dividing the entire width of the screen (640 pixels) by the number of data items (*HowMany*) divides the screen into *HowMany* columns. The lower left corner of the first bar is initialized to (0, 180) by these two statements:

```
start1 = 0
start2 = 180
```

The lower left corner of each successive bar is calculated by this expression:

```
start1 = start1 + INT(640 / HowMany)
```

Start2 always remains 180, so the base of each bar stays on that pixel line. But the x value, or *start1*, increases for each data item by the calculated amount. So, for five data items, the new *start1* value always adds 640/5 pixels, or 128 pixels, to the preceding bar's lower left corner location.

Some users like their bars to be solid and touching one another. If this is the case, the width value of the bar (variable *wide*) should equal 640/*HowMany* as well. However, this is another one of those parameters that varies with personal preference. I prefer some separation between bars. Hence, the width of each bar is slightly less than the maximum width.

```
wide = 640 \ (HowMany + 1)
```

Changing 1 to 2 or 3 or some other number would make each bar skinnier still.

Use STEP to signify coordinates relative to the last cursor location.

The new keyword seen here in the LINE statement is the STEP word just before the second (x2, y2) point. This second point fixes the upper right corner of each bar (*wide, −high*). The STEP keyword tells QuickBASIC that the values for *wide* and *−high* are to be treated as relative to the lower left corner of the bar. Without a STEP keyword, a coordinate (x, y) position is always "stepped off" from the (0, 0) position in the upper left corner of the screen. With a STEP keyword, a coordinate point is to be "stepped off" from the preceding point. In this case, the preceding point given to QuickBASIC is the lower left corner of the bar.

The final instructions in this program label the bars and loop until the user presses a key. You can store the labels as strings in a DATA statement just as you stored the original data itself in a DATA statement. The first loop can then read these strings into a specially dimensioned string array at the same time as it reads in the item values.

```
DIM names AS STRING
    .
    .
    .
READ names(counter)
```

This method generalizes the program so it requires less modification when new data is used. The PRINT statements can be replaced with another DO loop, which calculates the position to LOCATE the cursor, then PRINTs the *names(counter)* string value. If you feel up to the challenge, try this variation on your system now.

Review

This chapter completes your tour of the QuickBASIC programming language. You have learned the most important and common graphic techniques:

1. A graphic screen uses a (column, row) coordinate system relative to the upper left corner of the screen. This differs from text output which uses a (row, column) approach.

2. The number of individually addressable screen dots, or pixels, depends on both your video monitor and your graphics adapter. The SCREEN command sets the mode for graphic output for each different combination.

3. The LINE command can draw a line between any two points on the screen. The same command can be used with additional parameters to draw a rectangle whose opposite corner points are specified. The additional parameters enable you to set the color of the screen area enclosed by the rectangle, as well as the style of the line or rectangle.

4. The CIRCLE command can draw a complete circle or a circular arc anywhere on the screen. You must specify the circle's center, as well as its radius. For arcs, you must also specify the starting and ending angles. By negating the values for these angles, you can draw radial lines out to the arc's ends, creating visual pie slices.

Standard business graphics include both bar and pie charts. Programs included in this chapter demonstrate exactly how to use the LINE and CIRCLE commands to take a set of data values and draw these types of business graphs.

Quiz for Chapter 9

1. Graphic output is limited to a grid of points that is:

    a. 320 × 200 pixels
    b. 640 × 200 pixels
    c. 640 × 350 pixels
    d. Dependent on monitor/adapter

2. Text is output to a grid of characters that is:

    a. 25 × 80 characters
    b. 25 × 40 characters
    c. 43 × 80 characters
    d. Dependent on screen mode

3. Each graphic screen dot is called a:

    a. Pixie
    b. Pixture
    c. Pixel
    d. Pizel

4. Which command sets the graphic mode in QuickBASIC?

    a. GRAPHICS
    b. MODE
    c. SET
    d. SCREEN

5. What screen mode is the default?

    a. 0
    b. 1
    c. 2
    d. 3

6. Which statement is true?

    a. Graphic coordinate ordering is the reverse of text coordinates.
    b. Graphic coordinate ordering is the same as text coordinates.
    c. Graphic coordinate ordering is dependent on text coordinates.
    d. None of the above.

7. What are coordinates called when they are measured from the (0, 0) position in the upper left hand corner of the screen?

    a. Relative coordinates
    b. Absolute coordinates
    c. Measured coordinates
    d. Stepped coordinates

8. Which point is invalid in screen mode 2?

   a. (0, 0)
   b. (320, 100)
   c. (199, 199)
   d. (640, 200)

9. Which command draws a line completely along the screen diagonal in screen mode 1?

   a. LINE (0, 0) − (640, 200)
   b. LINE (0, 0) − (639, 199)
   c. LINE (0, 0) − (320, 200)
   d. LINE (319, 0) − (0, 199)

10. Which command draws an unfilled rectangle whose square area is 2500 square pixels?

    a. LINE (100,100) − (150,150), B
    b. LINE (100,100) − STEP (150,150), ,BF
    c. LINE STEP (100, 100) − (50, 50), ,B
    d. LINE (100, 100) − (50, 150), ,B

11. PI radians is equivalent to how many degrees?

    a. 90
    b. 180
    c. 270
    d. 360

12. Drawing a circular arc requires:

    a. Starting and ending angles
    b. A center point
    c. A radius
    d. All of the above

13. Drawing a pie slice requires angle values which are:

    a. Positive start, positive end
    b. Positive start, negative end
    c. Negative start, positive end
    d. Negative start, negative end

14. Which keyword enables you to specify coordinates that are relative to the preceding point, rather than relative to the (0,0) screen point?

    a. REL
    b. WRT
    c. STEP
    d. FROM

15. Which of the following is a valid hexadecimal value to be used for styling lines or rectangles?

    a. FFAB
    b. &FFAB
    c. &HFFAB
    d. 1000111110101111

3 | Designing Useful Application Programs

In Part 2, you learned the most crucial elements of the QuickBASIC program language. You saw many sample programs, which used variables, assignments, and flow of control commands. You learned how to create and access data files on disk. You learned how to manipulate character strings. And you learned how to create different sorts of graphic output from your data.

In this part, you will learn how to put those programming tools to work in an effective manner. You will learn the techniques used by professionals in designing, writing, testing, and debugging their programs.

Chapter 10 focuses on building a strong foundation for your QuickBASIC programs. In particular, you will learn how to design structured systems that make effective use of user-defined procedures and functions.

In **Chapter 11,** you will learn a host of tips and techniques aimed at ensuring that your individual programs are designed well. You will focus on methods for user-friendly dialogues, screen design, and error control.

Chapter 12, the final chapter, concentrates on the most effective ways to test and debug your programs. Careful explanations are provided for the powerful tools available from the Debug pulldown menu. You will also learn how to create .EXE files to make your programs available to users from the DOS prompt.

Learning the features and techniques presented in Part 3 will help to assure you of smooth programming with your new QuickBASIC skills.

Chapter **10** | # Building a Strong Foundation

In the previous five chapters, you learned how to construct individual QuickBASIC commands. And you learned how to solve a variety of problems by writing programs consisting of groups of these commands. That's all well and good, but it doesn't address the issue of which commands are best to use, or how to most effectively use the selected commands. Thus far, you have learned how to implement but not how to design a programming system.

This chapter treats the critical area of system planning and structure. You will learn how to analyze the elements of your application, and you will learn methods for organizing both your thinking and your QuickBASIC code to bear on those elements.

This chapter also begins to explain the most effective programming habits to develop, and you will learn more about this in Chapter 11. Acquiring these techniques will ensure that your actual development process is as smooth as possible. You will learn the most important methods used by professional programmers to successfully solve business, educational, and scientific problems with their programs.

Designing a Structured System

Your parents were right. Think before you act.

Planning always pays off. It enables you to do things more quickly, more easily, and more effectively. This is not necessarily true for the simplest

More to the point,
design before you
program!

programs written in QuickBASIC. Because of the powerful development environment, it is both tempting and possible to write simple programs with no plan. The debugging tools (see Chapter 12) can minimize
your struggles at making these programs work. However, more extensive application systems require a better approach.

Analyzing the Requirements of Your System

A complex system always has a recognizable structure. This structure
becomes visible when you analyze what the intended system must accomplish. Look at the data to be stored; look at the required outputs;
look at the necessary printed reports. Do this and you will begin to
realize the separate functions to be handled by your system. Figure 10.1
depicts these functional building blocks on which your programming
efforts will be based.

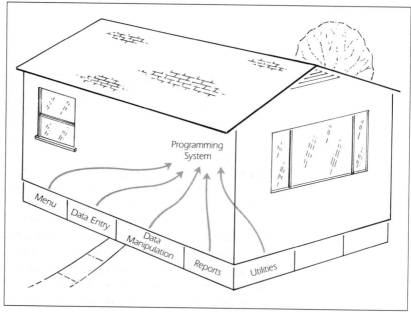

Figure 10.1 Functional Building Blocks of a
Programming System

Examples of these kinds of programs appeared throughout Part 2
of this book. In Chapter 6, you saw the MENU.BAS program. In study-
ing flow of control, you learned how this menu program enabled a user
to select which system function to perform next. This chapter will focus
on the techniques necessary to customize this example program for a
particular application environment.

In particular, an adjusted MENU2.BAS will be prepared in this chapter. It will contain examples of the building blocks seen in Figure 10.1. In general, a data entry program (like RANDOMWR.BAS in Chapter 7) reads data that is entered from the keyboard in response to screen prompting. Such a program then checks the data for validity and, if OK, stores that data in a data file.

Data manipulation programs handle the chores of retrieving, updating or deleting stored file information. Programs RANDOMRD.BAS and RANDOMCH.BAS in Chapter 7 were examples of these types of programs; they will be modified and used in this chapter.

Reporting programs sometimes include on-screen reports. That's certainly one point of view; in this discussion, reports will refer to hard-copy printed output. The reports can generate data on the fly, or they can contain organized information from data files, or they can contain both.

Utility programs represent a diffuse class of support routines. A program like STYLE.BAS (see Chapter 5), which analyzes text files, is such a program. So is the PRINTER.BAS program (see Chapter 8) for controlling special printer hardware features. So are the password and date validation programs developed in Part 2.

Designing with Structure Charts

A structure chart presents a visual map of the chores your application system must perform.

All application systems are made up of logically separate building blocks, or functions. Begin your design by drawing a *structure chart* of the system, outlining all major functions of the system. For example, a typical client/customer mailing list system might have the structure chart seen in Figure 10.2.

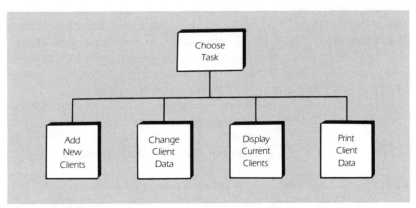

Figure 10.2 Structure Chart for a Typical Mailing List System

The boxes in this chart represent the major functions of this system; some but not all of the building blocks of Figure 10.1 are seen here. Resist any considerations about programming solutions yet. At this point, you are only thinking and designing. It is much easier to make adjustments now than after you begin writing QuickBASIC instructions.

Typically, you have discussions with intended users about what your computer system is supposed to do for them. After drawing this major system structure chart, check your discussion notes to be sure that you know which functional area is going to handle each necessary operational detail. You'll discover quickly if anything significant has been overlooked.

Each of these major functions can be decomposed into a series of subfunctions. Figure 10.3 does just that for the Add New Clients choice in Figure 10.2.

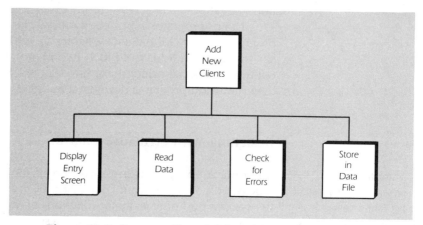

Figure 10.3 Structure Chart for the Add New Client Function

Modular programming makes the development chore much easier.

The goal of creating structure charts is to "modularize" your system. The term *modular programming* refers to the technique of writing distinct programs that perform unique chores. It's up to you to decide how to partition the system tasks into individual program modules. The structure charts can help greatly.

In general, you should think in terms of a separate program for each major function in your structure chart. Then, you can look for duplication of function, which can be isolated into its own program. For instance, both the Add New Clients and the Change Client Data modules of Figure 10.2 need code to handle the probable "Check for Errors" tasks.

If similar code in your application is very short, you can include the code in each module. This reduces the burden of establishing a separate module. However, if the programming steps are lengthy, tricky, complex, or simply common to many other modules, you may want to separate those steps into their own module.

Validating entered data is usually lengthy, so a separate error checking routine is reasonable. Figure 10.4 suggests that the Check For

Errors logic will be located in a unique code module, accessible to both the Add New Clients and Change Client Data modules.

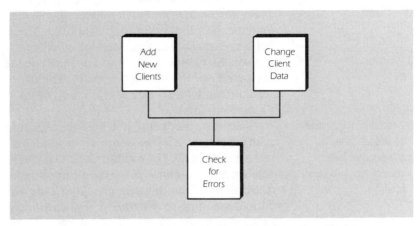

Figure 10.4 Separating Code Functions into New Modules

Choose code modularization over consolidation!

Sometimes, two very similar major tasks are consolidated into one program module. In that case, the program usually asks the user which task to perform. For example, one program could handle data entry and data change. In entering new data, the screen layout merely shows blank fields to fill in; in changing old data, the same screen layout could show the old data to be corrected. This reduces the number of modules of code but increases the complexity of the remaining modules. I strongly advise against this. If you're uncertain about whether to create a new module, or add code to an existing module, you should err on the side of modularization!

Guidelines for Structured Design

So far, you've focused on preparations for programming. In defining your separate program modules, follow these guidelines:

1. Start at the top level and work down.

2. Make sure that each module has an independent task.

3. Limit the size of modules.

4. Don't go overboard on modularization.

So far, the examples in this chapter have demonstrated guideline number 1. Although some system designers advocate a bottom-up approach to system development, my experience convinces me that a top-down approach is more successful. Working from the most general to the most specific always allows a system designer to know how everything fits in. No pieces are created that will not be used by your specific application puzzle.

Each module must be independent so that the context does not affect the job performed. In the example of error checking above, a date field can be validated in such a module. The job of validating the date field is reasonably independent of whether it is the date the client contact was first made (for the Add module) or the date the client was last contacted (for the Change module). The date validation logic can be a separate module, accessible from each of the two higher level Add and Change modules.

Dependent logic means embedded code. Independent logic usually means separate modules.

On the other hand, if the error checking logic is not independent of the modules that pass control to it, then it shouldn't reside in a separate module at all. For example, the client's business type field can be validated for an entry of S (Sole Proprietorship), P (Partnership), or C (Corporation). But the error checking logic may need to perform differently depending on whether a new corporation client is being added, or a former sole proprietor client has incorporated. In this case, you must write two separate versions of the primary logic; both the Add and the Change modules need their own versions.

The smaller the module, the easier it is to read, understand, revise, or debug. Some designers suggest that you write no individual program that exceeds one page in length. That's nice but a bit excessive. One- or two-page modules are perfectly readable and reasonably sized.

On the other hand, some programmers get caught up in the ease of writing, rewriting, reading, and debugging small modules. They begin to write small modules that are five or ten lines long. This is also excessive. Each separately written module carries its own measure of system overhead. Too many small modules can be bad for system performance.

Writing a Structured System

Individual programs in QuickBASIC stand completely on their own. You load them into memory from the File menu, then execute them from the Run menu. Program MENU2.BAS in Listing 10.1 is an example of such a program.

Listing 10.1 Main Menu Program in a Structured System

```
DECLARE SUB PrintClients ()
DECLARE SUB PrinterControl ()
DECLARE SUB Style ()
DECLARE SUB ChangeClients ()
DECLARE SUB ShowClients ()
```

```
DECLARE SUB AddClients ()
' Program MENU2.BAS
' Demonstrates a completely structured system
' Displays menu, accepts user choice, passes control to
    procedures
'
CONST FALSE = 0, TRUE = NOT FALSE
TYPE contact
  id AS LONG
  first AS STRING * 10
  last AS STRING * 15
  date AS STRING * 8
  marital AS STRING * 1
  grade AS INTEGER
  salary AS SINGLE
END TYPE
DIM eachline AS contact
CLS
FINISHED = FALSE
standard$ = "Your selection, please?"
message$ = standard$
DO WHILE NOT FINISHED
  CLS
  PRINT TAB(25); "Main Administrative System"
  LOCATE 5, 15
  PRINT TAB(15); "1    Change client data", CHR$(10)
  PRINT TAB(15); "2    Display current clients", CHR$(10)
  PRINT TAB(15); "3    Add new clients", CHR$(10)
  PRINT TAB(15); "4    Print client list", CHR$(10)
  PRINT TAB(15); "5    Control Printer Features", CHR$(10)
  PRINT TAB(15); "6    Style Analysis", CHR$(10)
  PRINT TAB(15); "Q    Quit", CHR$(10), CHR$(10)
  LOCATE 20, 1
  PRINT message$
  message$ = standard$
  choice$ = INPUT$(1)
  SELECT CASE choice$
    CASE "1"
      CALL ChangeClients
    CASE "2"
      CALL ShowClients
    CASE "3"
      CALL AddClients
    CASE "4"
      CALL PrintClients
    CASE "5"
      CALL PrinterControl
```

```
      CASE "6"
        CALL Style
      CASE "Q", "q"
        FINISHED = TRUE
      CASE ELSE
        LOCATE 18, 1
        message$ = "Invalid Choice! Please Select Again."
    END SELECT
  LOOP
  END
```

This is the main menu program in a demonstration system. It represents the coding for the Choose Task box in Figure 10.2; the results of running this selection program can be seen in Figure 10.5.

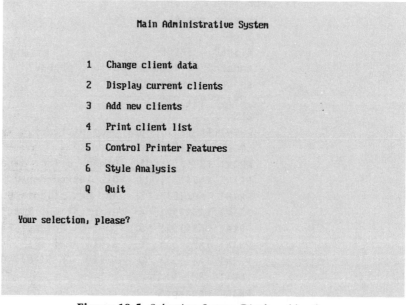

Figure 10.5 Selection Screen Displayed by the
MENU2.BAS Program

Use CALL to transfer control to other modules.

After a user has made one of the choices in Figure 10.5, the SELECT CASE statement controls the execution flow. The CALL statement is QuickBASIC's primary method of transferring control to code located outside of the current module. For example, the statement

```
CALL PrintClients
```

transfers the flow of control to a separate module called PrintClients. This enables your MENU2.BAS program to respond to a user entry of 4 (that is, they chose Print Client List) without having to embed all of the handling code within MENU2 itself. Using structured design techniques, the logic to produce the printed client list must be separate from, yet accessible to, the MENU2 program. But to do this, you must learn how to write a special form of program module called a *procedure*.

Using QuickBASIC Procedures

Modules that you CALL are called subprograms, or SUBs.

In order to write modules that can be accessed by a CALL statement, you must use a special form. This form is called a SUB, or subprogram, procedure. The simplest way to write such a separate procedure is to type the word SUB followed by the name of the procedure.

```
SUB PrintClient
```

When you press the Enter key, QuickBASIC clears the View window and displays its special SUB definition screen window (see Figure 10.6). This SUB definition window displays the keyword SUB followed by the complete subprogram name. The third line displayed is END SUB; the cursor rests on the blank line between these two lines. You are expected to enter all of the instructions that will make up the logic of the newly minted subprogram.

Listing 10.2 represents the resulting code for SUB module Print-Clients. Notice that I've chosen to use a record variable named *el* of TYPE contact. The actual TYPE statement appears in the main MENU2 program and is used by this as well as several other SUB modules.

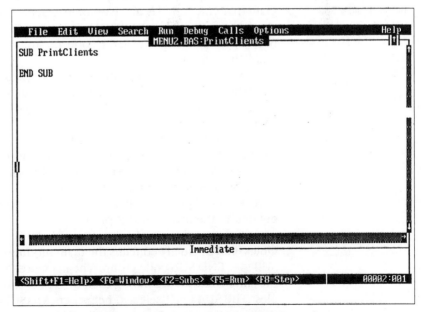

Figure 10.6 Creating a New SUB Procedure

Listing 10.2 The PrintClients SUB Procedure

```
SUB PrintClients
' Prints out the contents of the employee.dta file
'
DIM el AS contact
OPEN "employee.dta" FOR RANDOM AS #1 LEN = LEN(el)
OPEN "LPT1:" FOR OUTPUT AS #2
DONE = FALSE
recno = 1
CLS
PRINT #2, "CURRENT CLIENT LIST"
PRINT
maxrecs = LOF(1) \ LEN(el)
DO UNTIL recno > maxrecs
  GET #1, recno, el
  PRINT #2, el.id; el.first; el.last; el.date; el.marital;
    el.grade; el.salary
  recno = recno + 1
LOOP
CLOSE #1

END SUB
```

You can convert an existing stand-alone program into a SUB.

Each of the five other modules referenced by MENU2 are simple variations of programs you've seen earlier in this book. If the SUB program that you define is made up of instructions from an existing stand-alone program (such as RANDOMCH.BAS), you can use the editing techniques in Chapter 4 to move the code into the spaces between each SUB and END SUB lines.

At any time you like, when developing a modular system, you can press function key F2 to display the modular structure. Figure 10.7 shows the result of pressing F2 after each of the six SUB procedures have been defined.

All of the procedure code contained in each SUB module is actually stored with the main program that CALLs the SUBs. The SUB version of each group of code is virtually the same as the original stand-alone programs, except that the TYPE and CONST statements have been removed. They are not necessary in each SUB, because they are defined in the main MENU2 program.

As you can see in Listing 10.3, the MENU2.BAS file as stored by QuickBASIC actually contains the main module code, followed by each SUB . . . END SUB code group. The keywords SUB and END SUB have the simple task of separating each SUB procedure from all other modules. The SUB line itself also helps QuickBASIC to determine where to transfer control when you use the CALL statement.

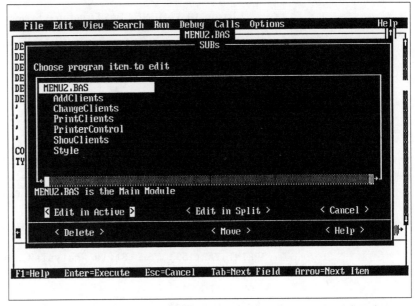

Figure 10.7 Example of How All Module Names Are Displayed
by Pressing F2

Listing 10.3 The Complete MENU2.BAS Structured
System Module

```
DECLARE SUB PrintClients ()
DECLARE SUB PrinterControl ()
DECLARE SUB Style ()
DECLARE SUB ChangeClients ()
DECLARE SUB ShowClients ()
DECLARE SUB AddClients ()
' Program MENU2.BAS
' Demonstrates a completely structured system
' Displays menu, accepts user choice, passes control to
    procedures
'
CONST FALSE = 0, TRUE = NOT FALSE
TYPE contact
  id AS LONG
  first AS STRING * 10
  last AS STRING * 15
  date AS STRING * 8
  marital AS STRING * 1
  grade AS INTEGER
  salary AS SINGLE
END TYPE
DIM eachline AS contact
```

(continued)

Listing 10.3 MENU2.BAS Structured System Module *(continued)*

```
CLS
FINISHED = FALSE
standard$ = "Your selection, please?"
message$ = standard$
DO WHILE NOT FINISHED
  CLS
  PRINT TAB(25); "Main Administrative System"
  LOCATE 5, 15
  PRINT TAB(15); "1   Change client data", CHR$(10)
  PRINT TAB(15); "2   Display current clients", CHR$(10)
  PRINT TAB(15); "3   Add new clients", CHR$(10)
  PRINT TAB(15); "4   Print client list", CHR$(10)
  PRINT TAB(15); "5   Control Printer Features", CHR$(10)
  PRINT TAB(15); "6   Style Analysis", CHR$(10)
  PRINT TAB(15); "Q   Quit", CHR$(10), CHR$(10)
  LOCATE 20, 1
  PRINT message$
  message$ = standard$
  choice$ = INPUT$(1)
  SELECT CASE choice$
    CASE "1"
      CALL ChangeClients
    CASE "2"
      CALL ShowClients
    CASE "3"
      CALL AddClients
    CASE "4"
      CALL PrintClients
    CASE "5"
      CALL PrinterControl
    CASE "6"
      CALL Style
    CASE "Q", "q"
      FINISHED = TRUE
    CASE ELSE
      LOCATE 18, 1
      message$ = "Invalid Choice! Please Select Again."
  END SELECT
LOOP
END

SUB AddClients
' Adds a complete new record to the existing employee.dta
    file
'
```

```
DIM eachline AS contact
CLS
OPEN "employee.dta" FOR RANDOM AS #1 LEN = LEN(eachline)
lastrec = LOF(1) \ LEN(eachline)
DONE = FALSE
DO
  CLS
  INPUT " Please enter new Employee's ID"; eachline.id
  IF eachline.id = 9999 THEN
    DONE = TRUE
  ELSE
    INPUT "                  and first name"; eachline.first
    INPUT "                   and lastname"; eachline.last
    INPUT "                 and date of hire"; eachline.date
    INPUT "          and marital status";
      eachline.marital
    INPUT "                  and pay grade"; eachline.grade
    INPUT "                     and salary"; eachline.salary
    lastrec = lastrec + 1
    PUT #1, lastrec, eachline
  END IF
LOOP UNTIL DONE
CLOSE #1

END SUB

SUB ChangeClients
' Modifies any specified client record
' All fields must be entered
'
DIM eachline AS contact
CLS
OPEN "employee.dta" FOR RANDOM AS #1 LEN = LEN(eachline)
DONE = FALSE
DO
  INPUT "Enter next record number to update:"; recno
  IF recno = 9999 THEN
    DONE = TRUE
  ELSE
    CLS
    GET #1, recno, eachline
    PRINT "Employee Number"; eachline.id, eachline.first;
      eachline.last
    PRINT
    PRINT "Date of Hire:"; eachline.date
    PRINT "Marital Status:"; eachline.marital
    PRINT "Pay Grade:"; eachline.grade
    PRINT USING "Salary $$####.##"; eachline.salary
```

(continued)

Listing 10.3 MENU2.BAS Structured System Module *(continued)*

```
    PRINT
    INPUT "Please enter any changes to employee ID";
      eachline.id
      INPUT "                          and first name";
      eachline.first
      INPUT "                          and lastname";
      eachline.last
      INPUT "                          and date of hire";
      eachline.date
      INPUT "                          and marital status";
      eachline.marital
      INPUT "                          and pay grade";
      eachline.grade
      INPUT "                              and salary";
      eachline.salary
      PRINT
      PUT #1, recno, eachline
    END IF
  LOOP UNTIL DONE
  CLOSE #1

  END SUB


  SUB PrintClients
  ' Prints out the contents of the employee.dta file
  '
  DIM el AS contact
  OPEN "employee.dta" FOR RANDOM AS #1 LEN = LEN(el)
  OPEN "LPT1:" FOR OUTPUT AS #2
  DONE = FALSE
  recno = 1
  CLS
  PRINT #2, "CURRENT CLIENT LIST"
  PRINT
  maxrecs = LOF(1) \ LEN(el)
  DO UNTIL recno > maxrecs
    GET #1, recno, el
    PRINT #2, el.id; el.first; el.last; el.date; el.marital;
      el.grade; el.salary
    recno = recno + 1
  LOOP
  CLOSE #1

  END SUB


  SUB PrinterControl
  ' Uses string functions to control special printer features.
```

```
'
CLS
OPEN "lpt1:" FOR OUTPUT AS #9
EpsonCompress$ = CHR$(15)
EpsonExpand$ = CHR$(18)
HPLaserCompress$ = CHR$(27) + "&k2S"
HPLaserExpand$ = CHR$(27) + "&k0S"
PRINT TAB(25); "Printer Control Program"
PRINT
PRINT "1  Compressed mode on IBM/Epson"
PRINT "2  Compressed mode on HP LaserJet"
PRINT
PRINT "3  Normal 10 pitch mode on IBM/Epson"
PRINT "4  Normal 10 pitch mode on HP LaserJet"
PRINT
INPUT "Select one, please: ", choice
SELECT CASE choice
  CASE 1
    PRINT #9, EpsonCompress$
    PRINT "OK. Epson printer now in compressed mode."
  CASE 2
    PRINT #9, HPLaserCompress$
    PRINT "OK. HP LaserJet now in compressed mode."
  CASE 3
    PRINT #9, EpsonExpand$
    PRINT "OK. Epson printer now in normal 10 pitch mode."
  CASE 4
    PRINT #9, HPLaserExpand$
    PRINT "OK. HP LaserJet now in normal 10 pitch mode."
  CASE ELSE
    PRINT "Invalid choice. No control code sent to printer."
END SELECT
CLOSE #9

END SUB

SUB ShowClients
' Retrieves all client information for specified record
      number
'
DIM eachline AS contact
CLS
OPEN "employee.dta" FOR RANDOM AS #1 LEN = LEN(eachline)
DONE = FALSE
DO
  INPUT "Enter next record number to retrieve:"; recno
  IF recno = 9999 THEN
```

(continued)

Listing 10.3 MENU2.BAS Structured System Module *(continued)*

```
      DONE = TRUE
   ELSE
     CLS
     GET #1, recno, eachline
     PRINT "Employee Number"; eachline.id, eachline.first;
       eachline.last
     PRINT
     PRINT "Date of Hire:"; eachline.date
     PRINT "Marital Status:"; eachline.marital
     PRINT "Pay Grade:"; eachline.grade
     PRINT USING "Salary $$####.##"; eachline.salary
     PRINT
   END IF
LOOP UNTIL DONE
CLOSE #1

END SUB

SUB Style
'Analyze any text file for stylistic characteristics
'
CLS
INPUT "Please enter file to analyze: "; file$
CLS
PRINT "Style Analysis for file: "; file$
OPEN file$ FOR INPUT AS #1
  word% = 0
  sentence% = 0
  fog% = 0
DO
  eachchar$ = INPUT$(1, #1)
  SELECT CASE eachchar$
    CASE " ", CHR$(13)
      word% = word% + 1
      IF wordlength% > 7 THEN
        fog% = fog% + 3
      ELSE
        fog% = fog% + 1
      END IF
      wordlength% = 0
     CASE "."
      sentence% = sentence% + 1
    CASE ";", ",", ":", CHR$(10)
    CASE ELSE
      wordlength% = wordlength% + 1
```

```
  END SELECT
LOOP UNTIL EOF(1)
averagefog% = fog% / sentence%
PRINT "Total number of words is "; word%
PRINT "Total number of sentences is "; sentence%
PRINT "Average fog count is "; averagefog%

END SUB
```

The transfer of control to a separate procedure follows a straightforward flow. Whenever QuickBASIC encounters a CALL *ProcedureName*, control is passed to the procedure. All statements in the procedure are executed (up to the END statement), then control is returned to the calling location. The instruction located just after the CALL instruction is the one executed next (see Figure 10.8).

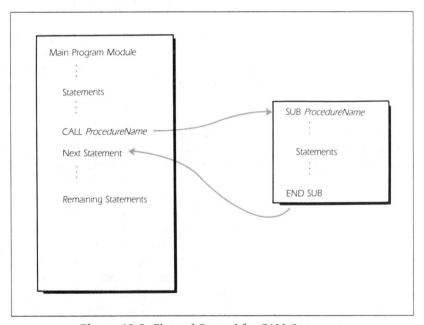

Figure 10.8 Flow of Control for CALL Statements

SUB procedures can CALL one another. And any QuickBASIC module can CALL procedures written in other languages.

There are several implications to this process. First, any one SUB procedure in a QuickBASIC program can CALL any other procedure. That's not shown in our sample system, but it becomes commonplace in more complex systems. Second, the CALL command can be used to transfer control to any properly prepared procedure. Although the mechanism for preparing other types of procedures is beyond the scope of this book, you can actually transfer control to procedures written in assembly language, C, or any other programming language.

You should also notice one other thing about the complete listing in Listing 10.3. The very first six lines are DECLARE statements, informing QuickBASIC of the names of the six "external" procedures used in program MENU2. QuickBASIC's Smart Editor put those lines into the code when I saved the module on disk; if you use your own separate word processor to write programs, you'll have to remember to include these DECLARE lines. One DECLARE statement is necessary for every code module that is to receive a transfer of control during program execution.

The example system presented in this chapter focuses on modularization. In actual practice, a SUB procedure can also use variable parameters to pass data to and from the procedure. Chapter 12 will treat this additional possibility in more depth. The next section explains parameters in the context of QuickBASIC's other type of procedure, the user-defined FUNCTION.

Writing QuickBASIC Functions

Chapter 8 presented a wide range of QuickBASIC string functions. In doing so, you learned that a built-in "function" is a little like a variable in that it acts like a single value. It is also a little like a program because it performs a number of processing steps to come up with its resultant single value. You are not limited to the built-in functions provided by QuickBASIC. You can write your own.

Use a FUNCTION for a module that determines a single output value.

Modularizing your system can sometimes result in a module that does not need to perform any input or output. Its task is simply to process some input data and produce some output data. The built-in string functions of Chapter 8 are like that. But what happens when you structure your system, and the function you need does not exist in QuickBASIC? Well, you just write your own FUNCTION. And you create a FUNCTION in the same fashion as you create a SUB procedure.

One of the program techniques shown in Chapter 8 is password encryption. A complete program was written to demonstrate how to accept a 5-byte password and store an encrypted version of it into a PASSWORD.DTA file. At that time, you were told that any application program that provided password control would have to include the same encryption logic.

This can lead to many separate copies of the same set of instructions. Clearly, a separate module is reasonable. A SUB procedure could easily be written to handle this chore; however, a FUNCTION is better in this case. You can write a FUNCTION whose purpose is to take in one value (that is, an entered password) and return an encrypted value. The FUNCTION name itself can then be used in a QuickBASIC expression, such as an IF statement.

Listing 10.4 lists the complete PASS2.BAS with the supporting FUNCTION encrypt$ procedure. Figure 10.9 displays the screen that results when storing a new password with PASS2. A user has typed in the password (56798) and the deceptive string "GIKNN" is stored in the

PASSWORD.DTA file. The key to this program rests in the FUNCTION encrypt$ statement.

Listing 10.4 Demonstration Code for User-Defined Functions

```
DECLARE FUNCTION encrypt$ (StringName$)
' PASS2.BAS demonstrates user defined functions
' Function ENCRYPT$ encodes the specified string
'
DIM pass AS STRING * 5
DIM StoredPass AS STRING * 5
CLS
PRINT TAB(20); "PASSWORD STORAGE AND RETRIEVAL
      DEMONSTRATION"; CHR$(10)
PRINT TAB(25); "1  Store New Password"; CHR$(10)
PRINT TAB(25); "2  Validate a Password"; CHR$(10)
INPUT "Select One: ", CHOICE
IF CHOICE = 1 THEN
   OPEN "password.dta" FOR OUTPUT AS #1
   PRINT
   INPUT "Enter new password: "; pass
   PRINT
   PRINT "String to be stored is "; encrypt$(pass)
   PRINT #1, encrypt$(pass)
ELSEIF CHOICE = 2 THEN
   OPEN "password.dta" FOR INPUT AS #1
   INPUT "Enter your password: "; pass
   INPUT #1, StoredPass
   IF StoredPass = encrypt$(pass) THEN
      PRINT "Password is OK"
   ELSE
      PRINT "Password is invalid"
   END IF
END IF
CLOSE #1
END

FUNCTION encrypt$ (StringName$)
'
NumChars = LEN(StringName$)
counter = 1
DO UNTIL counter > NumChars
  result$ = result$ + CHR$(ASC(MID$(StringName$, counter,
     1)) + counter + 17)
  counter = counter + 1
LOOP
```

```
encrypt$ = result$
END FUNCTION
```

```
                    PASSWORD STORAGE AND RETRIEVAL DEMONSTRATION

                        1   Store New Password

                        2   Validate a Password

        Select One: 1

        Enter new password: ? 56798

        String to be stored is GIKNN
```

```
        Press any key to continue
```

Figure 10.9 Screen Design for PASS2.BAS Program

Whenever encrypt$ is referenced in a program, control is transferred to the FUNCTION encrypt$ procedure. In this example, the PASS2 line that actually stores the encrypted password in the file is

```
PRINT #1, encrypt$(pass)
```

The value of *pass* is 56798; the value of *encrypt$(pass)* is "GIKNN". Referencing the name encrypt$ in the PRINT command is equivalent to executing the entire encryption sequence located inside the FUNCTION . . . END FUNCTION procedure. The end result is simply that string encrypt$ contains a 5-character encoded version of the value in *pass*. The encryption algorithm used in this function is somewhat different from that used in the demonstration program of Chapter 8.

Similarly, the code for validating a password (choice 2 in PASS2.BAS) references the encrypt$ function. In that portion of the program, the formerly encrypted value for the correct password is read into a variable called *StoredPass*.

```
INPUT #1, StoredPass
```

Then, the user's new entry for a password (which is stored in variable *pass*) is compared to it, after processing this password with the encrypt$ procedure.

```
IF StoredPass = encrypt$(pass) THEN
    PRINT "Password is OK"
ELSE
    PRINT "Password is invalid"
END IF
```

The same function is used in both storage and validation sequences. The sole purpose of the function is to return an encrypted string, given an unencrypted string. This *user-defined function* allows any code that uses it to be smaller and easier to read.

Distinguishing Between Parameters and Arguments

You should understand the distinction between the common terms *parameter* and *argument*. Let's take a look at the FUNCTION that is defined with the following line (see Listing 10.4):

```
FUNCTION encrypt$ (StringName$)
```

In this definition line, the parenthetical expression contains the variable *StringName$*. Yet, when you actually reference the function's name from a program such as PASS2.BAS, you use something else inside the parentheses (such as *pass*). Any variable name that appears in the parentheses on the definition line is called a *parameter*; when you actually write the reference to the FUNCTION in another program, the variable name you use is called an *argument*.

Parameters are place holders for the real data, called arguments. Parameters are the variable names used inside procedures; arguments are the names of the actual data used in the referencing programs.

The parameter is a place holder within a SUB or FUNCTION procedure for the real data, which comes later when the procedure is referenced. This distinction actually helps separate the variables used in a main program from the variables used to perform a task in a subprogram, such as a FUNCTION or a SUB procedure. This discussion applies to both equally. You will see SUB procedures that use several parameters in Chapter 12. This facility does not exist in most earlier versions of the BASIC language.

In this example, all of the instructions in the FUNCTION procedure use the place-holding variable called *StringName$*. When PASS2 actually references the encrypt$ function, the argument *pass* is given to the procedure to use. Each instruction in the procedure that uses *StringName$* will now actually use the value in *pass* to perform the logic.

This distinction is meaningful from a computer science point of view. In practice, it's not a big deal. Often, programmers use the same names for both the parameters and the arguments, blurring the distinction between the two. However, since there are a number of advanced subtleties regarding parameters and arguments, you might as well begin right now to develop a sense of their differences.

Applying Structured Programming Principles

All of the programs you've seen in this book have consisted of three basic program structures:

- Sequence
- Loops
- Choices

A sequence is any set of commands executed one after another. A loop repeatedly executes any set of commands until or while some conditional expression is TRUE. And a choice occurs when one or more alternative sets of commands are executed, also based on some conditional expression or value.

You can write any program using only sequences, repetition, and decisions.

The theory of structured programming asserts that all programs, no matter how complex, can be constructed of these three structures. You have now seen program after program containing sequences within loops or choices, loops within choices, and choices within loops. Each of your program modules will always use one or more of these structured building blocks.

Within each program, and within each of these building blocks, the fundamental principle of structured programming requires that

**Every program or structure should have one starting and
one ending point.**

What this means to you is that a well-written program in QuickBASIC can easily be read from top to bottom. No structure is arbitrarily started or ended in the middle. This book consciously avoids covering such commands as RETURN and EXIT because they are often used inappropriately. If you've programmed in other languages or versions of BASIC, you may already have written programs with multiple RETURN or EXIT statements. And they may have worked just fine. But they are not good programming technique.

Clarity is a prized goal for computer programmers. It is the basis for this principle. If a structure or program always begins and ends at the expected top or bottom, then debugging can always proceed in a consistent manner. You are never uncertain about the flow of control, and you can more effectively use the debugging tools provided by the QuickBASIC development environment.

Review

In Part 2, you learned the tools of the QuickBASIC programming language. In this chapter, you learned a number of guidelines for using those tools effectively.

1. You can design an application system as a collection of separately written application modules. Structure charts are used to analyze the major chores that your application must perform.

2. Modular programming relies on different programs for different chores. Modularization produces systems that are easier to read, modify, and debug.

3. Structured design always proceeds from the top level and works down. Each module has an independent task, and is neither excessively large (more than two pages) nor excessively small (fewer than five to ten lines).

4. The CALL statement enables a QuickBASIC module to transfer execution control to a separately written program called a SUB procedure. A SUB procedure is defined as the group of QuickBASIC instructions contained between SUB and END SUB statements.

5. A FUNCTION procedure receives an automatic transfer of execution control whenever its name is referenced within another QuickBASIC statement. Its instructions are executed and the final result is that the FUNCTION's name itself, like a simple variable, receives a value. The value is then used in the expression in place of the FUNCTION reference.

6. The fundamental principle of structured programming is that every program or structure should begin at the top, and end at the bottom.

Quiz for Chapter 10

1. A main menu program:

   a. Displays choices
   b. Prompts for a selection
   c. Transfers control
   d. All of the above

2. Which statement transfers control to an external procedure?

   a. GOTO
   b. XFER
   c. CALL
   d. DO

3. Which type of procedure can a QuickBASIC program pass control to by simply referencing the procedure's name inside an expression?

   a. Subroutine
   b. Function
   c. SUB
   d. Module

4. Which type of procedure can a QuickBASIC program pass control to by naming it in a CALL statement?

   a. Subroutine
   b. Function
   c. SUB
   d. Module

5. What visual technique is used to analyze the major chores of an application system?

   a. Bubble chart
   b. Structure chart
   c. Gantt chart
   d. Pert chart

6. Writing distinct programs to perform independent chores is called:

   a. Modular analysis
   b. Modular design
   c. Modular programming
   d. Structured design

7. Which of the following is an important guideline for structured design?

    a. Work top down
    b. Work bottom up
    c. Both (a) and (b)
    d. Neither (a) nor (b)

8. Which is true of modules in structured programming?

    a. The more modules, the better
    b. The fewer modules, the better
    c. The more closely related, the better
    d. The less closely related, the better

9. Which function key displays the names of all modules currently in memory?

    a. F2
    b. F4
    c. F6
    d. F8

10. Which of the following statements is true?

    a. SUB procedures are stored in separate files.
    b. Main modules require a PROGRAM statement.
    c. FUNCTION procedures are stored with main modules.
    d. FUNCTION procedures are stored in SUB files.

11. After a procedure completes execution, where does the flow of control continue?

    a. At the calling statement
    b. At the end of the SELECT CASE
    c. At the statement after the CALL
    d. At the next procedure

12. Which statement is required for every SUB or FUNCTION procedure?

    a. SUB
    b. FUNCTION
    c. CALL
    d. DECLARE

13. Which statement is automatically inserted in your program when you save the program module to disk?

    a. SUB
    b. FUNCTION
    c. CALL
    d. DECLARE

14. In the SUB definition, `SUB Sample(one#,two)`, what types of variables are *one#* and *two*?

    a. Parameters
    b. Arguments
    c. Integers
    d. Strings

15. Every structured program has:

    a. Choices
    b. Loops
    c. Sequences
    d. One starting and one ending point

| # Programming Tips and Techniques

Chapter 10 focused on the design of your application system. This chapter focuses on the implementation of your programs. You will learn a host of tips and techniques aimed at ensuring that your programs are both user-friendly and programmer-friendly. These are the two key subject areas of this chapter.

If your program is friendly to your users, they will be friendly to you.

A program that is *user*-friendly incorporates good screen design and flexible data entry and retrieval methods. It provides a variety of necessary reporting options. A user-friendly programming system also handles error situations smoothly, and offers clear documentation about the system's use.

A program that is *programmer*-friendly uses professional development techniques and adheres to a set of accepted programming habits. These kinds of programs also provide accurate and detailed documentation about both the overall system design and the internal programming logic.

Tips for Effective Program Development

In the last chapter, we discussed the types of programs you are likely to encounter in developing a typical application. Once you have decided to write a particular program, there are a number of approaches you can take.

Programming is an iterative process. Your analysis and your structure charts help you decide what should go into a program. You write it and try it out, often discovering that it isn't quite right. So you change it and try it out again. As you learned in Chapter 5, this development process continues until you are satisfied that the program works.

Since you learned in Chapter 10 about SUB programs, your systems will probably consist of programs that CALL one another. After you get the first program to work (like MENU2 in Chapter 10), you begin to write the SUB programs. You go through the same development cycle with each of them, running and testing them until they perform satisfactorily.

Sometimes, in testing a SUB program, you discover an omission in the CALLing program. In that case, you go back and make any necessary changes. And so the cycle goes from program to program as your total system evolves under your fingertips. The more programming experience you have, the fewer iterations are necessary to make the system perform as you envisioned. But nobody's system is perfect the first time, unless the programs in it are extremely small.

So don't be concerned about missteps in programming. It's the norm. The more mistakes you make, the faster you'll become a better programmer. Since mistakes are common, even for experienced programmers, the debugging methods of Chapter 12 are even more valuable to you. However, the techniques in this chapter can minimize the amount of debugging you must do, so they are equally important.

Good Programming Habits

Habits form by themselves. You might as well make them good ones.

Everybody develops habits. When you're programming, you might as well learn some good ones. They'll help rather than hinder your programming efforts.

Develop Your Programs in Steps

A typical computer user just wants a system that works! Programmers should realize this.

The best sequence of steps to follow in developing any program is

1. Make it work.

2. Make it look good.

3. Make it efficient.

Pretty screens and attractive report layouts are useless if the data on them is wrong. Programs that are faster than a speeding bullet don't please anybody if they don't produce the expected results. Step one—Make it work—is all-important. First, get your program logic to work correctly. While you are developing your code, it doesn't matter if output doesn't line up neatly, or if page breaks don't occur in the right place. Those will be easy to adjust later.

Use the PRINT command liberally during this development phase. Even if you will be writing data into a file, PRINTing the data to the screen first can quickly verify to you that the correct results have been produced. Then you can add the #1 or #2 file number to the command. Once the program logic—the loops, choices, and sequences—works correctly, you can take the next step.

Step two is concerned with making your program's output look good. Once users get the correct desired output, then they become more concerned with its appearance. The pressure is off with respect to getting results. The pressure is on to produce attractive results. But because this is a cosmetic chore only, it doesn't take a lot of time. So, why bother with it on the first pass?

First make your program work. Then make it look good.

During the development phase, you will make your job more difficult if you worry about appearance. Concentrate instead on getting your program's logic to work correctly. After it's working, you can easily go back into your code and adjust it for the sake of appearance. Add a LOCATE command here and there; or PRINT some additional output strings for labelling or prompting; or just add a few TAB and SPACE$ functions to your PRINT lines. And presto, you're done!

Well, not quite. Some users are not satisfied when the correct results are presented to them in attractively laid out reports. They complain about slow program response. If that is the case, you can consider moving on to step three. I say "consider", because a slow system that works well is better than a fast system that works poorly. Also, it takes time to rewrite programs in a more efficient manner. You won't always have the luxury of improving the efficiency of one program while another program has yet to be written at all.

Worry about accuracy before worrying about efficiency.

If you're an experienced programmer, you were probably thinking of improvements in efficiency while you worked on steps one and two. But if you're relatively new to programming, you should put off this third step until your entire system is complete. It usually turns out that if an entire system is sluggish the cause can be traced to one or two code modules. After determining which modules are the culprits, you can concentrate your efforts and time on those modules. Improving any others will not be worth the work.

Figure 11.1 illustrates the separate and distinct purpose of each step of program development. If you're a beginning or intermediate programmer, take these steps in sequence. It's going to be easiest that way. As you gain more experience and develop programming forethought, you'll find yourself increasingly able to merge the steps successfully.

Make Your Programs More Readable

QuickBASIC's Smart Editor helps a lot in the area of readability. It adds spaces between operators and operands as you type each line. However, you can do even more to make your programs readable. As you've seen

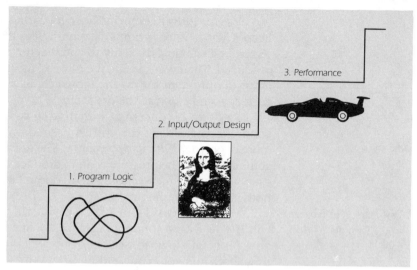

Figure 11.1 Distinct Purpose of Each Step in
Program Development

in all programs in this book, indentation is used consistently for code appearing within compound statements. In fact, when a DO or IF or SELECT CASE statement appears within another compound statement, the indentation level is increased once again.

QuickBASIC does not care how many blank spaces appear at the beginning of a command line. So this indentation is for *your* benefit, not QuickBASIC's. Indentation reveals the structure of a program. This allows you to understand the sequence, loop, and choice structures as they have been put together in any program.

Blank lines are often inserted as well. QuickBASIC ignores them too; their real purpose is to make portions of your program stand out. Again, this is just cosmetic. Indentation, blank spaces, and blank lines are all directed at improving program readability. This is critical for others who will read and work with your code. But it is just as important for you when you return two weeks, or two years later, to work with your own programs.

Document What Your Programs Do

Document how your overall system works and how to use it. Explain both the obvious and the non-obvious, as well as what your program will do with

There are three kinds of documentation that can be prepared with and for your systems. It's kind of sad that some systems do not include even one kind of documentation. One reason is that programmers sometimes get caught up in the excitement of writing programs. They easily get involved in the creative act of making the computer do what they want. In that respect, programming is a lot like composing music or creating art. In contrast, unfortunately, documenting what your pro-

expected and unanticipated inputs.

gram does is more like writing a book report than reading the book. Hardly anybody likes to do it.

But everybody ought to document their programs. If you do, the quality of your system will improve, and you will probably save many hours of frustration in the future. Documenting your work in words is just as important as designing your work with structure charts. Both techniques will make the building and maintaining of your system much easier.

Careful documentation is one obvious way to distinguish a professional from a hacker. A professional prepares three types of documentation before, during, and after programs are developed. *System documentation* explains the overall system, *program documentation* addresses the nitty-gritty elements, and *user documentation* explains how to use the system.

Preparing System Documentation

The more documentation, the fewer eventual bugs.

For the most part, your system documentation can be developed during the design phase. Ideally, it should be complete before the first program is written. It should include the following four elements:

1. *Basic system purpose:* State the overall system function in one or two sentences.

2. *Overall system structure:* Prepare structure charts for the primary system chores. Explain the individual role of each module.

3. *Interface definition:* Explain all parameters used by SUB and FUNCTION procedures. Also explain what expectations each procedure has, such as a user-defined TYPE being created in the CALLing program.

4. *Validation criteria:* Specify all tests that must be applied to input data to verify its validity. For example, does the data have to be within a certain range, or be one of a set of choices, or be found in an existing file record?

Preparing Program Documentation

As you write your individual programs, you should incorporate the following elements into your documentation:

1. *Program listings:* The actual instruction listing of the programs that are running in your system is the ultimate source of system explanation and clarification. Keep current listings of each source module for quick reference.

2. *File structures:* Prepare some visual depiction of the contents of each data file. Explain what each field does, and include samples of the type of data stored in the file.

3. *Logic descriptions:* Describe all logic sequences. Obvious code needs only a sentence describing its purpose. Tricky sequences require further explanations. If you wrote these before programming, make sure to rewrite them as you adjust the design and the actual code.

4. *Comments in the code:* Place the program name in a comment on the first line of the program itself. You can easily identify the printed listings. Also include a brief description of what the program does. Where necessary, add comments throughout the code to explain individual instructions.

   A particularly advantageous type of comment to include is the "audit" comment. Whenever you change a working program, enter a comment line listing both the date and nature of the change. This assures an audit trail of modifications that will be useful later if a working system begins to develop bugs.

Preparing User Documentation

The preceding two sections dealt with documentation aimed at the developers and maintainers of the software. Don't forget the people who use the software. Attending to the following two areas will lead you to include useful information in the user's manual.

1. *Listen and watch as users learn:* Pay attention to the questions they ask and the mistakes they make. Watch for difficulties encountered or assumptions made.

2. *Anticipate what can go wrong:* Programming for errors is one thing; writing clear error messages is another. Then again, some things are not under your control, such as power failures. Explain what to do when things go wrong; for example, you can tell users how to print a copy of the screen, or how to discover what files are open.

Make Your Programs More Understandable

Program clarity is dependent upon how you name your variables, organize your statements, and lay out entire modules.

Documenting your programs is the best thing you can do to make them easy to understand. Explain in simple English what your program is doing, how it uses variables, and how its logic works. Clear English is more comprehensible than the best computer program. Add as much as possible to your program in the form of comments.

The next best guideline to follow for clarity is the fundamental principle of structured programming: each module or programming structure should start at the top and end at the bottom. Side trips to SUB or FUNCTION procedures are OK, since the flow of control returns to the calling program. But control transfers that never return, such as EXIT, are unacceptably difficult to follow and to understand.

Nomenclature is another tool that you can use to make your programs more understandable. File names like EMPLOYEE.DTA and CLIENTS.DTA are likely to contain information about employees and clients. When a file has a name such as one of these, the file's use and contents are immediately obvious to someone reading an OPEN statement in a QuickBASIC program. If you have multiple files with similar contents, adjust the names accordingly. For instance, a file containing sales statistics could be SALES.DTA; several years' worth of files could be SALES89.DTA, SALES90.DTA, and so forth.

Similarly, you should assign descriptive names to variables that suggest their role in the program. For instance, the programs in this book use names like *last, address, city, state, zip,* and *phone.* The contents of these variables are intuitively obvious. Contrast this with programs using alternative naming conventions like *I, J,* and *K,* or *A1, A2,* and *A3.* You should use this suggestive naming technique for simple variables as well as the more complex user-defined groups defined with the TYPE statement.

Shorthand is meant for dictation. Avoid it when naming variables and procedures.

When you give names to your SUB and FUNCTION procedures, you can also help the cause of readability. Naming a procedure PrintClients is much clearer than naming it PC. Remember that variables and procedure names can be as long as 40 characters; use as many as you need.

Make Your Programs Obey the Golden Rule

Figure 11.2 depicts the Golden Rule of Programming. This rule says that you should write your programs for others in the same careful and professional manner that you'd like others to follow when they write programs for you. It's usually pretty easy to identify what you don't like about somebody else's program. Try to remember those things you've encountered in the past when you write your own code. Ignore advice that runs counter to the suggestions of this section. Alternative suggestions may have some merit, but not enough, in my opinion, to warrant the sacrifices in understandability.

For instance, some writers suggest that you use shorthand variable names, eliminate blank lines and documentation lines, and forget about indentation levels. Yes, doing those things will speed up the interpretation or compilation of your programs. However, this gain is small compared to the loss of readability and understandability of the resultant code.

Such well-meaning advice is always offered in the name of improved performance or efficiency. But in the real world, the *human* side of the human-machine interaction is the important side. Pay attention to it first. Experienced programmers know how tough it can be to figure out somebody else's program without adequate documentation, without indentations, and with occasional "tricks" built into the code.

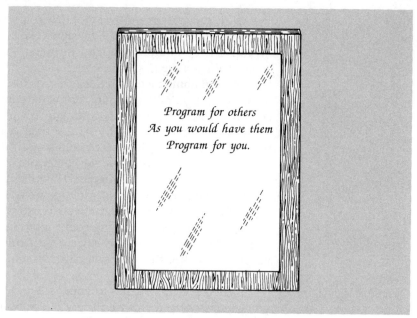

*Program for others
As you would have them
Program for you.*

Figure 11.2 The Golden Rule of Programming

A program may run 10 percent faster because of a series of well-intentioned shortcuts, but it may require an extra week to understand it. This is wrong! Clear thinking, clear planning, and clear programming all go hand in hand. Changes for correction or enhancement will be easy only if a program is put together effectively. If you must have better performance, think first of a faster computer or a faster hard disk. Let programming tricks and shortcuts be the last recourse.

So stick with the Golden Rule of Programming. Be kind to future programmers who will work with the code you write today. After all, it may be you.

Techniques for User-Friendly Programs

Don't you think that side notes like this make a book more user friendly?!

User-friendly is an overused term that simply means "easy to use." Unfortunately, some application systems use this term to describe any product, regardless of whether or not it really is user-friendly. Your software will be user-friendly if you use a majority of the techniques described in this section.

Making Your Programs User-Friendly

Think about computer systems you have personally used. Which did you like? Which did you hate? Which were easy to use, and why? If you can identify the features that make a system comfortable or uncomfortable, you can include or avoid the same features in the programs you write.

Three general characteristics make up a user-friendly program:

1. *Intuitiveness:* Your programs should work the way a user would guess they would work. If most users expect to press function key F1 for on-line help, don't ask them to press Alt-F9 in your system.

2. *Unobtrusiveness:* Your program logic should help, not hinder, your users. Your system may be designed around a series of menus containing many options. Experienced users may not need these any longer; the system should have alternative mechanisms available to make system use easier on these advanced users.

3. *Consistency:* The same input should lead to the same output throughout all the parts of your program. Users prize predictability in their computer systems.

The following sections provide examples that illustrate the usefulness of these guidelines.

Dealing with Long Running Programs

Let users know when a program is going to take a long time.

Some programs are going to be slow on any computer. A three dimensional biological or missile simulation will take a while, and often doesn't even require any screen or keyboard interaction. A long report that reads sequentially through a 20,000 record data file is going to take a long time, no matter how fast your printer is. Most people will accept these situations, if only they have some idea of how long the operation will take.

The simplest way to warn the user is to clear the screen (CLS) and tell the user that the program is going to take a long time. Use a PRINT statement for a simple output message. Depending on the expected length of the program, suggest going out for coffee, or lunch, or the night. It's a good idea to estimate the time requirements first and offer the user a way out. You can provide a controlled choice, specifying whether to go ahead with the operation or to cancel it. This is important since most users will choose not to begin long operations in the morning; to do so might cause them to lose the use of their computer for the rest of the day.

When users elect to go ahead with the long running process, they will find the display of a progress counter helpful. Suppose a file with thousands of records is being processed. Using a *counter* variable as shown in the many example programs in this book is a good idea. The exact number of records in the file is

```
NumRecs = LOF(1) / LEN(eachline)
```

where *eachline* is a variable of the user-defined TYPE set up earlier in the program. You can display the program's running progress by incorporating these statements into the primary processing loop:

```
CLS
LOCATE 5,1
PRINT "There are ";NumRecs;" records to process."
PRINT "Now processing record number "; Counter
```

The program will be done when it completes all the records, but the user will be able to look at the screen at any time and assess the program's progress.

Naturally, you can get much fancier. QuickBASIC includes a TIME$ function which returns the current time of day. You can use this function to estimate the program's progress. For example, you know how many records have to be processed (that is, NumRecs). For any value of *counter*, you can determine how many seconds have elapsed since the beginning of the loop. Invoke TIME$ before the loop and convert the string digits to numbers. Then invoke TIME$ from within the loop, convert digits to numbers, and perform appropriate subtractions, adjusting for hours, minutes, and seconds.

You can then estimate the amount of time per loop iteration; this is roughly the time to process one record. Doing a little bit of calculation and knowing how many records remain, should enable you to display a message indicating approximately how much time remains before the program completes. With an IF statement, you can limit how often the calculation is made and how often a "time remaining" message is displayed.

The logic of this process for displaying the time remaining in a program can be pretty jazzy. Take a few minutes now to try it out. Just set up an example counting loop to test out your calculation logic. If you're in a mood more for reading than for writing, take a look at the THRMOMTR.BAS program in Listing 11.1.

Assuming that your output screen can display graphics, you can provide an even more visually pleasing display. This program produces an on-screen thermometer that fills up as the records are processed. Figure 11.3 displays the output from this program at a point approximately 70 percent through the loop. The maximum number of records is first calculated and displayed at the top of the thermometer. The outline of the thermometer itself is drawn with a CIRCLE and a LINE statement.

Display ongoing progress information during time-consuming program operations.

Listing 11.1 THRMOMTR.BAS—Displaying a Thermometer to Measure Program Progress

```
' THRMOMTR.BAS draws a progress thermometer on the screen
'
```

```
' Demonstration assumptions:
'         1. Screen height of thermometer is 100 pixels
'         (SCREEN 2)
'         2. File size exceeds 100 records
'
CLS
TYPE contact
  id AS LONG
  first AS STRING * 10
  last AS STRING * 15
  date AS STRING * 8
  marital AS STRING * 1
  grade AS INTEGER
  salary AS SINGLE
END TYPE
DIM eachline AS contact
CLS
OPEN "clients.dta" FOR RANDOM AS #1 LEN = LEN(eachline)
DONE = FALSE
SCREEN 2
NumRecs = LOF(1) / LEN(eachline)
LINE (305, 150) - STEP(30, -100), , B
CIRCLE (320, 150), 30, 2
LOCATE 7, 43
PRINT INT(NumRecs)
LINE (360, 140) - (360, 60), , , &HF0F0
LINE (350, 70) - (360, 60), , , &HF0F0
LINE (370, 70) - (360, 60), , , &HF0F0
counter = 1
GrowIt! = NumRecs / 100
AddOne = 1
DO UNTIL counter > NumRecs
   IF counter MOD GrowIt = 0 THEN
       LINE (305, 150) - STEP(30, -AddOne), , BF
       AddOne = AddOne + 1
   END IF
   counter = counter + 1
LOOP
END

NumRecs = LOF(1) / LEN(eachline)
LINE (305, 150) - STEP(30, -100), , B
CIRCLE (320, 150), 30, 2
LOCATE 7, 43
PRINT INT(NumRecs)
```

Next, successively filled rectangles are drawn with the LINE,,BF state-

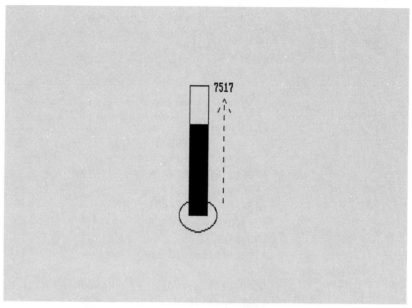

Figure 11.3 Graphic Output Partway Through
THRMOMTR.BAS

ment. But they are not drawn for each value of the *counter*. This would
be unnecessary program overhead, since the progress level in the thermometer does not change for every increase in the value of *counter*. In
fact, a variable called *GrowIt!* is used to manage the growth in the thermometer's liquid level. One screen pixel is used to represent 100 iterations through the loop.

```
GrowIt! = NumRecs / 100
```

Graphic progress displays are intuitively understood.

The counting loop ranges from 1 to NumRecs, but the nested IF statement assures that a new higher liquid level is only drawn every 100
iterations. For this purpose, the QuickBASIC MOD function is used.

```
IF counter MOD GrowIt = 0 THEN
    LINE (305, 150) - STEP(30, -AddOne), , BF
    AddOne = AddOne + 1
END IF
```

This works because the MOD function has a zero value only when the
value on its left side (*counter*) is evenly divisible by the value on its right
side (*GrowIt*). Three fixed LINE statements precede the loop to draw the
vertical dashed arrow, located beside the thermometer.

```
LINE (360, 140) - (360, 60), , , &HF0F0
LINE (350, 70) - (360, 60), , , &HF0F0
LINE (370, 70) - (360, 60), , , &HF0F0
```

The size and location of this arrow are fixed. If you feel more like writing code now, you could modify the THRMOMTR.BAS program to make the dashed arrow grow vertically as the level of the thermometer's liquid grows. To do this, you'll have to move the three LINE statements into the loop, and replace some of the fixed numbers with variables. These new variables then must depend on information in the loop.

Protecting Your Users from Problems

Catch data errors at the time of input.

There are many steps you can take to reduce the number of your user's headaches. Probably the best known technique is validating input data when it is first entered. But you can anticipate and avoid many other situations.

For example, lengthy printed reports often have to be restarted when a paper jam occurs after 10 or 15 pages have been printed. Your program can anticipate this problem by INPUTting from the user the record number, ID number, or even page number at which to begin printing. The program can calculate where to begin in the file. If your printer is liable to jam up frequently, this technique can reduce the amount of time during which such a jam can occur.

For that matter, users don't always need a printout of all possible records in a file. Allowing the user to specify both a starting point and an ending point gives your program flexibility. Additionally, it reduces the time spent by the program in outputting information that is not needed.

Designing Input and Output Screens

When people first meet you, they form an immediate impression of you based on appearance. While this certainly doesn't consider all your other virtues, it is a fact of life. The design of your input and output screens can help to create a similar first impression of your program in the eyes of your users.

Screen design encompasses three areas. First, the screen *appearance* deals with how easy a screen is to read. Ask yourself, how readily does a user perceive and understand what input is being requested? How clearly does output stand out? It must always be clear what data is being requested and what data is being delivered by a program.

Secondly, screen *operation* deals with how easy a screen is to work with. Are you required to enter all fields again when an error is discovered, or can you correct only the one field found to be in error? If you see an error on the screen you're still working with, can you correct it on the spot, or is it too late?

Thirdly, screen *dialogue* deals with how smoothly one screen flows into the next. Even with one screen, some interactions between users and your program require inputs followed by outputs followed by more inputs. The order and nature of the dialogue should be natural and comfortable. If you are asking for the entry of a name and address, don't ask for the zip code field before the city and state. It's simply not the way people are used to thinking.

Be consistent, and make your screens easy to read.

Here are some tips for producing well-designed screens for your programs:

1. *Leave lots of white space.* A screen which is solidly filled with fields is difficult to read. This is just like a program with no blank lines, indentations, or spaces between operands and operators.

2. *Use a consistent format.* Always use a title on the top line so a user who walks away and then returns can quickly identify what program is running and where he or she left off. Some programmers also display the current date and time on the top line. If you do that, place them in the same place (such as the upper corners) on all screens.

   Error messages should also appear in a consistent, reserved portion of the screen. Your user will automatically look there if something goes wrong. Whether this portion is on the bottom or the top of the screen is unimportant (although I prefer the bottom of the screen); consistency is the important thing.

3. *Use consistent terminology.* If you call a field "Customer ID" on one screen, don't call it "Account Number" on another screen. In addition, label your screen areas with names familiar to the users.

4. *Use correct spelling.* Your screens are like personal billboards advertising your work. If they contain misspellings, inconsistent capitalization, or poor punctuation, users will see them over and over again, and your reputation will suffer accordingly.

5. *Use proper abbreviations.* If there is plenty of space on your screens, try not to use abbreviations at all. However, screens are usually limited, and headings, field labels, and descriptions must often be abbreviated. Be sure to select phrases that either will be obvious to anyone, or at least are well-known to the intended users.

6. *Use helpful error messages.* They should be clear, polite, and helpful. Describe the problem and what must be done to correct it. "Bad input," which is commonly used, is virtually useless. "Invalid Employee ID. Please reenter." is both explicit and helpful. A user should not have to look in the manual to find out what to do when an error message appears.

7. *Use consistent keystrokes.* Making menu choices and selecting screen options are extremely common user operations. If the Esc key exits on one screen, don't use the F10 key to cancel an opera-

tion on another screen. If you use letters for menu choices on one screen, don't use numbers on another menu.

Don't make your screens overly gaudy or overly complex.

8. *Don't overuse color or highlighting.* Use color or other forms of emphasis for occasional screen fields or groupings. Whatever you choose should be "easy on the eyes."

9. *Limit the options.* A menu list becomes difficult to read when it has more than eight or nine choices. Consider subdividing long menus; you've probably seen menus on which one of the choices leads to another submenu of choices. Or, perhaps you've seen a scrolling window of choices with a mouse or down arrow that enables you to bring additional choices into view.

Of course, you don't have to follow all of these suggestions. But do consider them seriously, for each one represents years of trial-and-error experience with real programs, real users, and real bugs.

Review

You learned many guidelines, principles, and suggestions about programming in this chapter. You learned numerous tips for effective program development and a broad range of techniques for writing user-friendly programs.

1. You should develop programs in these steps:

   Step 1: Make the program work.

   Step 2: Make the output look good.

   Step 3: Make the program run faster.

   Step one is always important. Step two is easy and can be added quickly after the program works. Step three is optional according to your available development time and the importance of program speed.

2. Good programming habits consist of methods for 1) making your programs more readable; 2) documenting what your system does, how each program works, and how to use the programs; 3) making your programs more understandable to other programmers; 4) making your programs obey the Golden Rule of Programming.

3. User-friendly programs are intuitive, unobtrusive, and consistent. They contain aids such as 1) apprising the user of progress in long running programs; 2) methods of protecting the user from anticipated problems; 3) screens that are easy to read, are easy to work with, and contain smooth and natural dialogues.

Quiz for Chapter 11

1. Which statement is most true?

    a. Programming is irritating
    b. Programming is interactive
    c. Programming is iterative
    d. Programming is imitative

2. Which is most important?

    a. Making your program efficient
    b. Making your program attractive
    c. Making your program interactive
    d. Making your program work

3. Which is easiest to do?

    a. Make your program efficient
    b. Make your program attractive
    c. Make your program interactive
    d. Make your program work

4. Which of the following does not make your programs more readable?

    a. Blank spaces
    b. Indentations
    c. Blank looks
    d. Blank lines

5. Which is the least useful form of computer documentation?

    a. System documentation
    b. Program documentation
    c. Cost documentation
    d. User documentation

6. Which of the following should be included in system documentation?

    a. Basic purpose
    b. Overall structure
    c. Validation criteria
    d. All of the above

7. Which of the following should be included in program documentation?

    a. Program listings and file structures
    b. Logic descriptions
    c. Comments in the code
    d. All of the above

8. Which of the following should you use as a primary source for information to include in user documentation?

   a. Questions users ask
   b. Mistakes users make
   c. Both (a) and (b)
   d. Neither (a) nor (b)

9. Giving names that imply their use to which of the following can make a program more understandable?

   a. Variables
   b. Files
   c. Procedures
   d. All of the above

10. Which of the following traits is not found in a user-friendly program?

    a. Intuitiveness
    b. Unobtrusiveness
    c. Humor
    d. Consistency

11. What type of program most needs a progress display?

    a. Complicated
    b. Lengthy
    c. Business
    d. Scientific

12. Programs should help to protect users from:

    a. Anticipated problems
    b. Expected bugs
    c. File failures
    d. System crashes

13. Screen design encompasses all but which of the following areas?

    a. Appearance
    b. Operation
    c. Dialogue
    d. Performance

14. Only one of the following is not a guideline for screen design. Which is it?

    a. Use consistent keystrokes
    b. Use consistent terminology
    c. Use consistent format
    d. Use consistent white space

15. Only one of the following is not a guideline for screen design. Which is it?

    a. Use correct spelling
    b. Limit the colors
    c. Limit the messages
    d. Limit the options

12 | Testing, Debugging, and Running Your Programs

In Chapter 10, you learned how best to design your programs. And in Chapter 11, you learned how to successfully write those programs. But neither of those steps is enough. They are necessary, but if you believe the advice given in those chapters, you must take additional steps before turning your programs over to their eventual users.

Some programmers can be very methodical about designing and programming; their systems are clear, organized, and user-friendly. But they simply don't always work. Although it would be silly to assert that your system will never fail, a number of techniques do exist for program and system testing that will reduce the number of bugs, and that will assure positive acceptance of your work.

Eliminate the obvious bugs with careful testing methods.

In the program development cycle, a final phase comes after the original design and the actual programming. This phase consists of testing and debugging, coupled with rewriting, then further testing and debugging, and it ends with a working, running system. Sure, more bugs may be later found by system users. But they won't be the obvious or anticipated ones.

This chapter deals with the three aspects of this final phase: testing, debugging, and running. You will learn a range of techniques aimed at assuring a successful series of tests, and at eliminating as many program and system bugs as possible. You will learn many methods, some general and some specific to QuickBASIC, used by professional programmers to correct bugs found in their programs. Lastly, you will learn how to take any program developed successfully in QuickBASIC and make it run from a DOS command prompt, independent of the Quick-BASIC development environment.

Testing Your Programs

Just as you learned the value of top-down structure design in Chapter 10, so will you learn the value of top-down program testing in this section. You will also learn how to do it effectively in QuickBASIC, and how to use test files and scripts to help you in your efforts.

Understanding the Mechanics of Top-Down Testing

Top-down testing means that you start at the top program module and work downward.

Top-down means simply that you start your testing with the main menu module first. Then, you work your way through all SUB and FUNC-TION procedures which are executed in your system. First, all SUBs called from your main menu program should be tested. Next, all procedures invoked from other procedures are tested.

You may wonder, though, how to test a program when the programs that it calls haven't been written yet. This is done with a technique known as *stub programming*. In this technique you replace each intended procedure with a simpler "stub" procedure. The main program can then be tested without all support procedures needing to be written. Each subordinate program will simply print a message instead of performing its eventual task.

For example, suppose the selection part of a main menu program looks like this:

```
SELECT CASE choice$
  CASE "1"
    CALL ChangeClients
  CASE "2"
    CALL ShowClients
  CASE "3"
    CALL AddClients
  CASE "4"
    CALL PrintClients
  CASE "Q", "q"
    FINISHED = TRUE
  CASE ELSE
    LOCATE 18, 1
    message$ = "Invalid Choice! Please Select Again."
END SELECT
```

After you've finished writing the code for this module, you would normally begin writing the code for each of these four SUB modules. But don't do that yet. Instead, type in only the following four program "stubs":

```
SUB ChangeClients
Print "ChangeClients stub"
END SUB

SUB ShowClients
Print "ShowClients stub"
END SUB

SUB "AddClients"
Print "AddClients stub"
END SUB

SUB "PrintClients"
Print "PrintClients stub"
SUB
```

You can now test all of the main module's possible chores, from displaying its menu to accepting a user choice to passing control to each of several subprograms. That's all you need to do to verify that the main module is coded correctly.

Next, you can move on to the various procedures in your system. However, to test them, you may need to replace some stubs with code that really does a job. But it doesn't have to be the final, fancy job. For instance, let's assume that you've specified your user-defined type in the main program:

Use simple stub programs for quick and effective testing.

```
TYPE contact
  id AS LONG
  first AS STRING * 10
  last AS STRING * 15
  date AS STRING * 8
  marital AS STRING * 1
  grade AS INTEGER
  salary AS SINGLE
END TYPE
DIM eachline AS contact
```

In that case, a modest adjustment to the data entry stub (AddClients) might look like this:

```
SUB "AddClients"
Print "AddClients stub"
OPEN "employee.dta" FOR RANDOM AS #1 LEN = LEN(eachline)
```

```
INPUT " ID"; eachline.id
INPUT " First name"; eachline.first
INPUT " Last name"; eachline.last
INPUT " Hire Date"; eachline.date
INPUT " Marital"; eachline.marital
INPUT " Grade"; eachline.grade
INPUT " Salary"; eachline.salary
RecNum = LOF(1) \ LEN(eachline) + 1
PUT #1, RecNum, eachline
CLOSE #1
END SUB
```

This is now a complete, working data entry program. It isn't elegant or pretty, it does no data validation, and it allows only one record to be entered each time you run it. But, for all its simplicity, it does let you put test data into the file. You can now continue to test and further develop other modules in your system.

As you progress in your testing, you can expand other module stubs as necessary in this fashion. Until you must write and test a particular module for itself, you only need to write the minimum "stub" code for that module. This reduces the complexity of your task. It enables you to concentrate on writing, testing, and debugging one module at a time.

The Advantages of Top-Down Testing

Top-down testing eliminates bugs early and confirms design correctness.

What's the point of this method? Why should you follow the structure chart, testing the highest level program first and working your way down? Why should you use program stubs as substitutes for lower-level modules that haven't yet been completely written? There are a number of advantages.

First, you can begin to carry out testing before a system's final design and coding are even completed. It's easier to find bugs when there are fewer untested modules that could contain the problem. Writing and testing one module at a time helps.

Second, you can develop a prototype of your final system very quickly. Once you've successfully written and tested the main menu program, and written simple stub programs for the principal procedures, you can begin to show it to users. That makes them happy, because they can see real progress going on. Remember the importance of providing progress information during program execution? It's just as important to provide it during program development.

Also, these same users can begin to give you useful feedback about the system's appearance and flow. It's easier for users to understand a system from a working prototype. Computer documentation is often incomprehensible to people unfamiliar and uncomfortable with the language of a computer programmer or system designer.

The third benefit of top-down testing is extremely important: major design flaws can be discovered early. Sometimes (heaven forbid!), users are so unhappy with a programming system that they simply quit using the system at all. Simple bugs don't justify this response. Usually, this happens when the system designer never really understood how the system was supposed to work.

However, if you develop your system from the top down, and your users review your efforts as you go along, you greatly reduce the chances of discovering too late that your programs solved the wrong application problem. Don't be afraid of the user's early feedback. It will get you and keep you on the right track, and it will increase the likelihood of your system being well received.

A last benefit has to do with full scale testing. If you've thoroughly tested each individual program in this suggested top-down manner, you can be fairly confident of your overall system. You will need to do very little total-system testing. On the other hand, it is extremely difficult to test a 50-module system all at once, and to determine which module is responsible for an apparent bug.

Top-down testing is both a strategy and a philosophy of testing. If you've never done it before, it may take a little time and effort to become comfortable with it, but the payoff is worth it.

Using Test Scripts and Test Files

Use test scripts to anticipate possible inputs.

In order to effectively test your programs, you need a methodical approach. Such an approach specifies a set of data to use when testing your programs. This data should mimic the different possibilities anticipated when your users actually run the programs. If your program expects inputs from the keyboard, then you must define a set of possible keyboard inputs. This set of data is called a *test script*. If your program processes inputs from a data file, then you must set up a file that contains a range of possible field values. This file is then called a *test file*.

A test script concentrates primarily on your program's editing and validation logic. However, it also must test everything else, from menu choices to data updating to report selection criteria. You can use such a test script to test your system's error-handling ability, as well as its ability to process all expected data properly. A test file is similar to a test script, except that it usually involves a much larger amount of test data. Several techniques will serve you well in this testing phase.

Outline Your Expected Tests

Sit down before programming and write down what tests you will run. Many programmers write programs, then sit down and invent their test on the fly. This approach is too haphazard to ensure thoroughness.

Write down sample groups of input data, and then write down what you expect the system response to be. In the first place, you are likely to produce a more complete set of test data before programming has prejudiced your view of the system than after. In the second place, thinking in advance exactly what the program should do with various inputs will make the writing of the program easier.

Include Both Correct and Incorrect Data

This sounds obvious, but it is not followed often enough. Programmers are notorious for testing a program with "normal" data and then getting upset when a user tells them the program didn't work (with what the programmers term "weird" data). This explains why some organizations actually hire different people to write and test programs separately.

Test for both expected and unexpected values.

You can't test every possible input combination, but you can test sample combinations. Don't be random; be thorough. Cover as many conditions as possible. Some input data can have one field in error; other input scripts can specify several or even all fields in error. Since error situations are usually less frequent, and well defined, you usually can and should test all or nearly all of them.

Always Test the Limit Conditions

Go to the outside limits of data expectation. Your users will; sometimes they'll enter out-of-limits data accidentally, and sometimes they'll do it purposely to "see what happens."

For example, if your program is supposed to ensure that salary never exceeds $2000,

```
IF salary! > 2000 THEN
```

then your script should validate this with values for *salary!* of 1999, 2000, and 2001.

If your test file contains 25 records, and the user is asked to enter a record number (RecNum), test the program with a RecNum equal to 25, 50, 0, and −10. Always test numeric fields for zero and negative entries, as well as values that simply are bigger or smaller than the possible maximum or minimum values.

The general idea is to test for what could possibly be entered, not for what you anticipate will be entered. Test numeric fields for character input; test character strings for numeric input; test strings used as dates for leap year; test for every conceivable class of input.

Save Test Files and Scripts

Save test scripts and files for future testing. Later

Test scripts are valuable. Don't throw them away after you've gotten the system working. Very few programming systems remain static. After be-

code modifications will require revalidation that your system still works.

ing used for a while, desirable changes and enhancements become apparent. Users request them, and you or the next programmer may have to adjust the code to handle them.

When you make changes to a system later, it would be nice to be able to run a known, complete set of tests to make sure that everything still works as before. Running the same tests, and obtaining the same results, is a simple yet efficient way of assuring this goal.

Debugging Your Programs

"My program has a bug." You've heard that one before. It's a little like "Sorry, our computer is down." You can't do anything about it, and it's sometimes accompanied by a giggle or a regretful look. Programmers occasionally view bugs as cute little creatures that creep into their code when they're not looking. If they saw bugs as mistakes or defects, they might put more energy into avoiding them.

Debugging is part analysis and part detective work; it is partly creative and partly mechanical. It is wholly satisfying to mold a computer program to your desires, to fix it when it doesn't work correctly, and to discover exactly why it is performing in a particular way. Nevertheless, it is even more satisfying to have the program work right the first time, and never to require any debugging effort at all.

This section addresses general debugging techniques that you can use, as well as specific QuickBASIC tools at your disposal. In the following example of these debugging techniques, you will learn more about preparing SUB procedures that use multiple parameters.

Applying General Debugging Techniques

Your skill at finding bugs will increase as you become more experienced with writing and debugging QuickBASIC programs. There are a number of fundamental techniques that you can use immediately:

1. *Think.* Yes, you've heard this before: Think before you act. Think before you design. Think before you program. And now, think before you spend time using any of the following debugging techniques. Try to remember what recent change you added to the code. Try to mentally visualize the flow of control in the program. Try to revisit the logic you put in place.

2. *Isolate the bug.* Run the program several times. Does the same error happen in the same way, at the same time, given the same inputs or test script? Repeatable errors are the easiest to solve. Intermittent errors are much more elusive.

Speed up debugging by isolating the responsible code.

Note what parts of the program seemed to have worked prior to observing the bug. Then note what seems to happen after the bug shows up. This helps to pin down the approximate location in your code of the problem. By eliminating from consideration those parts of your program that seem to work correctly, you can concentrate your energies on the suspicious parts of the program.

3. *Do desk checking.* This involves reading through your program modules, line by line, and assessing exactly what the program should do when it runs. If you understand each command, and know what data is being input to that command, you can predict the result of each successive line in your program modules. You can then see where the actual result (when you run the program) deviates from the predicted one. Turning QuickBASIC's trace feature ON (see the Full Debug menu in Appendix C) can perform the same process dynamically.

4. *Ask a colleague for help.* An impartial outsider can often spot errors that you repeatedly overlook. Also, showing your code to another person often forces you to look at the instructions so carefully that you discover the error yourself.

5. *Look at intermediate results.* At various points during your program's execution, you can look at the values of variables, expressions, or even the contents of data files. If you understand the eventual results, the intermediate values can suggest what portions of the logic may not be working properly. To do these things, you can take advantage of QuickBASIC's watch expressions and breakpoints (see the next section).

6. *Check for test data.* Your program may be fine, but your supposedly "correct" test data may have been entered incorrectly.

7. *Get away from it all.* Go play racquetball or tennis, or set up a backgammon or chess game. You can do anything to forget about the #@$%!# bug; the bug will probably be easier to understand and solve when you come back refreshed.

Hiding Places for Tough Bugs

If you can't uncover a bug quickly, take a look at some of the following more subtle possibilities:

1. Improper module interface

2. Insufficient input validation

3. Procedures that change variable values

4. Faulty end-of-loop or end-of-file logic

The problem of improper module interfaces has to do with assumptions. Sometimes, a SUB or FUNCTION procedure assumes that the CALLing module has set up the value of a variable or even opened up a file. Sometimes, the CALLing module assumes these things will be taken care of by the procedure. Verify all such assumptions.

As for insufficient input validation, a data entry program may not catch an error in the quality of input. Later, this same data may be retrieved by another working program that will fail because it is trying to process data which, according to the system design, could not possibly be in the data file. An example might be a salary value that is negative. A missing validation IF for negative values could enable such a keyboard typo to get placed into an employee file.

Sometimes procedures change variable values. Once a procedure is called or referenced, it can possibly change the value of a variable defined elsewhere. In the example below, a procedure uses variables defined as specific parameters. Any of these could be changed erroneously within the procedure; the bug could then show up in the main calling module.

Test for "off by one" errors in DO . . . LOOP constructions.

Last, faulty end-of-loop or end-of-file logic could be the problem. Examine all loops for proper terminating conditions. Both beginning and ending logic should be checked closely. For example, consider the following loop:

```
counter = 1
DO WHILE counter < 100
counter = counter + 1
LOOP
```

It will execute only 99 times, not 100. And this loop:

```
recnum = 1
DO WHILE NOT EOF(1)
GET #1, recnum, eachline
PRINT eachline.first
LOOP
```

is of the infamous "infinite" variety, since the recnum variable is never changed within the loop, and the end of file condition (EOF) is never reached.

Using the QuickBASIC Debug Pulldown Menu

In Chapter 11, you saw a program called THRMOMTR.BAS, which placed a graphic thermometer on the screen. Located at a fixed point, and occupying a fixed size, it demonstrated how to provide visual feedback on the progress of a lengthy program. Let's take that program and generalize it so that its functionality is available to any program you write.

We'll rewrite the logic of the program as a SUB procedure. In the process, you'll see how parameters can be used effectively. The intention will be to define a procedure with five input parameters. They will specify the proposed thermometer's screen height and width in pixels. In addition, you will be able to specify pixel values for the base (x,y) location of the thermometer. Last, you will provide a fifth parameter for the maximum value of the thermometer's counter. Listing 12.1 shows the first attempt at modifying the Chapter 11 program to create a test module as well as the new SUB procedure itself. Figure 12.1 shows the results of running this logic.

Listing 12.1 Program that Is a First Attempt at a Generalized Progress Thermometer

```
DECLARE SUB thermo (ht!, wd!, x!, y!, Max!)
' SUB THERMO draws a progress thermometer on the screen
'
' Required Parameters:
'        1. Thermometer height in pixels (SCREEN 2 assumed)
'        2. Thermometer width in pixels
'        3. Base location (x, y) of thermometer's 'mercury'
'        circle
'        4. Maximum value for the thermometer's counter.

' Assumptions:
'        1. Height counter File size exceeds 100 records
'        2. Mercury ball is 50% larger than thermometer's
'        width
CLS
TYPE contact
  id AS LONG
  first AS STRING * 10
  last AS STRING * 15
  date AS STRING * 8
  marital AS STRING * 1
  grade AS INTEGER
  salary AS SINGLE
END TYPE
DIM eachline AS contact
CLS
OPEN "clients.dta" FOR RANDOM AS #1 LEN = LEN(eachline)
DONE = FALSE
SCREEN 2
NumRecs = LOF(1) / LEN(eachline)
CALL thermo(100, 30, 360, 150, 7000)
```

```
END

SUB thermo (ht, wd, x, y, Max) STATIC
GrowIt = Max / 100
AddOne = 1
IF FirstTime = 0 THEN
  FirstTime = 1
  LINE (x - wd / 2, y) - STEP(wd, -ht), , B
  LOCATE 7, 43
  PRINT INT(NumRecs)
  LINE (x + wd, y - 2 * wd) - (x + wd, y - 2 * wd - ht), , ,
      &HF0F0
  LINE (350, 70) - (360, 60), , , &HF0F0
  LINE (370, 70) - (360, 60), , , &HF0F0
  CIRCLE (320, 150), 30, 2
END IF
counter = 1
DO UNTIL counter > NumRecs
   IF counter MOD GrowIt = 0 THEN
       LINE (305, 150) - STEP(30, -AddOne), , BF
       AddOne = AddOne + 1
   END IF
   counter = counter + 1
LOOP

END SUB
```

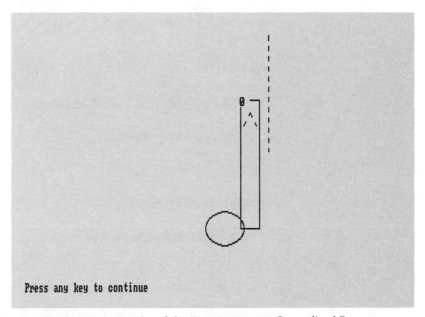

Figure 12.1 Results of the First Attempt at Generalized Progress
Thermometer

The results are not too good! But, then again, they are not really unexpected. Only one of the four LINE statements was changed from the original Chapter 11 program. The generalized SUB should use position coordinates for every LINE and CIRCLE statement; these should depend on the input parameter values ht, wt, x, and y. So, even though the first result is somewhat shocking, it's immediately apparent that the next step is to correct all the LINE statements and the CIRCLE statement. They must all depend on a user's specified location and size; the original fixed numbers won't do in a generalized program.

Correlate output symptoms to the statements that produce them.

The next thing to notice is the *0* that displays; we want the top of the thermometer to display the number of records in the sample data file (we know from Chapter 11 that there are over 7000 records). So, knowing this, you look at the CALL line in the main module:

```
CALL thermo(100, 30, 360, 150, 7000)
```

In this first test, 7000 was entered as the fifth argument. Why was 0 displayed? Because the SUB procedure erroneously prints NumRecs, not the fifth input parameter Max:

```
PRINT INT(NumRecs)
```

Within the SUB procedure, there is no variable known as NumRecs. Only variable names specified within the SUB itself, or in the parameter list, are known to the SUB. In addition, since the loop is controlled by NumRecs (which never changes from 0), the thermometer never fills. So, another problem has been resolved; this PRINT line should be changed to

```
PRINT INT(Max)
```

and the loop expression should be changed from

```
DO UNTIL counter > NumRecs
```

to

```
DO UNTIL counter > Max
```

Several changes later, we run the test program again, this time testing out the thermometer in a new position on the screen.

```
CALL thermo(150, 45, 160, 166, NumRecs)
```

This tests out a thermometer with height equal to 150 pixels, width equal to 45 pixels, and base location at (160, 166). NumRecs is calculated in the CALLing program as the exact number of records in the file, so it is now used properly as the fifth argument submitted to the SUB procedure. Any reference to this value in the SUB must be to the parameter name known to it (Max).

This time, as shown in Figure 12.2, the thermometer appears nearly correct. The number of records (7517) is printed at the top, the outline of the thermometer looks good, and the "liquid" level rises visually. If you impatiently concluded that you are done, you are wrong. With these program adjustments, the liquid height only rises to about two thirds of the entire thermometer's height, even after all the records are processed.

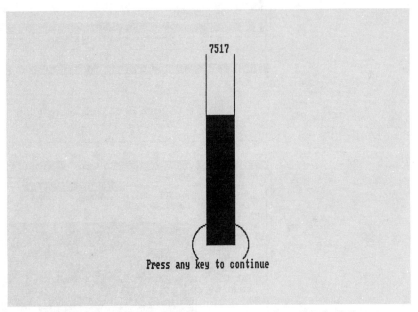

Figure 12.2 Subtle Logical Flaw in Liquid Level Calculation

In the QuickBASIC development environment, the message **Press any key to continue** appears when a program completes. As you can see, the liquid level in Figure 12.2 stopped well short of the correct height. It's time to use some of QuickBASIC's power debugging tools.

Figure 12.3 shows the Debug pulldown menu. In attempting to figure out this last logical error, we will try several things on this menu. First, we successively place the cursor on variable names *counter* and *AddOne* in SUB thermo. Then, we pull down this menu, and select Instant Watch. You can also use a shortcut key (Shift-F9) or a shortcut mouse press (Shift-right button); in either case, a dialog box like the one in Figure 12.4 appears. Selecting the ⟨*Add Watch*⟩ choice at the bottom of the dialog box causes each of those variables to be added to the Watch window (see Chapter 3).

Add Watch allows you to specify any simple variable name or complex QuickBASIC expression.

Instant Watch automatically shows you the current value of the expression the cursor happens to be on or highlighting. You can quickly add it to the Watch window by pressing Enter.

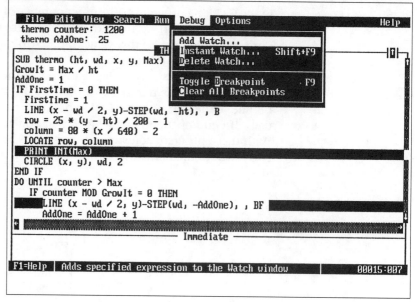

Figure 12.3 The Debug Pulldown Menu

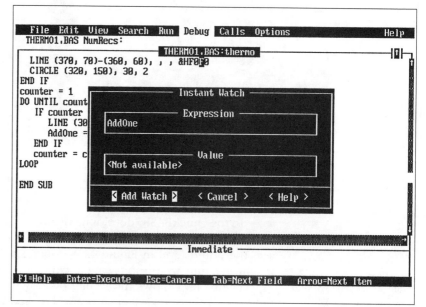

Figure 12.4 Using Watch Expressions and Breakpoints

As the program progresses, you can watch the changing values of these two variables. In order to stop the program at opportune times, then move the cursor to two separate statements in the procedure. First, select the PRINT INT(Max) line and choose *Toggle Breakpoint* on the Debug menu (or press F9). This highlights the line chosen as a breakpoint (see Figure 12.3). When this instruction executes, QuickBASIC will pause and allow you to look at the status of various expressions. Set another highlighted breakpoint at the LINE statement inside the loop.

At the point Figure 12.3 was captured, the loop had run through approximately one sixth of the file records (1200 out of 7517). This is consistent with the pixel height of the thermometer (150); the AddOne height of the liquid level is at 25 (one sixth of the total 150). So, adding further information about other variables to the Watch window leads to the realization that the *GrowIt* variable is not correct. Quickly, this leads to the first statement in the thermo procedure. Instead of the Max value being divided by a fixed 100 pixels (as it was in the stand-alone Chapter 11 program), it should be divided by the desired height of the thermometer, as in

```
GrowIt = Max / ht
```

The final SUB procedure appears in Listing 12.2 and can now be used by any program module you now write.

Pressing F8 after a breakpoint will cause your program to continue executing one statement at a time. Pressing F5 after a breakpoint will cause your program to continue executing at full speed up to the end of the program, or to the next breakpoint.

Listing 12.2 Completely Debugged SUB Thermo

```
SUB thermo (ht, wd, x, y, Max) STATIC
GrowIt = Max / ht
AddOne = 1
IF FirstTime = 0 THEN
  FirstTime = 1
  LINE (x - wd / 2, y) - STEP(wd, -ht), , B
  row = 25 * (y - ht) / 200 - 1
  column = 80 * (x / 640) - 2
  LOCATE row, column
  PRINT INT(Max)
  CIRCLE (x, y), wd, 2
END IF
DO UNTIL counter > Max
   IF counter MOD GrowIt = 0 THEN
      LINE (x - wd / 2, y) - STEP(wd, -AddOne), , BF
      AddOne = AddOne + 1
   END IF
   counter = counter + 1
LOOP

END SUB
```

As you debug, you can remove a Watch expression from the Watch window with the *Delete Watch* choice on the pulldown menu. Do this after you no longer need the expression displayed. (Only eight expressions can be shown in the Watch window.) You can also clear breakpoints with the *Clear All Breakpoints* choice. These debugging tools are useful when you are trying to figure out problems. As soon as you eliminate a potential problem, delete the watch or remove the breakpoints. They only serve to slow up your continued debugging efforts.

Running Your Debugged QuickBASIC Programs Under DOS

In Chapter 4, you studied the STYLE.BAS program, which analyzed any text file for word quantity and sentence quality. That demonstration program asked for the file name to be analyzed.

```
INPUT "Please enter file to analyze: "; file$
CLS
PRINT "Style Analysis for file: "; file$
OPEN file$ FOR INPUT AS #1
```

The rest of the program uses the *file$* you specify. Many programs work this way, interactively asking the user for information as it is needed. However, a user often knows both the questions to be asked and the answers to be given. Under DOS, some programs can be initiated with anticipated answers being provided as parameters along with the program name. For instance, it would be nice to simply be able to enter

```
STYLE c:\wp\chap12
```

at the DOS C⟩ prompt to obtain an analysis of this chapter you are now reading.

However, as it stands, you must first bring up the QuickBASIC development environment, then OPEN the STYLE.BAS program. Only then can you run the program, answering the question posed by the INPUT statement about the desired file name to analyze.

Two steps can be taken to shorten this overall process. First, the INPUT statement can be replaced with the following assignment statement:

```
file$ = COMMAND$
```

Use COMMAND$ in QuickBASIC to simulate DOS command line parameters.

The special COMMAND$ function obtains the parameter(s) entered on the DOS command line; in this example, the only anticipated parameter is the file name. Since it is directly assigned to the *file$* variable, it no longer must be INPUT after program execution begins. The INPUT command is useful for quick development and testing of a program within the QuickBASIC development environment. It is easiest if you use the COMMAND$ function only after developing, debugging, and finalizing the code for a program that can accept arguments at the DOS level such as this one.

Automate QuickBASIC programs with the /RUN switch.

QuickBASIC can be initiated with a number of special command switches, recognizable at the DOS command prompt. If you enter the following command to DOS:

```
QB /RUN STYLE /CMD c:\wp\chap12
```

you are asking DOS to bring up the QuickBASIC development environment. The /RUN switch then is passed to QuickBASIC and asks it to execute the STYLE.BAS program. The /CMD switch then passes the "c:\wp\chap12" string to the COMMAND$ function, which is used to initialize the value of the *file$* variable at the program's beginning.

This alternative has the advantage of minimizing the knowledge of QuickBASIC required in a user. However, it does still require that the entire QuickBASIC system be available on a user's system. Because of this, a powerful option is built into the QuickBASIC system: the choice on the RUN pulldown menu called ⟨*Make EXE File*⟩.

When you choose this option, you receive the dialog box seen in Figure 12.5. Press Enter, and the entire program in memory is compiled. This means that the program's QuickBASIC instructions are translated directly into machine instructions and stored in an independently executable .EXE file. Such a file can be invoked separately at any DOS command prompt. You can now simply enter

```
STYLE c:\wp\chap12
```

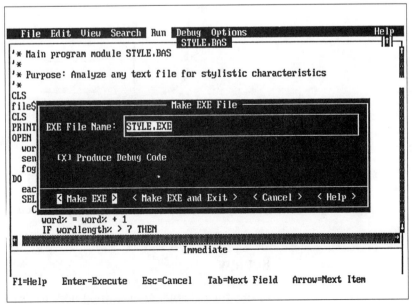

Figure 12.5 Compiling a Program in QuickBASIC

Compiled QuickBASIC programs require only that your system contain the run-time libraries BRUN45.LIB and BCOM45.LIB.

DOS passes control to the STYLE.EXE program, which accepts the first command line parameter `c:\wp\chap12` and passes it to the now independent, compiled QuickBASIC program. Although Quick-BASIC is no longer required, two run-time libraries (BRUN45.LIB and BCOM45.LIB) must be available on your system. If they are not in the current hard disk directory, or on the current QuickBASIC diskette, you will be asked to enter the complete path name to the directory (or diskette) that contains them.

Figure 12.6 summarizes the three execution possibilities just discussed. In this summary, Situation A is the standard situation seen throughout this book. You write, test, and run a program from within the QuickBASIC development environment. Situation B allows you to specify what QuickBASIC program to open and run at the same time that you direct DOS to run the QuickBASIC development environment. Situation C allows you to run a compiled program directly from DOS, requiring only two run-time libraries at most.

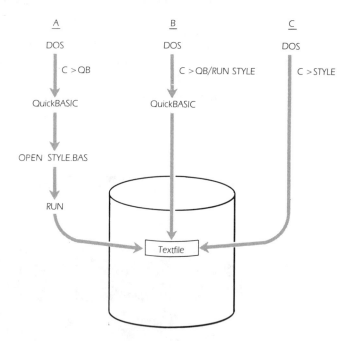

Figure 12.6 QuickBASIC Execution Alternatives

Review

In this final chapter, you learned how to test your programs properly. You also learned how to fix problems that arise, and how to successfully run fully debugged programs from a DOS command prompt. You learned the following key points:

1. Top-down testing is the most effective way of validating your program modules. Using simple and short modules called "stubs" enables you to test modules without having to write completely all procedures called by the modules.

2. Top-down testing has several benefits: it can be started before final design and coding are completed, it provides a prototype by which users can view the evolving system, and it allows major design flaws to be recognized early.

3. Test scripts and test files provide a thorough and methodical approach to testing your program logic.

4. Numerous general debugging techniques exist, including thinking, bug isolation, desk checking, colleague consulting, intermediate result checking, and data checking.

5. Subtle bugs are often discovered due to improper module interfaces, insufficient input validation, variable modification in procedures, and faulty end-of-loop or end-of-file logic.

6. The Debug menu provides a facility to watch the values of Quick-BASIC variables or expressions, as well as to pause the program on specified command lines called breakpoints.

7. Any QuickBASIC program can be compiled by using the ⟨*Make EXE File*⟩ choice on the Run pulldown menu. This enables you to run the program from a DOS command line, without having to have or to bring up the QuickBASIC development environment.

Quiz for Chapter 12

1. Testing your system in a modular fashion, beginning with the main menu module first, is called:

   a. Modular testing
   b. Top-down testing
   c. Bottom-up testing
   d. Stub testing

2. Incomplete subprogram modules that are used to enable testing to proceed quickly are best called:

   a. Stumps
   b. Stubs
   c. Modules
   d. Procedures

3. Which of the following is not a benefit of top-down testing?

   a. Testing before system completion
   b. Early design flaw discovery
   c. Feedback from system prototype
   d. Smaller test scripts and files

4. Which of the following is not part of a test script?

   a. An outline of expected tests
   b. Correct and incorrect data
   c. Logic listing for validations
   d. Data for limit conditions

5. Which of the following is a general debugging technique?

   a. Thinking
   b. Isolation
   c. Looking at intermediate values
   d. All of the above

6. Which of the following is not a general debugging technique?

   a. Desk checking
   b. Colleague checking
   c. Test data checking
   d. Design checking

7. Which of the following is not a subtle potential bug?

   a. Improper module interface
   b. Insufficient input validation
   c. Variable name spelling
   d. Faulty end-of-loop logic

8. Which pulldown menu contains debugging options?

    a. Run
    b. Debug
    c. Options
    d. File

9. Which is not a debugging option?

    a. Watch expression
    b. Breakpoint
    c. Instant watch
    d. View

10. Which feature pauses program execution during debugging?

    a. Pause
    b. SLEEP
    c. Breakpoint
    d. None of the above

11. What switch is used when invoking QuickBASIC from DOS to specify a program name to automatically open and run?

    a. Load
    b. Open
    c. Run
    d. Call

12. Compiling a program can be done with which of these Run menu choices?

    a. Compile a file
    b. Make EXE File
    c. Build EXE
    d. DOS Build

13. A stand-alone compiled QuickBASIC program requires which of the following run-time libraries?

    a. BCOM45.LIB
    b. BC.LIB
    c. LINK.LIB
    d. LIB.EXE

14. Which function key steps your program through execution, one statement at a time?

    a. F2
    b. F4
    c. F6
    d. F8

15. Which function key continues execution of your program up until the next breakpoint, or until the end of the program?

    a. F3
    b. F5
    c. F7
    d. F9

Appendix A | Glossary of General Terms

The first appendix is a glossary of general computer terms used in the DOS and QuickBASIC environments. Appendix B contains an explanation of all the QuickBASIC statements and functions, including the most advanced ones, and Appendix C describes the complete Full menu choices.

Absolute coordinates The distance in pixels on a screen in two directions, x and y, measured from left to right and from top to bottom. The upper left corner of a screen has an (x, y) position of (0, 0). Absolute and physical coordinates are the same. (*Compare* Logical coordinates.)

Address A specific memory location, or a specific track/sector disk location.

Algorithm A logical series of steps taken to solve a problem.

Animation 1) A graphic technique for making a screen figure appear to move. 2) A QuickBASIC debugging technique for highlighting each program line as it executes.

Argument A constant, variable, or expression that is provided to a QuickBASIC procedure. (*Compare* Parameter.)

Arithmetic conversion The process of changing the data format of a number (for example, from floating point to integer).

Array A homogenous set of data items, uniformly numbered.

Array bounds The maximum and minimum values for the numbering of the elements of an array.

ASCII American Standard Code for Information Interchange. A set of characters and special symbols agreed upon by convention.

Aspect ratio The width-to-height ratio for a display monitor.

Assignment The act of giving a value to a variable.

Attributes The characteristics of each display location on a video monitor, or of each printing position on a printer.

Automatic variable A temporary variable used by QuickBASIC procedures. Its value is not saved during recursive calls.

Base name The primary portion of a file's name. It includes up to eight characters located to the left of the period.

Batch A group of DOS commands or programs to run.

Binary A numerical system allowing only two values, 0 or 1.

Binary file A file containing ASCII control codes, as well as standard printing characters.

Block A group of QuickBASIC statements or declarations.

Breakpoint A program line at which your program will pause.

Byte The fundamental storage item, consisting of eight computer bits (0's or 1's), and containing the numerical code for an ASCII character or code.

Call by reference To pass an argument's address to a procedure, so that the original argument's value can be directly modified by the procedure.

Call by value To pass only the value of an argument to a procedure. A temporary storage location is used by the procedure for purposes of working with this copied value.

CGA Color Graphics Adapter. A video board that displays text, graphics, and color. Usually used for 25 x 80 text displays, or for color graphics containing a resolution of a maximum of 640 x 200 pixels.

Character string A contiguous series of ASCII characters.

Check box A QuickBASIC option on a screen that can have two values: *on* or *off*. The "box" is a pair of square brackets that contain an *x* if the option is currently set on.

Click To press and release a mouse button.

Clipboard A memory area containing the most recently cut or copied text.

Command button A selectable portion of a dialog box used to confirm (⟨*OK*⟩), escape (⟨*Cancel*⟩), or obtain context-sensitive help (⟨*Help*⟩).

Compilation The translation of QuickBASIC program lines into a binary form of executable instructions that can be understood directly by the hardware.

Compiler A program that translates English language QuickBASIC instructions into executable machine language instructions.

Compound statement A QuickBASIC statement requiring more than one line.

Constant An unchanging value.

Context-sensitive Relating to the currently highlighted screen item.

Current directory The first directory that QuickBASIC uses to search for files, and the directory used to store new programs which are written.

Current drive The default disk used for all input and output.

Cursor The blinking line or solid box which indicates the next screen location where typed characters will appear.

Data Information used by a program while running.

Data file A named area on a disk which contains a related set of numbers and/or text data.

Debugging The process of determining the location and nature of a program malfunction.

Declaration The act of assigning a type of data to a variable or procedure name.

Default The assumed value, unless otherwise set, for a variable or a QuickBASIC setting.

Development environment The complete set of QuickBASIC menus and windows in which you write, test, debug, and run your programs.

Device A specific piece of computing machinery, usually with a well-defined task, such as a plotter or a printer.

Dialog box An on-screen window that shows information and solicits additional data entry or option selection.

Dimension The number of subscripts in an array.

Directory The name given to a group of files on a disk.

Document Any text file in QuickBASIC that is not treated as a program file when loaded. All of QuickBASIC's Smart Editor features are turned off for document editing.

Double click To press a mouse button twice in rapid succession.

Double precision A high precision representation of numerical data, occupying eight bytes.

Drag To move an object on the screen by selecting it with a mouse, then moving the mouse while keeping button one depressed.

Dynamic array An array which is assigned actual memory locations only when the program that uses it actually runs.

EGA Enhanced Graphics Adapter. A video board that displays text, graphics, and color. Usually used for 25 x 80 text displays, or for color graphics using the common 640 x 350 resolution (although more highly resolved video modes are possible). Both text and graphics are typically higher resolution than its historical predecessor, the CGA.

Enabled event An event that is actively tested for with an ON *event* statement.

Escape sequences Control codes sent to a device. The first code is usually an ASCII 27 character, the ESC character.

Event An occurrence, such as a keyboard choice or mouse selection.

Executable file A compiled QuickBASIC program that can be run at a DOS command prompt simply by typing the file name.

Execute To run a program, or to run a statement in the QuickBASIC Immediate window.

Expression A combination of variables, constants, and QuickBASIC operators that can be evaluated to a single value.

Field A single data item; one element in a record.

Free form A type of data entry using field separators. Fields can be of variable size.

Function A type of QuickBASIC procedure that executes a series of instructions, usually resulting in one value.

Global Available throughout a program and its support modules.

Highlighting A video display in which the usual relationship of the colors is reversed, signifying that a command, choice, or textual portion has been selected for the next QuickBASIC operation.

Hyperlink A selectable, triangle-bracketed, text portion of a help screen that produces a new display of textual information.

IEEE Institute of Electrical and Electronics Engineers. QuickBASIC supports a special standard format defined by the IEEE that produces more accurate arithmetical operations.

Immediate window The lowest visible window in the QuickBASIC development environment screen. Statements entered in this window are executed when the Enter key is pressed.

Include file A file of QuickBASIC instructions that can be added into any program during compilation by using the $INCLUDE metacommand.

Indentation level On the screen, the width of the left margin beside instructions that are nested within a compound QuickBASIC statement, such as an IF or a DO statement.

Infinite loop An unending repetition of QuickBASIC statements.

Input focus The portion of the screen that processes the next key or the next mouse button pressed.

Insert mode A mode of text entry in which newly typed characters slip into existing text without replacing any portion of it. (*Compare* Overtype mode.)

Integer A whole number falling within the range −32,768 to +32,767.

Interactive Involving a dialog between program and user.

Interpreter A program that translates and runs each program statement as it is read.

Keyword Any one of the special names reserved for statements, operators, or functions.

Label The name of a defined location in a QuickBASIC program.

Library A .LIB file that contains compiled object files.

Linking The process of connecting references in a QuickBASIC program to all referenced variables, modules, and library routines.

List box A window containing a series of items requiring selection.

Local Limited in scope to a module or a block of code.

Logical coordinates An x, y pair of values that defines screen locations for graphic plotting. Programs often use logical coordinates that are then translated into absolute coordinates which vary according to the display adapter and video monitor. (*Compare* Absolute coordinates, Physical coordinates.)

Long integer A whole number requiring four bytes of storage (rather than the two used by a standard integer), and having a range of approximately −2 billion to +2 billion.

Main module The block of code that contains the first program statement to execute.

Menu bar The line at the top of the QuickBASIC development environment screen that contains the main menu action possibilities (the titles of the pulldown menus).

Metacommands Special instructions to the compiler that direct the compilation process itself, rather than the statements contained in the program which direct the execution of the program.

Modular programming A system of programming that relies upon defining separate but related groups of code, each designed to perform a specific task.

Module A collection of QuickBASIC statements serving a specific purpose and stored in a separate DOS file.

Module-level code Any program statements contained inside a QuickBASIC module but not contained inside a SUB or FUNCTION module.

Mouse A hand-held pointing device that moves on a flat surface. Its representation on screen (the mouse pointer) is used to select and control screen items.

Mouse pointer Also called *mouse cursor*. A reverse video rectangle that appears on screen when a mouse has been installed and that represents the current mouse position.

Mutually exclusive Non-overlapping.

Object file The intermediate file of translated code produced by a compiler. It contains relocatable code that can be linked later with other translated code to form an executable .EXE file.

Operand A variable value or constant that is acted upon by an operator in a QuickBASIC expression.

Operator A symbol (or symbols) used to indicate which arithmetic or logical operations are to be performed on an expression's operands.

Output screen The monitor display showing the results of running a program from within the QuickBASIC development environment.

Overtype mode A mode of text entry in which newly typed characters replace existing characters at the point of the cursor. (*Compare* Insert mode.)

Parameter The name of the place-holding variable used for SUB and FUNCTION procedures. (*Compare* Argument.)

Path The list of directories that DOS will search to find executable (.COM, .EXE, and .BAT) files.

Parsing The process of the character-by-character scanning of a program by a language such as QuickBASIC.

Physical coordinates The actual pixel coordinates, or absolute coordinates, on the screen. The upper left corner of the screen has an x, y location of (0, 0). (*Compare* Logical coordinates.)

Pixel Each individual dot of light on a video monitor.

Place marker One of up to four lines (numbered 0 to 3) in your program which can be immediately made into the current line by entering Ctrl-Q-n (n = 0 to 3).

Precedence The order in which multiple program operators are evaluated in an expression.

Procedure A generic term for a FUNCTION or SUB subprogram.

Program A combination of QuickBASIC statements, subprograms, and other modules that form an executable set of instructions.

Program stepping Highlighting and executing one instruction at a time.

Pulldown menu A vertical list of QuickBASIC command choices that appears just below an entry on the main menu bar when that entry has been selected.

QB Advisor The on-line system program which provides context-sensitive help.

Quick library A collection of independently defined QuickBASIC procedures.

Random access file A file whose records can be read in any order.

Record A collection of uniquely named data items (fields) stored together in a file.

Recursion The technique of having a program calling itself during execution.

Reference bar The bottom line of the QuickBASIC development environment screen listing active key assignments and brief information about the results of the next keypress.

Reserved words Individual names reserved by QuickBASIC and DOS for commands and language operations.

Run To execute a program.

Scope The range of statements and modules over which an argument or parameter is defined.

Scroll bars Vertical and horizontal bars appearing on the right side and bottom, respectively, of a screen window. They enable you to scroll the window text.

Scrolling Bringing a portion of your file that is not currently visible in a screen window up or down or across so that it is visible.

Search and replace An editing feature that allows you to replace any specified string of characters in your module with a second string of characters.

Selection cursor The extended highlighting that delineates text which is to be cut or copied in the next specified QuickBASIC operation.

Semantics The logical meaning of a statement, rather than the grammatical structure of the statement. (*Compare* Syntax.)

Simple variable A string, numerical, or user-defined type of non-array data.

Single precision Floating point accuracy of numerical data to four bytes, or seven decimal places.

Smart Editor The on-line program editor in the QuickBASIC development environment that incorporates automatic capitalization of keywords and syntax checking.

Source file A file containing QuickBASIC program statements.

Statement A QuickBASIC instruction, either single-line or multiline in nature.

Static array An array with memory allocated at the time of compilation.

String A constant series of characters, or a variable containing a series of characters.

Subprogram A separately defined group of QuickBASIC instructions (either a SUB or FUNCTION procedure) that can be invoked during program execution from other QuickBASIC instructions.

Subroutine A block of BASIC code that can be invoked from other statements. It is more limited in nature than QuickBASIC's newer subprogram types.

Subscript An integer specifying which array element is to be accessed.

Symbol A named memory location.

Syntax The grammatical requirements, or rules, for constructing a QuickBASIC statement. (*Compare* Semantics.)

Text box A small data entry window presented within a dialog box.

Tiling The process of designing a graphic pattern with the PAINT command for the purpose of filling in a screen figure.

Title bar The top line of a screen window, which displays the name of the window.

Toggle A selectable screen choice, or an assigned function key, that switches the value of a system option between on and off.

Trapping The detection of an event occurrence. Trapping usually includes a programmed response to the event.

Type The assumed or defined nature of a numerical variable.

Type checking A compiler feature that ensures that procedure call argument types are correct, or that an operator's operands are correct.

User-defined type A complex data structure containing multiple numerical and/or string variables. This kind of record is defined with a QuickBASIC TYPE statement.

Variable A named memory location whose value can change during a program's execution.

VGA Video Graphics Array. A very high resolution text, graphic, and color display that uses square pixels.

View window The primary screen window in which program text editing occurs.

Watch window A debugging window that can display the values of expressions and variables during program execution.

Watchpoint A program expression that is constantly evaluated during program execution. Execution pauses when the expression becomes true.

Window A rectangular portion of the screen.

B | QuickBASIC Statements and Functions

This appendix offers concise descriptions of and syntax for each statement and function found in QuickBASIC 4.5. The descriptions give more than merely syntax and an objective definition of purpose, however. They explain the *best usage* of each command and include explanations of each parameter and other parts of the command.

ABS Function

Best Command Usage
Calculating the absolute value of a numerical expression.

Syntax
ABS(numerical-expression)

ASC Function

Best Command Usage
Obtaining the ASCII code for the first character in a string expression.

Syntax
ASC(stringexpression)

ATN Function

Best Command Usage

Obtaining the arctangent of a numerical expression.

Syntax

ATN(numerical-expression)

BEEP Statement

Best Command Usage

Sounding an alarm during program operation.

Syntax

BEEP

BLOAD Statement

Best Command Usage

Rapidly reloading a byte-for-byte memory image previously saved with a BSAVE command.

Syntax

BLOAD filespec[,offset]

filespec: string expression naming the source file or device for the memory image.

offset: memory address in the data segment at which to begin loading this image file.

BSAVE Statement

Best Command Usage

Storing a memory image of data or programs. This statement allows rapid restoration of a program state or a screen image during later program execution.

Syntax

BSAVE filespec,offset,length

filespec: string expression naming the destination file or device for the memory image.

offset: memory address offset in the data segment at which to begin copying bytes into the destination image file.

length: number of bytes to copy.

CALL Statement

Best Command Usage

Transferring control to another procedure, either in QuickBASIC (in which case the procedure would be a SUB) or in another programming language. CALL facilitates structured, modular program design (See Chapter 10).

Syntax

[CALL] name[(argumentlist)]

name: name of the SUB or alternate programming language procedure.

argumentlist: the parameter names or values passed to the SUB.

Other CALL Statements

CALL INT86OLD

This statement allows earlier QuickBASIC programs to make DOS system service calls.

CALL ABSOLUTE

This statement allows QuickBASIC programs to call machine language procedures.

CALL INTERRUPT

This statement allows newer QuickBASIC programs to make DOS system service calls.

CDBL Function

Best Command Usage

Converting a numerical expression to double precision. Used to increase accuracy when the final calculated result is to be in double precision.

Syntax

CDBL(numerical-expression)

CHAIN Statement

Best Command Usage

Irrevocably transferring control to another program. It is not advisable to use this statement because it does not lend itself readily to well-structured code development.

Syntax

CHAIN filespec

filespec: string expression naming the program that is to receive continuing execution control.

CHDIR Statement

Best Command Usage

Changing the current DOS directory for the specified drive.

Syntax

CHDIR pathspec

pathspec: string expression specifying drive and directory name.

CHR$ Function

Best Command Usage
Converting ASCII codes to characters.

Syntax
CHR$(code)
code: ASCII value between 0 and 255.

CINT Function

Best Command Usage
Converting more complex integer expressions to simple integers. CINT is used to simplify arithmetic calculations. Rounding, as opposed to truncation, is used.

Syntax
CINT(numerical-expression)

CIRCLE Statement

Best Command Usage
Drawing complete circles or ellipses. Also, drawing such figures with wedges removed for graphic presentations in business applications.

Syntax
CIRCLE [STEP]
        (x, y),radius[,[color][,[start][,[end][,aspect]]]]
(x, y): actual screen coordinates of the center.
radius: numerical value for geometric radius or elliptical axis.
STEP: indicates that the *x* and *y* values are relative offsets from the current cursor position.
start/end: angles for arc drawing.
color: screen color attribute.
aspect: screen width to height ratio.

CLEAR Statement

Best Command Usage
This is a quick and complete way to reset all program variables, to close all open files, and to set the stack size.

Syntax
CLEAR [,,stack]
stack: number of bytes to set aside for your program's stack. The extra commas are required for compatibility with BASICA.

CLNG Function

Best Command Usage
Converting any numerical expression to a 4-byte (long) integer. CLNG uses the technique of rounding.

Syntax
CLNG(numerical-expression)

CLOSE Statement

Best Command Usage
Formally sending an end-of-file code when no more data is to be written to a file. This statement also releases all associated system file buffer space.

Syntax
CLOSE [#filenumber[,# filenumber] . . .]
filenumber: numerical ID of an open file. If no file numbers are entered, QuickBASIC closes all open files and devices.

CLS Statement

Best Command Usage
Clearing the screen just prior to displaying any new and logically distinct group of output data.

Syntax
CLS [{0 ¦ 1 ¦ 2}]
0: clears all text and graphics.
1: clears all active graphics.
2: clears only text.
No arguments: clears either graphics only or text only, depending on the prior VIEW statement.

COLOR Statement

Best Command Usage
Selecting foreground, background, and border colors. Use a limited number of variations to call attention to portions of your output. Different colors can be assigned to separate logical groups of data, separate functional areas of the screen, and to cases of data output that are exceptions.

Syntax
SCREEN mode 0:
COLOR [foreground][,[background][,border]]
foreground: text color (0-31 non-blinking, 16-31 blinking).
background: screen color (0-7).
border: color of the screen's edge (0-15).

SCREEN mode 1:
COLOR [background][,palette]
background: screen color (0-15).
palette: 0 = green, red, and brown.
1 = cyan, magenta, and bright white.
SCREEN modes 7-10:
COLOR [foreground][,background]
foreground: line-drawing color (0-15, except in Mode 10).
background: screen color (variable ranges).
SCREEN modes 11-13:
COLOR [foreground]
foreground: line-drawing color (variable ranges).

COM(n) Statement

Best Command Usage
Turning on, turning off, or pausing the processing of interrupts from a serial communications port.

Syntax
COM(n) ON
COM(n) OFF
COM(n) STOP
n: serial port number (1 or 2).

COMMAND$ Function

Best Command Usage
Enabling your program to parse (analyze) the parameters typed in at the DOS command line when the program was run. This function also is used during development to simulate DOS parameters when the program is actually run from the development environment. (*See* Run menu.)

Syntax
COMMAND$

COMMON Statement

Best Command Usage
This is an old-style programming technique for sharing variables between different code modules. It is not recommended for effective structured programming, because it lends itself too readily to subtle effects caused by interaction of modules.

Syntax
COMMON [SHARED][/blockname/] variablelist
variablelist: names of variables to be made available across different code modules.
SHARED and */blockname/:* support naming of a block of variables.

CONST Statement

Best Command Usage

Defining a program constant value as a symbol name. This statement makes later program changes to the constant a considerably easier task; only the CONST statement needs to be changed, not the multiple references to the constant located throughout the code.

Syntax

CONST constantname = expression [,constantname = expression] . . .
constantname: any legitimate BASIC variable.
expression: any legitimate combination of arithmetic or logical operators and operands, except for exponentiation.

COS Function

Best Command Usage

Obtaining the geometric cosine of an angle.

Syntax

COS(numerical-expression)
numerical-expression: any expression which evaluates to the desired angle, given in radians.

CSNG Function

Best Command Usage

Converting numerical expressions to single precision values.

Syntax

CSNG(numerical-expression)

CSRLIN Function

Best Command Usage

Obtaining the current line (row) position of the cursor during program operation.

Syntax

CSRLIN

CVDMBF *See* CVSMBF.

CVI, CVS, CVL, CVD Function

Best Command Usage

Converting strings which contain numerical values to numbers.

Syntax

CVI(2-byte-string)
CVS(4-byte-string)
CVL(4-byte-string)
CVD(8-byte-string)

CVSMBF, CVDMBF Function

Best Command Usage

Converting strings that contain Microsoft binary format numbers to IEEE-format numbers.

Syntax

CVSMBF(4-byte-string)
CVDMBF(8-byte-string)

DATA Statement

Best Command Usage

Defining a series of known numerical and string constants to be used during program execution by READ statements.

Syntax

DATA constant[,constant] . . .
constant: any legal numerical or string value.

DATE$ Statement/Function

Best Command Usage

As a statement, setting the current date. As a function, obtaining the current date.

Syntax

DATE$ [= stringexpression]
stringexpression: used when setting the current date in a Quick-BASIC statement. Must be *mm-dd-yy, mm-dd-yyyy, mm/dd/yy,* or *mm/dd/yyyy,* where *mm* and *dd* are the month and day, and *yy* or *yyyy* is the year.

DECLARE Statement

Best Command Usage

Informing QuickBASIC that your program will invoke SUB procedures without a CALL keyword. It also tells QuickBASIC that your program may invoke FUNCTION procedures defined in another module, or non-QuickBASIC procedures written in other programming languages. Most importantly, it requests the compiler to check both the number and type of parameters used when procedures are invoked.

Syntax

DECLARE {FUNCTION ¦ SUB} name [([parameterlist])]
name: name of the procedure.
parameterlist: specifies both the number and type of parameters
required to invoke the procedure.

DEF FN Statement

Best Command Usage

None. Avoid this construction. Instead, use the FUNCTION statement in
QuickBASIC 4.5. DEF FN should be retained only when needed for
compatibility with earlier BASIC versions.

Syntax

As a single-line statement:
DEF FNname[(parameterlist)] = expression
As a block statement:
DEF FNname[(parameterlist)]
[statements]
FNname = expression
[statements]
END DEF

DEF SEG Statement

Best Command Usage

Setting the current segment address for the program's later use of the
PEEK function or the BLOAD, BSAVE, CALL ABSOLUTE, or POKE statements.

Syntax

DEF SEG [= address]
address: beginning segment address (0-65,535). If no address is
specified, then the BASIC data segment is used.

DEFtype Statement

Best Command Usage

Setting default data type for variables, DEF FN functions, and FUNC-
TION procedures. Facilitates easy determination of variable type by visual inspection.

Syntax

DEFINT   letterrange [,letterrange] . . .
DEFSNG   letterrange [,letterrange] . . .
DEFDBL   letterrange [,letterrange] . . .
DEFLNG   letterrange [,letterrange] . . .
DEFSTR   letterrange [,letterrange] . . .

letterrange: letter1[-letter2] The last three letters of the keyword (INT, SNG, DBL, LNG, or STR) specify the data type.

DIM Statement

Best Command Usage
Allocating space for a named array of data. DIM is necessary for multidimensional, variable-range arrays. Using the upper and lower bounds feature enables your program to use familiar values and reduces debugging effort.

Syntax
DIM [SHARED] variable[(subscripts)] [AS type]
      [,variable[(subscripts)] [AS type] . . .
variable: any BASIC data name.
SHARED: allows all procedures in this module to access this variable.
subscripts: specifies the dimensions (lower TO upper).
AS *type:* declares the data type of the array elements.

DO . . . LOOP Statement

Best Command Usage
Repeating a group of QuickBASIC statements while or until a logical expression is true. This statement is used to control the execution of a series of similar steps, usually with one or only a few minor changes during each execution sequence. This is the preferred QuickBASIC looping construction, because it allows for testing of the controlling expression either at the beginning or at the end of the loop.

Syntax
    DO [{WHILE ¦ UNTIL} booleanexpression]
      [statements]
      LOOP
or
    DO
      [statements]
      LOOP [{WHILE ¦ UNTIL} booleanexpression]
booleanexpression: logical expression that evaluates to true or false.
statements: any number of single or multiline QuickBASIC statements.

DRAW Statement

Best Command Usage
Creating and drawing graphic objects for a special purpose. Use the macro language capabilities of this command to control image definition, as well as color, angle, and scaling.

Syntax

DRAW stringexpression
stringexpression: series of macro drawing commands.

END Statement

Best Command Usage

Specifying the physical end of a BASIC program, procedure, or block.

Syntax

END [{DEF ¦ FUNCTION ¦ IF ¦ SELECT ¦ SUB ¦ TYPE}]

ENVIRON$ Statement/Function

Best Command Usage

As a statement, creating or updating a DOS environmental variable's contents. As a function, obtaining the contents of a DOS environmental string variable.

Syntax

As a statement:
ENVIRON "EnvironVarName = text"
As a function:
ENVIRON$(environmentstring)
ENVIRON$(n)
environmentstring: name of the desired environment string.
n: relative number of the desired string from the DOS environment list of string entries.

EOF Function

Best Command Usage

Testing for end-of-file condition during sequential file record processing. EOF maintains control when all individual records have been processed. It has a value of true or false.

Syntax

EOF(filenumber)
filenumber: ID number of an open file.

ERASE Statement

Best Command Usage

Resetting to blanks or zeroes the elements of static arrays. It also deallocates the storage assigned to dynamic arrays.

Syntax

ERASE arrayname [,arrayname] . . .
arrayname: name of the array.

ERDEV, ERDEV$ Function

Best Command Usage
Determining the error code (ERDEV) or the device name (ERDEV$) of a
device reporting an error.

Syntax
    ERDEV
    ERDEV$

ERL, ERR Function

Best Command Usage
Rapid debugging support by specifying the line number containing the
error (ERL) and the QuickBASIC error code (ERR).

Syntax
    ERR
    ERL

ERROR Statement

Best Command Usage
Obtaining the QuickBASIC error message associated with an error code.
ERROR also can be used to generate your own unique set of new error
codes.

Syntax
    ERROR integerexpression
    integerexpression: 1-255, returns error message.
                    〉255, creates new error code.

EXIT Statement

Best Command Usage
Providing immediate termination of the processing of a loop or procedure.

Syntax
    EXIT {DEF | DO | FOR | FUNCTION | SUB}

EXP Function

Best Command Usage
Calculating the exponential power value (*e* raised to the power specified
in the single argument).

Syntax
    EXP(numerical-expression)
    numerical-expression: The power (< 88.02969) to which to raise *e*.

FIELD Statement

Best Command Usage
Providing space for variables in a random access file buffer. However, you should avoid this technique in favor of a user-defined record type of structure.

Syntax
FIELD #filenumber, fieldwidth AS stringvariable
[,fieldwidth AS stringvariable] . . .
filenumber: number of an open file.
fieldwidth: number of bytes in the field.
stringvariable: name of the program variable.

FILEATTR Function

Best Command Usage
Determining the DOS file handle or the file usage mode (input, output, random, append, or binary).

Syntax
FILEATTR(filenumber,attribute)
filenumber: number of an open file.
attribute: indicates whether to return mode (1) or handle (2) information.

FILES Statement

Best Command Usage
Displaying the names of files residing on the specified drive/directory.

Syntax
FILES [filespec]
filespec: string variable or constant specifying a full DOS path name. If no parameter is specified, files in the current directory are shown.

FIX Function

Best Command Usage
Correctly returning the integer portion of a numerical expression when the expression has a negative value. This function fixes the internal processing error experienced by the INT function.

Syntax
FIX(numerical-expression)

FOR . . . NEXT Statement

Best Command Usage

Repeating a group of statements a known number of times. This is sometimes called a 'counting' loop.

Syntax

```
FOR  counter = start TO end [STEP increment]
    [statements]
NEXT counter
```

counter: variable used to keep track of the repetitions.
start/end: initial and final values of the counter variable.
increment: amount by which to increment the counter variable each time the loop is executed.

FRE Function

Best Command Usage

Obtaining the amount of available system memory.

Syntax

```
FRE(stringexpression)
FRE(numerical-expression)
```

stringexpression: a string type that requests memory compaction. FRE returns with total free space.
numerical-expression: requests maximum non-string dimensioning space (-1), remaining unused stack space (-2), or the next free string storage area.

FREEFILE Function

Best Command Usage

Obtaining the next valid yet unused file number. FREEFILE should be used by independently written procedures to minimize the possibility that subprograms might accidentally open files already in use.

Syntax

```
FREEFILE
```

FUNCTION . . . END FUNCTION Statement

Best Command Usage

Defining the name, parameters, and code that make up the body of a FUNCTION procedure. This statement should be used for repetitive blocks of code that result in a single value.

Syntax

```
FUNCTION  name [(parameterlist)][STATIC]
    [statements]
```

        name = expression
            [statements]
        END FUNCTION
name: name of this block of code.
(parameterlist): input parameters to the function.
expression: value returned by the function.
STATIC: retains local variable storage.

GET Statement

Best Command Usage
Performing random access retrieval from a disk file. Also, GET is a command to store a graphic screen image into an array for later redisplay with the PUT command.

Syntax
For random access retrieval:
        GET #filenumber[,[recordnumber][,variable]]
        filenumber: number of an open file.
        recordnumber: record number (for random access files) or beginning byte number (for binary mode files).
For storing graphic images:
        GET [STEP](x1, y1) − [STEP](x2, y2),arrayname[indices]
        x1, y1 − x2, y2: diagonally opposite screen coordinates of the rectangle spanning the portion of the screen to save.
        STEP: indicates that *x* and *y* are relative to the last point plotted.

GOSUB . . . RETURN Statement

Best Command Usage
None. Avoid this old-style construction in favor of QuickBASIC 4.5's newer SUB and FUNCTION procedures.

Syntax
        GOSUB {linelabel1 ¦ linenumber1}
            [statements]Block
            RETURN [linelabel2 ¦ linenumber2]
        linelabel1/linenumber1: label or number of the first line of the subroutine.
        linelabel2/linenumber2: label or number of the line number at which to return execution.

GOTO Statement

Best Command Usage
None. Avoid this statement completely, in favor of more structured code.

Syntax

GOTO {linelabel | linenumber}
linelabel/linenumber: label or line number of the line in the current procedure or subroutine to execute next.

HEX$ Function

Best Command Usage

Obtaining the hexadecimal string equivalent of a decimal expression.

Syntax

HEX$(expression)
expression: decimal numerical expression.

IF . . . THEN . . . ELSE Statement

Best Command Usage

Implementing simple decision making in your programs. *Important:* use only block IF . . . THEN . . . ELSE statements. Single-line, they are terribly hard to read and debug—avoid them like the plague!

Syntax

IF booleanexpression1 THEN
    [statementblock-1]
[ELSEIF booleanexpression2 THEN
    [statementblock-2] . . . ELSE
    [statementblock-n]]
END IF
booleanexpression: any logical expression evaluating to true or false.
statementblock: legal QuickBASIC statements.

INKEY$ Function

Best Command Usage

Obtaining a code representing the key pressed at the keyboard. This function typically is used for menu and list selection, using special purpose keys.

Syntax

INKEY$

INP Function

Best Command Usage

Making decisions in programs based on data read in from a communications port.

Syntax

INP(port)

port: port ID number.

INPUT Statement

Best Command Usage

Enabling program prompting for user input, and subsequent reading of data values from the keyboard.

Syntax

INPUT [;] ["promptstring"{; ¦ ,}]variablelist

variablelist: names of variables to receive the data typed in by the user.

promptstring: displays a message of your choosing to the user.

; (after "INPUT": keeps the cursor on the same line.

; (after "prompstring"): prints a question mark at the end of the prompting message.

INPUT$ Function

Best Command Usage

Assigning to variables the values found in a disk file or other sequential device.

Syntax

INPUT$(n[,#filenumber])

n: number of bytes to read from the file (if file number is used), or from the DOS standard input device.

INSTR Function

Best Command Usage

Locating the position in one string that matches another specified string.

Syntax

INSTR([start,]stringexpression1,stringexpression2)

stringexpression1: string to be searched.

stringexpression2: string to match.

start: optional character position at which to begin the matching search.

INT Function

Best Command Usage

Truncating a numerical expression and returning the integer portion.

Syntax

INT(numerical-expression)

IOCTL, IOCTL$ Statement/Function

Best Command Usage

Sending or receiving control information to or from a device driver.

Syntax

As a function:

IOCTL$(#filenumber)

filenumber: number of an open device.

As a statement:

IOCTL #filenumber, string

filenumber: number of an open device.

string: control code string to be sent.

KEY[(n)] Statement

Best Command Usage

Customizing your function keys to your application program's needs.

Syntax

KEY LIST

This statement displays current values on the screen.

KEY {ON ¦ OFF}

This statement turns on or off the truncated bottom line soft-key display.

KEY(n) {ON ¦ OFF ¦ STOP}

This statement turns on, turns off, or buffers the trapping of special keypresses.

KEY n,stringexpression

This statement assigns soft-key string values.

n: number of a specific key.

stringexpression: the characters transmitted to your program whenever an assigned soft-key has been pressed.

KILL Statement

Best Command Usage

Deletes a DOS disk file.

Syntax

KILL filespec

filespec: identifies the file to erase.

LBOUND Function

Best Command Usage
Obtaining the lowest possible subscript value for one of the dimensions of an array.

Syntax
LBOUND(array[,dimension])
array: name of the array.
dimension: number of the array dimension.

LCASE$ Function

Best Command Usage
Converting a string expression to lower case.

Syntax
LCASE$(stringexpression)
stringexpression: any string constant or variable.

LEFT$ Function

Best Command Usage
Obtaining the leftmost substring in a string expression.

Syntax
LEFT$(stringexpression,n)
stringexpression: the original string expression.
n: number of characters, beginning with position 1, to return.

LEN Function

Best Command Usage
Obtaining the length of a string. LEN also obtains the number of bytes required by a QuickBASIC variable.

Syntax
LEN(stringexpression)
LEN(variable)
stringexpression: the subject string.
variable: the subject variable name.

LET Statement

Best Command Usage
Assigning a value to a variable.

Syntax
[LET] variable = expression

LINE Statement

Best Command Usage
Drawing a line or a rectangle on the screen; also, for input.

Syntax
For drawing:

    LINE [STEP] (x1, y1)] − [STEP] (x2, y2)

                [,[color][,[B[F]][,style]]]

(x2, y2): coordinates of the end of the line.

(x1, y1): coordinates of the start of the line.

STEP: specifies that the screen coordinates are relative.

color, B, BF, and *style:* these control color and styling.

For input:

    LINE INPUT # [;]["promptstring";]stringvariable

The above statement reads an entire line of input from the keyboard into *stringvariable.* If # is specified, the line is read from a sequential file.

LOC Function

Best Command Usage
Obtaining the current byte position within a file. LOC also obtains the number of characters waiting to be read from an input queue.

Syntax

    LOC(filenumber)

filenumber: number of an open file or device.

LOCATE Statement

Best Command Usage
Repositioning the screen cursor.

Syntax

    LOCATE [row][,[column][,[cursor][,[start,stop]]]]

row/column: these tell where to position the cursor.

Cursor/start/stop: these specify the visibility and shape of the cursor.

LOCK . . . UNLOCK Statement

Best Command Usage
Controlling multiuser network access to files under DOS 3.1 and later.

Syntax

    LOCK #filenumber [,{record ¦[start] TO end}]

      [statements]

    UNLOCK #filenumber [,{record ¦ [start] TO end}]

filenumber: number of an open file.
record/start/end: range of records or bytes to be locked.

LOF Function

Best Command Usage
Obtaining the length of a file in bytes.

Syntax
LOF(filenumber)
filenumber: number of an open file.

LOG Function

Best Command Usage
Obtaining the natural logarithm of a numerical expression.

Syntax
LOG(numerical-expression)
numerical-expression: a positive value.

LPOS Function

Best Command Usage
Obtaining the current position of the line printer's print head.

Syntax
LPOS(n)
n: printer port number.

LPRINT, LPRINT USING Statement

Best Command Usage
Standard printing to the LPT1 printer.

Syntax
LPRINT [expressionlist][{; ¦ ,}] LPRINT USING formatstring; expressionlist[{; ¦ ,}]
expressionlist: variables or expressions to print.
formatstring: string literal or variable specifying a special format to use for outputting data.

LSET Statement

Best Command Usage
Left-justifying string data for output purposes.

Syntax
LSET {stringvariable = stringexpression}

stringvariable: any string variable.

stringexpression: value assigned to stringvariable after leading space characters have been removed.

LTRIM$ Function

Best Command Usage
Immediately removing leading spaces.

Syntax
LTRIM$(stringexpression)

MID$ Statement/Function

Best Command Usage
As a function, obtaining a substring of a larger string. As a statement, replacing a substring of a string with a new substring.

Syntax
MID$(stringvariable,start[,length]) [= stringexpression]
stringvariable: name of the original string.
start: beginning position of the substring.
length: number of characters in the substring.
stringexpression: replacement characters.

MKD$, MKI$, MKL$, MKS$ Function

Best Command Usage
These are old-style conversion functions. Avoid these in favor of newer record type variables.

Syntax
MKI$(integerexpression)
MKS$(single-precision-expression)
MKL$(long-integer-expression)
MKD$(double-precision-expression)

MKDIR Statement

Best Command Usage
Creating new file groupings (that is, directories) while in a QuickBASIC program.

Syntax
MKDIR pathspec
pathspec: string expression identifying the directory to be created.

MKDMBF$ *See* MKSMBF$.

MKI$, MKL$, MKS$ *See* MKD$.

MKSMBF$, MKDMBF$ Function

Best Command Usage
Converting an IEEE-formatted number to a string containing a Microsoft binary formatted number.

Syntax
MKSMBF$(single-precision-expression)
MKDMBF$(double-precision-expression)

NAME Statement

Best Command Usage
Changing the name of a disk file or directory. Also, moving the file to a new location on the same drive, possibly with a new name simultaneously.

Syntax
NAME oldfilename AS newfilename
oldfilename: name of an existing file.
newfilename: new name for the old file.

OCT$ Function

Best Command Usage
Obtaining a string representing the octal value of a numerical expression.

Syntax
OCT$(numerical-expression)

ON Statement

Best Command Usage
Conditional trapping of numerous program and system events.

Syntax
ON ERROR GOTO line
ON event GOSUB procname {linenumber | linelabel}
event {ON | OFF | STOP}
event: one of a host of possibilities for system activities, such as a keypress or joystick trigger, or communications port data reception.
procname: name of the procedure gaining control.
linenumber/linelabel: number or name of the linc which receives control.

OPEN Statement

Best Command Usage
Opening a file to allow program read/write access; also, opening a communications channel.

Syntax
Opening a file:
OPEN file [FOR mode] [ACCESS access] [lock] AS #filenum [LEN
    = reclen]
    file: path name of specified file (or device name).
    mode: random, input, output, append, or binary.
    access/lock: networking specifications.
    filenum: integer file ID number.
    reclen: 128 (random access) or 512 (sequential).
Opening a communications channel:
    OPEN COM

OPTION BASE Statement

Best Command Usage
None. Avoid this statement. Use the DIM statement to specify lower and upper bounds for array subscripts.

Syntax
    OPTION BASE n
    n: lower dimension value (0 or 1).

OUT Statement

Best Command Usage
Sending control codes to a hardware I/O port.

Syntax
    OUT port, data
    port: integer ID for the I/O port.
    data: integer expression (0-255) representing the data code to send out the port.

PAINT Statement

Best Command Usage
Filling a graphic object on the screen with a color or pattern.

Syntax
    PAINT [STEP] (x, y)[,[paint] [,[bordercolor] [,background]]]
    x, y: coordinates of any point in the area to be filled.

STEP: specifies that *x* and *y* are relative to the most recently drawn point.
paint: number of the desired fill color.
bordercolor: color of the screen border rectangle.
background: controls the algorithm for defining the edges of area to be filled.

PALETTE, PALETTE USING Statement

Best Command Usage
Mapping the more extensive color possibilities of EGA, VGA, and MCGA adapters to the more limited set of color attributes used by QuickBASIC's CIRCLE, COLOR, DRAW and LINE statements.

Syntax
PALETTE [attribute,color]
PALETTE USING array-name [(array-index)]
attribute: attribute to be changed.
color: color assigned to the attribute.
array-name/array-index: group of values used to change multiple assignments with a single statement.

PCOPY Statement

Best Command Usage
Copying the contents of one screen page to another. Used for rapid and programmed screen switches.

Syntax
PCOPY sourcepage, destinationpage
sourcepage: integer specifying the source page number.
destinationpage: integer specifying the destination page number.

PEEK Function

Best Command Usage
Investigating the byte contents of specified memory locations.

Syntax
PEEK(address)
address: offset address of the desired byte location.

PEN Statement/Function

Best Command Usage
As a statement, enabling, disabling, or buffering lightpen event trapping. As a function, reading current lightpen coordinates.

Syntax

PEN {ON | OFF | STOP}
PEN(n)
n: number indicating which lightpen value is to be returned.

PLAY Statement

Best Command Usage

Generating music with the computer's speaker. Also enabling, disabling, or buffering the playing of music.

Syntax

PLAY {ON | OFF | STOP}
PLAY commandstring
commandstring: string of codes indicating octave, tone, duration, tempo, and operation.

PMAP Function

Best Command Usage

Converting logical view coordinates to actual physical coordinates, or vice versa.

Syntax

PMAP(expression, function)
expression: the x or y coordinate to be mapped.
function: integer (0-3) indicating the desired type of mapping.

POINT Function

Best Command Usage

Obtaining the coordinates or color of a screen pixel.

Syntax

POINT (x, y)
POINT (number)
(x, y): coordinates of the target pixel.
number: integer (0, 1, 2, or 3) indicating, respectively, whether to return physical *x* or *y* or logical *x* or *y* coordinates.

POKE Statement

Best Command Usage

Patching a program by writing a new value to a byte location.

Syntax

POKE address,byte
address: memory offset to write into.
byte: data value (0-255) to write into the specified byte location.

POS Function

Best Command Usage
Obtaining the current cursor column value.

Syntax
POS(0)

PRESET Statement

Best Command Usage
Drawing an individual pixel on the screen and setting its color attribute. The same as PSET, except that the default color used is the background color.

Syntax
PRESET [STEP](x, y)[,color]
x, y: pixel coordinates to draw.
STEP: specifies that *x* and *y* are relative to the current cursor location.
color: color attribute to use.

PRINT Statement

Best Command Usage
Sending output to the screen.

Syntax
PRINT# [USING stringexpression] [expressionlist][{, ¦ ;}]
expressionlist: numerical or string expressions to be shown on the screen.
stringexpression: format of the output information.
#: number of the sequential output file.

PSET Statement

Best Command Usage
Drawing an individual pixel on the screen and setting its color attribute. The same as PRESET, except that the default color used is the foreground color.

Syntax
PSET [STEP](x, y)[,color]
x, y: pixel coordinates to draw.
STEP: specifies that *x* and *y* are relative to the current cursor location.
color: color attribute to use.

PUT Statement

Best Command Usage
Writing data to a random access record, or an absolute byte location, in a file. Also, writing a graphic screen image which was originally stored with the GET statement.

Syntax
Writing to a file:

PUT #filenumber[,[recordnumber][,variable]]
PUT #filenumber
    [,{recordnumber ¦ recordnumber,variable ¦ ,variable}]

filenumber: number of an open file.
recordnumber: record number (random access file) or byte number (binary file) to which to write data.
variable: the data to be written.

Redrawing a graphic image:

PUT [STEP] (x, y),arrayname[(indices)] [,actionverb]

x, y: coordinates of top left corner of the image to be drawn.
STEP: indicates that the coordinates are relative.
arrayname: name of array containing graphic image.
indices: these retrieve a partial image beginning with the specifed array position.
actionverb: action to control merging of stored image with existing screen image.

RANDOMIZE Statement

Best Command Usage
Resetting the random number generator. Use this to avoid a repeated number sequence with the RND function.

Syntax

RANDOMIZE [expression]

expression: any QuickBASIC expression. Use TIMER for a conveniently changing expression.

READ Statement

Best Command Usage
Copying values from successive DATA statements and assigns them to program variables.

Syntax

READ variablelist

variablelist: series of QuickBASIC variable names.

REDIM Statement

Best Command Usage
Changing the space allocated to a dynamically defined array.

Syntax
REDIM [SHARED] variable(subscripts)[AS type]
[,variable(subscripts)[AS type]] . . .
variable: name of a numerical or string variable.
SHARED: indicates that all procedures in this module can access this variable.
subscripts: array dimensions.
AS type: declares a data type for array elements.

REM Statement

Best Command Usage
Inserting documentation into your program listings.

Syntax
REM remark
remark
remark: any character text.

RESET Statement

Best Command Usage
Closing all disk files.

Syntax
RESET

RESTORE Statement

Best Command Usage
Reusing some or all of your DATA statements.

Syntax
RESTORE [{linelabel ¦ linenumber}]
linelabel/linenumber: label or line number of the next DATA statement to use by the next READ statement.

RESUME Statement

Best Command Usage
Debugging support. RESUME continues program execution after an error trapping routine has run.

Syntax
> RESUME [0]
> RESUME NEXT
> RESUME {linelabel ¦ linenumber}
> *0:* resume at the statement that caused the error.
> *NEXT:* resume at the statement immediately following the one that caused the error.
> *linelabel/linenumber:* resume at specific line number or label.

RETURN Statement

Best Command Usage
Returning control from a subroutine to the invoking program.

Syntax
> RETURN [{linelabel ¦ linenumber}]
> *linelabel/linenumber:* line number or label in the module-level code to execute next. If this is omitted, the statement following the GOSUB is executed next.

RIGHT$ Function

Best Command Usage
Obtaining the rightmost *n* characters of a string.

Syntax
> RIGHT$(stringexpression,n)
> *stringexpression:* a string constant, string variable, or string expression.
> *n:* number of characters desired.

RMDIR Statement

Best Command Usage
Removing an empty DOS directory.

Syntax
> RMDIR pathspec
> *pathspec:* specifies the directory to be removed.

RND Function

Best Command Usage
Obtaining a single-precision random number between 0 and 1.

Syntax
> RND[(n)]
> *n:* return the next random number in sequence ($n > 0$), the last number generated ($n = 0$), or the same random number ($n < 0$). If

the argument is omitted, the RND function returns the next number in the random number sequence.

RSET Statement

Best Command Usage
Right-justifying string data for output purposes.

Syntax
RSET {stringvariable = stringexpression}
stringvariable: any string variable.
stringexpression: value assigned to stringvariable after trailing space characters have been removed.

RTRIM$ Function

Best Command Usage
Immediately removing trailing spaces.

Syntax
RTRIM$(stringexpression)

RUN Statement

Best Command Usage
Immediately running the currently loaded memory program, or a specified alternate program.

Syntax
RUN [{linenumber ¦ filespec}]
linenumber: line number at which to begin executing.
filespec: name of file to load and run.

SADD Function

Best Command Usage
Obtaining the near pointer for a specified string.

Syntax
SADD(stringvariable)
stringvariable: target string.

SCREEN Statement/Function

Best Command Usage
As a statement, specifying the type of display screen. As a function, reading the color or character at a specified screen location.

Syntax

As a statement:

    SCREEN [mode] [,[colorswitch]][,[apage]][,[vpage]]
    mode: integer that indicates a screen mode for a particular display
    and adapter combination.
    colorswitch/apage/vpage: see your User's Manual.

As a function:

    SCREEN (row,column[,colorflag])
    row,column: x, y pixel coordinates.
    colorflag: asks for color or ASCII code of the character at that
    coordinate.

SEEK Statement/Function

Best Command Usage

As a statement, setting the file position for the next read or write. As a
function, obtaining the current file position.

Syntax

As a statement:

    SEEK #filenumber,position
    filenumber: integer number of the file.
    position: byte or record offset for the next read or write.

As a function:

    SEEK(filenumber)

SELECT CASE Statement

Best Command Usage

Controlling a multiway decision point in a program.

Syntax

    SELECT CASE testexpression
        [CASE expressionlist1]
            [statementblock-1]
        [CASE expressionlist2]
            [statementblock-2]

            . . .

        [CASE ELSE
            [statementblock-n]]
    END SELECT
    testexpression: any numerical or string expression.
    expressionlist: any expression of the same type as testexpression.
    statementblock: group of single line or multiline statements.

SETMEM Function

Best Command Usage

Increasing or decreasing the amount of memory used by the far heap. SETMEN typically is needed when library routines written in other languages are included in Quick libraries or are linked to compiled Quick-BASIC programs.

Syntax

SETMEM(numerical-expression)
numerical-expression: influences the extent of increase or decrease in heap space.

SGN Function

Best Command Usage

Obtaining the sign of a numerical expression.

Syntax

SGN(numerical-expression)
numerical-expression: if positive, **+1** is returned; if zero, **0** is returned; if negative, **−1** is returned.

SHARED Statement

Best Command Usage

Sharing module level variables without passing them to a SUB or FUNCTION procedure through standard parameter techniques. Avoid this mechanism; it contradicts structured programming principles and makes your code much more difficult to understand and debug.

Syntax

SHARED variable [AS type] [,variable [AS type]] . . .
variable: name of module-level variable or array.
AS type: specifies data type.

SHELL Statement

Best Command Usage

Running a DOS command or a .COM, .EXE, or .BAT program from within a QuickBASIC program.

Syntax

SHELL [commandstring]
commandstring: string expression containing the program or command name, as well as any program parameter values. If there is no *commandstring* this statement produces a secondary DOS command processor only.

SIN Function

Best Command Usage
Obtaining the sine of an angle given in radians.

Syntax
SIN(numerical-expression)
numerical-expression: the angle in radians.

SLEEP Statement

Best Command Usage
Causing a controlled processing pause. SLEEP temporarily suspends execution of the calling execution.

Syntax
SLEEP [seconds]
seconds: time to pause calling program. If omitted, pauses until any keypress.

SOUND Statement

Best Command Usage
Generating variable tones through the computer's speaker.

Syntax
SOUND frequency,duration
frequency: integer expression representing the frequency of the sound in cycles per second.
duration: integer number of system clock ticks for which the sound lasts.

SPACE$ Function

Best Command Usage
Initializing a string to a precise number of blank spaces.

Syntax
SPACE$(n)
n: integer number of desired spaces.

SPC Function

Best Command Usage
Assisting in output layout by producing a controlled number of blank spaces during a PRINT or LPRINT statement.

Syntax
SPC(n)
n: integer number of desired spaces.

SQR Function

Best Command Usage
Obtaining the square root of a numerical expression.

Syntax
SQR(numerical-expression)
numerical-expression: any non-negative numerical expression.

STATIC Statement

Best Command Usage
Ensuring that procedural variables are truly independent of variables in calling modules or procedures, even though there may exist other variables with the same names.

Syntax
STATIC variable[( )][AS type][,variable[( )][AS type] . . .
variable: name of any array or QuickBASIC variable.
AS type: type of data.

STICK Function

Best Command Usage
Obtaining the *x* and *y* coordinates of the two joysticks.

Syntax
STICK(n)
n: integer. *0* and *1* request, respectively, the *x* and *y* values for joystick A; *2* and *3* request the *x* and *y* values for joystick B.

STOP Statement

Best Command Usage
Terminating the running program.

Syntax
STOP

STR$ Function

Best Command Usage
Converting a numerical expression to a string representation for the typical purposes of output formatting.

Syntax
STR$(numerical-expression)

STRIG(n) Statement

Best Command Usage
Obtaining joystick trigger status.

Syntax
STRIG(n)

STRING$ Function

Best Command Usage
Generating a string for output formatting consisting of one character repeated a fixed number of times.

Syntax
STRING$(m,n)
STRING$(m,stringexpression)
m: length of the generated string.
n: ASCII code of the character to repeat in the generated string.
stringexpression: existing string whose first character is used as the repeating character in the generated string.

SUB . . . END SUB Statement

Best Command Usage
Delineating the beginning and end of a subprogram.

Syntax
SUB globalname[parameterlist][STATIC]
    [statements]
[EXIT SUB]
    [statements]
END SUB
globalname: unique name for this subprogram.
parameterlist: list of variables and arrays passed to the SUB when it is called.
STATIC: localizes variable values.

SWAP Statement

Best Command Usage
Exchanging the values of two variables to reduce required programming code.

Syntax
SWAP variable1,variable2
variable1/variable2: any QuickBASIC variables of the same type.

SYSTEM Statement

Best Command Usage
Closing open files and returning control to the operating system.

Syntax
SYSTEM

TAB Function

Best Command Usage
Adjusting the horizontal print location during output printing.

Syntax
TAB(column)
column: integer specifying the horizontal position at which to print the next output characters.

TAN Function

Best Command Usage
Obtaining the tangent of an angle.

Syntax
TAN(numerical-expression)
numerical-expression: numerical angle in radians.

TIME$ Statement/Function

Best Command Usage
As a statement, setting the current time. As a function, obtaining the current time.

Syntax
As a statement:
TIME$ = stringexpression
stringexpression: string representation of the time to be set (*hh,
hh:mm,* or *hh:mm:ss*)
As a function:
TIME$

TIMER Statement

Best Command Usage
Accessing and controlling timer interrupt information.

Syntax
TIMER [{ON | OFF |STOP}]

TRON, TROFF Statement

Best Command Usage
Enabling or disabling visual program line tracing.

Syntax
TRON
TROFF

TYPE Statement

Best Command Usage
Creating sophisticated user-defined data types. The TYPE statement facilitates powerful extensions to the fundamental structures of the language.

Syntax
TYPE usertype
    elementname AS typename
    [elementname AS typename]
    .
    .
    .
END TYPE
usertype: unique name for the newly created data type structure.
elementname: identifies each individual kind of data element.
typename: either integer, long, single, double, string*n or a previously created user-defined type.

UBOUND Function

Best Command Usage
Obtaining the maximum upper bound of an array dimension.

Syntax
UBOUND(array[,dimension])
array: name of the array.
dimension: dimension number of interest.

UCASE$ Function

Best Command Usage
Converting any string expression to upper-case characters.

Syntax
UCASE$(stringexpression)

UEVENT Statement

Best Command Usage
Enabling, disabling, or buffering user-defined events.

Syntax
UEVENT {ON | OFF | STOP}

UNLOCK Statement

Best Command Usage
Releasing an existing file or record lock when operating in a multiuser networked system under DOS 3.1 and above.

Syntax
UNLOCK # filenumber [,{record | [start] TO end}]
filenumber: number of an open file.
record/start/end: range of records or bytes to be unlocked.

VAL Function

Best Command Usage
Converting a string containing digits to a numerical value.

Syntax
VAL(stringexpression)

VARPTR, VARSEG Function

Best Command Usage
Obtaining the memory offset (VARPTR) and segment (VARSEG) addresses of specified variables.

Syntax
VARPTR(variablename)
VARSEG(variablename)
variablename: any legal BASIC variable.

VARPTR$ Function

Best Command Usage
Obtaining a string representation of a variable's address as required for compiled use of the DRAW and PLAY statements.

Syntax
VARPTR$(variablename)

VARSEG *See* VARPTR.

VIEW Statement

Best Command Usage
Restricting graphic or text output to a viewport (rectangular subportion) on your physical screen.

Syntax
For restricting graphic output:
VIEW [[SCREEN] (x1, y1)-(x2, y2) [,[color][,border]]]
For restricting text output:
VIEW PRINT [topline TO bottomline]
x1, y1 and *x2, y2:* coordinates of diagonally opposite corners of the viewport.
SCREEN: indicates that the *x, y* pairs are relative to the actual physical screen, not relative to an already established viewport.
color/border: color of the viewport and the border rectangle around the viewport.
topline/bottomline: top and bottom line numbers in the text viewport.

WAIT Statement

Best Command Usage
Pausing a program until a specified bit pattern is received at one of your computer's input ports.

Syntax
WAIT portnumber,and-expression[,xor-expression]
portnumber: number of the input port.
and-expression: a bit pattern to AND with the data received from the port.
xor-expression: a bit pattern to XOR with the data received from the port.

WHILE . . . WEND Statement

Best Command Usage
Repeating a group of statements so long as a logical expression remains true.

Syntax
WHILE condition
    [statements]
WEND
condition: logical true or false expression.
statements: any number of BASIC statements to be executed while the specified condition remains true.

WIDTH Statement

Best Command Usage

Setting the actual, or imposing an artificial, width of a file or device for output purposes.

Syntax

WIDTH [columns][,lines]
WIDTH {#filenumber ¦ device},width
WIDTH LPRINT width
columns/lines: screen output dimensions.
#filenumber: integer file ID number.
device: DOS device ID.
width: number of output columns.

WINDOW Statement

Best Command Usage

Adjusting the logical dimensions of the current viewport to allow customized programs which output to logical x, y coordinates rather than absolute screen positions.

Syntax

WINDOW [[SCREEN] (x1, y1) − (x2, y2)]
x1, y1 and *x2, y2:* new logical coordinates for the screen corners.
SCREEN: reverses screen direction of the y axis.

WRITE # Statement

Best Command Usage

Outputting automatically comma-delimited file data.

Syntax

WRITE #filenumber[,expressionlist]
filenumber: integer ID of the open file.
expressionlist: list of output variables or expressions.

C | QuickBASIC's Full Menus

This appendix provides capsule descriptions of all commands found on the Full menus in QuickBASIC's development environment. Full menus, as opposed to the more limited but more common Easy menus, present a more sophisticated and more extensive set of command choices. You may select between these two kinds of menus during system installation. You can also change from one to the other while online by making a toggle choice from the Options pulldown menu.

Both Easy and Full menus offer the same set of critical commands. Full menus offer an additional set of choices. This appendix presents the menu commands in this two-fold manner as well. Under each menu it discusses the types of commands contained on the menu, then presents the choices common to both the Easy and the Full menus, and, last, discusses the choices present on the Full menu only.

The order of the menus in this appendix—File, Edit, View, Search, Run, Debug, Call, Options, and Help—is based on the order of the menus appearing in the menu bar.

The File Menu

The File menu provides commands that work with entire files at a time in QuickBASIC. The following commands may be selected from this menu.

Easy and Full Menu Choices

New Program Creates a new program file and erases any currently loaded program from the memory work area.

Open Program Displays files in selectable list of directories and drives. Permits selection of any individual file to be read into memory to be worked on.

Save As Enables you to direct QuickBASIC to save the currently loaded file. It also allows you to specify the name of the disk file to be written.

Print Enables you to print any part(s) of your work.

Exit Leaves the QuickBASIC environment, reminds you to save currently loaded files, and returns to the DOS prompt.

Full Menu Choices Only

Merge Combines the textual contents of two files.

Save Automatically saves to disk a copy of the file in the active View window.

Save All Automatically saves to disk copies of all currently loaded files.

Create File Creates a new disk file (program, include, or document) and makes it a part of the current main program set.

Load File Loads into memory an existing disk file (program, include, or document type).

Unload File Removes a file (program, include, or document type) from those currently in memory.

DOS Shell Runs a copy of the DOS command interpreter while still under the auspices of the QuickBASIC development environment.

The Edit Menu

The Edit menu provides commands that enable you to manipulate the text in your QuickBASIC files and procedures. The following commands may be selected from this menu.

Easy and Full Menu Choices

Cut Erases currently selected text. Places a copy of the erased text into a memory buffer known as the clipboard.

Copy Copies the currently selected text to the special memory buffer known as the clipboard.

Paste Adds a copy of the textual contents of the clipboard at the current location of the cursor.

Full Menu Choices Only

Undo Reverses the effect of your last selected operation. This choice typically is used to restore text which has been deleted.

Clear Permanently erases selected text, while retaining the current contents of the clipboard.

New SUB Creates a new SUB procedure and attaches it internally to the module being worked on in the currently active window.

New FUNCTION Creates a new FUNCTION procedure and attaches it internally to the module being worked on in the currently active window.

The View Menu

The View menu provides commands that enable you to display and edit your individual files and SUB/FUNCTION procedures. The following commands may be selected from this menu.

Easy and Full Menu Choices

SUBs Enables you to select a file or procedure to activate in the current or split View window. It displays all loaded files and procedures.

Output Screen Toggles between the QuickBASIC development screen and the program output screen.

Included Lines Toggles the display of the contents of referenced include files. It does not permit editing of the include text.

Full Menu Choices Only

Next SUB Activates the next stored QuickBASIC procedure for editing in the currently active View window.

Split Toggles the availability of a second View window.

Next Statement Immediately moves the cursor to, and highlights, the next statement to be executed.

Included File Loads all referenced include files for both viewing and possible editing.

The Search Menu

The Search menu provides commands that enable you to locate and optionally replace specific text strings in your loaded files and procedures. The following commands may be selected from this menu.

Easy and Full Menu Choices

Find Searches for a specified text string in the active window, the current module, or in all loaded modules.

Change Provides a search and replace facility for QuickBASIC text editing.

Full Menu Choices Only

Selected Text Searches in the active window for a text string matching the currently selected text string.

Repeat Last Find Continues searching for the next occurrence of the text specified in the *Selected Text* command.

Label Searches for a program line label in the active window, the current window, or in all modules.

The Run Menu

The Run menu provides commands that enable you to test out, run, and compile your QuickBASIC programs. The following commands may be selected from this menu.

Easy and Full Menu Choices

Start Begins to execute the currently loaded program.

Restart Resets the current statement to the first one in your program and resets all variable values.

Continue Resumes program execution at the statement at which it was previously paused.

Make EXE File Compiles and links the current program.

Full Menu Choices Only

Modify COMMAND$ Enables you to edit the parameter string that would be passed to your program if it were run at the DOS command prompt.

Make Library Creates or updates a customized QuickBASIC Quick library.

Set Main Module Enables you to specify which of two or more loaded modules is to be the first one executed when you Start your program.

The Debug Menu

The Debug menu provides commands that assist you in discovering where errors exist in your programs and what they are. The following commands may be selected from this menu.

Easy and Full Menu Choices

Add Watch Incorporates a new variable or expression into the Watch window for viewing during program execution.

Instant Watch Immediately displays the value of a variable or an expression.

Delete Watch Erases a watched variable or expression from the Watch window.

Toggle Breakpoint Sets or clears a breakpoint at the current line.

Clear All Breakpoints Removes all existing breakpoint indicators.

Full Menu Choices Only

Watchpoint Enables you to set a logical expression which, when it becomes true, causes program execution to suspend.

Delete All Watch Erases all Watch window entries at once.

Trace On/Off Toggles on and off an execution mode that causes a program to run very slowly, highlighting each statement in your View window as that statement executes.

History On/Off Toggles on and off a record-keeping mode during which the twenty most recently executed statements are recorded and can be called up on your screen for display.

Break on Errors Pauses execution at the most recently activated ON ERROR command, if one exists in your program.

Set Next Statement Makes the currently highlighted program line into the next line to be executed when program execution resumes.

The Calls Menu

The Calls menu is available only when the Full menus mode is active. It displays the names of all procedures in the flow of execution control that have led to the current point of execution.

The Options Menu

The Options menu provides a set of miscellaneous commands that enable you to further customize your QuickBASIC development environment. The following commands may be selected from this menu.

Easy and Full Menu Choices

Display Controls and customizes various features of your QuickBASIC development environment screen.

Set Paths Sets search paths for QuickBASIC file types.

Full Menus Toggles on and off the alternative Full or Easy menu displays.

Full Menu Choices Only

Right Mouse Customizes the assignment of an installed mouse's button two. Button two normally calls up context-sensitive help, but can be switched with this toggle command to request that QuickBASIC execute the current program from its beginning to the current line.

Syntax Checking Toggles on and off the automatic syntax checking mode of the QuickBASIC smart editor.

The Help Menu

The Help provides commands that provide you with access to QuickBASIC's on-line context-sensitive help text. The following commands may be selected from this menu:

Easy and Full Menu Choices

Index Provides access to an alphabetized list of QuickBASIC keywords, as well as more detailed help about any one of them.

Contents Offers a selectable hierarchy of help topics.

Topic Provides detailed help about the variable, keyword, or QuickBASIC screen element currently highlighted.

Help on Help Displays information about the on-line help system itself.

Full Menu Choices Only

None.

Answers to Quizzes

1 | 1-b, 2-a, 3-c, 4-d, 5-c, 6-c, 7-d, 8-c, 9-c, 10-c, 11-b, 12-c, 13-d,
14-c, 15-d

2 | 1-c, 2-b, 3-b, 4-a, 5-b, 6-a, 7-c, 8-b, 9-d, 10-d, 11-b, 12-d, 13-d,
14-c, 15-b

3 | 1-d, 2-c, 3-c, 4-d, 5-b, 6-c, 7-c, 8-b, 9-b, 10-b, 11-c, 12-b, 13-b,
14-b, 15-c

4 | 1-c, 2-b, 3-c, 4-a, 5-c, 6-c, 7-c, 8-d, 9-b, 10-c, 11-d, 12-b, 13-b,
14-c, 15-b

5 | 1-d, 2-b, 3-c, 4-b, 5-c, 6-d, 7-d, 8-d, 9-c, 10-c, 11-b, 12-a, 13-c,
14-d, 15-c

6 | 1-a, 2-c, 3-d, 4-b, 5-d, 6-b, 7-d, 8-b, 9-d, 10-c, 11-d, 12-c, 13-b, 14-d, 15-d

7 | 1-d, 2-b, 3-c, 4-c, 5-b, 6-a, 7-b, 8-a, 9-d, 10-d, 11-b, 12-c, 13-b, 14-b, 15-b

8 | 1-c, 2-a, 3-b, 4-c, 5-b, 6-d, 7-a, 8-d, 9-d, 10-d, 11-d, 12-b, 13-d, 14-b, 15-c

9 | 1-d, 2-d, 3-c, 4-d, 5-a, 6-a, 7-b, 8-d, 9-d, 10-d, 11-b, 12-d, 13-d, 14-c, 15-c

10 | 1-d, 2-c, 3-b, 4-c, 5-b, 6-c, 7-a, 8-d, 9-a, 10-c, 11-c, 12-d, 13-d, 14-a, 15-d

11 | 1-c, 2-d, 3-b, 4-c, 5-c, 6-d, 7-d, 8-c, 9-d, 10-c, 11-b, 12-a, 13-d, 14-d, 15-c

12 | 1-b, 2-b, 3-d, 4-c, 5-d, 6-d, 7-c, 8-b, 9-d, 10-c, 11-c, 12-b, 13-a, 14-d, 15-b

Index

Understanding C

Carl Townsend

This is an entry-level tutorial providing the novice C programmer with a complete overview of the language in the MS-DOS® environment. Using the successful Understanding Series format which features key terms, marginal notes, and end-of-chapter questions and answers, the book can be used with the Turbo C or QuickC compilers as well as with other ANSI C compilers on the market.

Topics covered include:

- The C Language
- C Data Types
- Arithmetic Operations and Expressions
- The User Interface: Input and Output
- Program Control: Conditional and Loop Structures
- Using Pointers
- Using Functions and Macros
- Managing Variable Storage
- Building Arrays
- Using Data Structure
- Files and Other Types of Input and Output
- Using Graphics
- Using BIOS Services
- Structured Programming
- Appendices: Turbo C/QuickC Comparison, Glossary, ASCII Character Set, C Operators, C Data Types, C Keywords, Tips

288 Pages, 7 x 9, Softbound
ISBN: 0-672-27278-4
No. 27278, $17.95

Understanding HyperTalk™

Dan Shafer

Understanding HyperTalk brings the power and fascination of programming in HyperTalk to those Macintosh® owners who want to customize their environment with Apple®'s HyperCard™, Version 1.2.
This book will be useful to people who are deciding whether to buy HyperCard and to people who want to teach themselves or others Hyper-Card programming and stacks.

Topics covered include:

- Programming Basics
- Object-Oriented Programming Ideas
- HyperTalk Basics
- HyperTalk Building Blocks
- System Messages
- Input, Output, and Control
- Card Management
- Field and Text Management
- User Interface: Dialog and Menus
- Graphics and Visual Effects
- Sound and Music
- Math Functions and Operators
- Properties and Their Management
- Extending HyperTalk

288 Pages, 7 x 9, Softbound
ISBN: 0-672-27283-0
No. 27283, $17.95

Understanding Local Area Networks

Stan Schatt

This tutorial on the latest local area network technologies provides an in-depth description of the major LANs on the market as well as a conceptual framework to help the reader understand how LANs communicate with mainframe computers. It details why they are important to business and how they are configured to transmit information from one location to another.

Topics covered include:

- An Overview of the IBM PC and Local Area Networks
- The Basics of a Local Area Network
- Gateways
- The IBM PC Network and Token Ring Network
- Novell's Local Area Network Systems
- 3Com's Local Area Networks
- AT & T's STARLAN and ISN
- Corvus's Local Area Network
- Other Networks and Pseudo-Networks
- A Guide to Networkable Software
- Local Area Network Selection and Managment

276 Pages, 7 x 9, Softbound
ISBN: 0-672-27063-3
No. 27063, $17.95

Understanding Microsoft® Windows

Katherine Stuart Ewing

Readers having little or no experience with Microsoft Windows and those users who want more complete information than is supplied in the documentation will benefit from this book. Using the successful Understanding Series format, the book is equally suitable as a text, study guide, or supplemental reference.

Topics covered include:

- Operating Systems and Operating Environments
- Installing and Using Windows
- Understanding Desktop Applications
- Understanding Paint
- Understanding Write
- Understanding Non-Windows Applications
- Understanding the Control Panel
- Windows Potpourri
- Appendices: The WIN. INI File, PIF Files, Version 2.0 Revisions, Glossary, Answers to Review Questions

300 Pages, 7 x 9, Softbound
ISBN: 0-672-27279-2
No. 27279, $17.95

The Waite Group's Understanding MS-DOS®

Kate O'Day and John Angermeyer

MS-DOS is a very powerful and intricate operating system with millions of users. This operating system can be explored by beginning programmers in a hands-on approach at the keyboard.

Understanding MS-DOS introduces the use and operation of this popular operating system for those with little previous experience in computer hardware or software. The fundamentals of the operating system such as EDLIN, tree-structured directories and pathnames, and such advanced features as redirection and filtering are presented in a way that is easy to understand and use.

Topics covered include:

■ Organizing Data and Files
■ Redirecting Input and Output
■ Using the Text Editor EDLIN to Create and Edit Files
■ Special Function Keys and Key Combinations
■ Creating Batch Files of Often-Repeated Commands
■ Create and Use Tree-Structured Directories

240 Pages, 7 x 9, Softbound
ISBN: 0-672-27067-6
No. 27067, $17.95

Understanding WordPerfect® Version 5.0

Vincent Alfieri

Perfect for self-study or classroom use, this newest addition to the Understanding Series clearly and concisely introduces word processing in general and WordPerfect specifically.

The book uses the successful series format of chapter introductions, marginal notes, clear illustrations, and review questions and answers to introduce the many features of WordPerfect.

Topics covered include:

■ Getting Started
■ Moving the Cursor
■ Entering the Text
■ Saving, Retrieving, and Joining
■ Deleting, Moving, and Copying
■ Printing and Printers
■ Special Effects: Fonts and Characters
■ Line Formatting, Tabs, and Indents
■ Page Formatting and Forms
■ Useful Work Savers
■ Managing Files
■ Text and Math Columns
■ Editoring Niceties
■ Form Letters
■ Other Features
■ Appendices: WordPerfect Executive, Glossary, WordPerfect Codes, Answers to Quizzes

304 Pages, 7 x 9, Softbound
ISBN: 0-672-27277-6
No. 27277, $17.95

Understanding dBASE IV™

Judd Robbins

Appropriate for the beginning-to-intermediate user of dBASE IV, this book introduces its broad capabilities and features. The concise explanations and clear presentation will also appeal to the millions of dBASE III PLUS users ready to upgrade their software.

The book concentrates on the end-user features of dBASE IV, particularly the Control Center, a pull-down menu approach to data base management. It provides a step-by-step discussion of the Query by Example (QBE) facility; the Forms Generator, and the Report and Label Generator tools. Sample screen sequences for typical business applications and review questions and answers are included in each chapter.

Topics covered include:

■ Introduction to dBASE IV
■ Creating a Database
■ Using the Control Center
■ Using Query by Example
■ The Forms Generator
■ The Report and Label Generator
■ Structured Query Language

304 Pages, 7 x 9, Softbound
ISBN: 0-672-27284-9
No. 27284, $18.95

Mastering Turbo Assembler®

Tom Swan

A hands-on tutorial combined with an advanced-level reference make this book an excellent resource for MS-DOS programmers using Borland's newest language product —Turbo Assembler. Beginning with a sound tutorial on assembly language and the binary number system, the book progresses to subjects such as data storage techniques, input and output, macros, file handling, programming interrupts, and debugging.

Topics covered include:

■ First Steps
■ A Bit of Binary
■ Mastering Assembly Language
■ Minding the Data Store
■ Input and Output
■ Macros
■ Using a Math Coprocessor
■ Advanced Topics
■ Modular Assemblies
■ Mixing Assembly Language and Pascal
■ Mixing Assembly Language and C
■ Assembly Language Reference
■ Appendices: Bibliography, Answers to Questions, Index, Tear-out Reference Card

600 Pages, 7 ½ x 9 ¾, Softbound
ISBN: 0-672-48435-8
No. 48435, $24.95

The Waite Group's Turbo C® Programming for the PC, Revised Edition

Robert Lafore

This entry-level text teaches readers the C language while also helping them write useful and marketable programs for the IBM PC, XT, AT, and PS/2. The second edition has been expanded and updated to include Borland's new Turbo C Version 2.0. It explains the Compiler's powerful integrated environment and highlights the new graphics and debugger features.

Topics covered include:

- Getting Started
- C Building Blocks
- Loops, Decisions, Functions
- Arrays and Strings, Pointers
- Keyboard and Cursor
- Structures, Unions, and ROM BIOS
- Memory and the Monochrome Display
- Graphics
- Direct CGA and EGA Color Graphics
- Files and Larger Programs
- Advanced Variables
- Appendices: Reference, Supplementary Programs, Hexadecimal Numbering, Bibliography, ASCII Chart, The Turbo C Debugger, Answers to Questions and Exercises

700 Pages, 7 ½ x 9 ¾, Softbound
ISBN: 0-672-22660-X
No. 22660, $24.95

The Waite Group's Turbo C® Bible

Nabajioti Barkakati

Turbo C Bible is a complete user-friendly reference for programmers using Borland International's Turbo C compiler. Easy-to-understand tutorials point out the different purposes and appropriate uses of each function. Then the purpose, syntax, example call, includes, common uses, returns, comments, cautions and pitfalls, and cross-reference for each is explained.

Topics covered include:

- Turbo C 1.0 Compiler Features and Options
- Process Control
- Variable-Length Argument Lists
- Memory Allocation and Management
- Buffer Manipulation
- Data Conversion and Math Routines
- Character Classification and Conversion
- String Comparison and Manipulation
- Searching and Sorting
- Time and Input/Output Routines
- File and Directory Manipulation
- System Calls
- Drawing and Animation

950 Pages, 7 ½ x 9 ¾, Softbound
ISBN: 0-672-22631-6
No. 22631, $24.95

C: Step-by-Step

Mitchell Waite and Stephen Prata, The Waite Group

The first title in the Howard W. Sams Computer Science Series, this entry-level text follows an orderly, methodical fashion to teach the basics of C programming. Designed specifically for a one or two semester course in C programming, with exercises and quizzes throughout.

Topics covered include:

- Character Strings and Formatted Input/Output
- Operators, Expressions, and Statements
- Looping in C
- If Statements, Relational, and Logical Operators
- Character Input/Output and Redirection
- Functions, Arrays, and Pointers
- Character Strings and String Functions
- File Input/Output
- Storage Classes and Program Development
- Structures and Other Data Forms
- Bit Manipulation
- The C Preprocessor and the C Library

600 Pages, 7 ½ x 9 ¾, Softbound
ISBN: 0-672-22651-0
No. 22651, $27.95

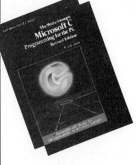

The Waite Group's Microsoft® C Programming for the PC, Revised Edition

Robert Lafore

This entry-level programming book assumes no previous knowledge of C as it moves quickly through the fundamentals of the language using step-by-step, hands-on tutorials. The new edition is based on the 5.1 compiler and includes a chapter on the newest graphics features, the newest updates to Codeview, ANSI C prototyping, VGA graphics, MCGA control, and details on the QuickC optimizing compiler.

Topics covered include:

- Getting Started
- C Building Blocks
- Loops, Decisions, Functions
- Arrays, Strings, and Pointers
- Keyboard and Cursor
- Structures, Unions, and ROM BIOS
- Memory and the Monochrome Display
- Library Graphics
- Direct CGA, EGA, and VGA Color Graphics
- New Microsoft Graphics Functions
- Files
- Larger Programs and Advanced Variables

750 Pages, 7 ½ x 9 ¾, Softbound
ISBN: 0-672-22661-8
No. 22661, $24.95

To Order Companion Diskettes

If you have found *Understanding Microsoft® QuickBASIC* useful, you'll be glad to learn that every one of the excellent programs developed in this book is contained on a companion diskette. Save time, energy, and money, and avoid the drudgery of typing these programs—use companion diskettes.

The 5¼-inch diskette is prepared for IBM-compatible computers running under DOS 2.1 or higher and formatted to 360K. The 3½-inch diskette is prepared for IBM-compatible computers running under DOS 3.1 or higher and formatted to 720K.

The diskette may be purchased with check or money order. Make checks and money orders payable to Computer Options. (No cash, please.) Use the order form below to order this or any of the other fine materials produced by Judd Robbins.

Send this form with your payment to:

Computer Options
198 Amherst Avenue
Berkeley, CA 94708

Howard W. Sams & Company assumes no liability with respect to the use or accuracy of the information contained on these diskettes.

- -

Diskette Order Form

Robbins, *Understanding Microsoft® QuickBASIC,* #27287

(Please print)

Name _____ Company _____

Address _____

City _____ State _____ Zip_____

Country _____ Phone (_____)_____

Place of Book Purchase_____

QuickBASIC companion disks

_____ 5¼" Disks (DOS 2.1 or higher) @ $19.95 each: $ _____ + $2.50* = $_____

_____ 3½" Disks (DOS 3.1 or higher) @ $19.95 each: $ _____ + $2.50* = $_____

Introduction to DOS Audio Cassette Training   (includes workbook and 2 audio cassettes)

_____ @ $19.95 each: $ _____ + $2.50* = $_____

Total for products $_____

California residents add 7% sales tax $_____

Total enclosed $_____

Method of Payment: Check# _____ M.O.# _____

All orders will be shipped U.S. Postal Service First Class. Please allow four weeks for delivery. Orders can be shipped Federal Express at the purchaser's expense.

*Shipping and Handling